TRANSFER PROCESSES IN TECHNICAL CHANGE

TRANSFER PROCESSES IN TECHNICAL CHANGE

edited by

FRANK BRADBURY
Technological Economics
Research Unit
University of Stirling

PAUL JERVIS
Oxford Centre for Management Studies
University of Oxford

RON JOHNSTON
Department of Liberal Studies in Science
University of Manchester

ALAN PEARSON
Manchester Business School
University of Manchester

SIJTHOFF & NOORDHOFF   1978
Alphen aan den Rijn — The Netherlands

ISBN 90 286 0347 6

Printed in The Netherlands.

D
607.2
TRA

FOREWORD

In the post-war world the overwhelming importance of technical change has been universally recognised. Whether in relation to military affairs, industrial production, consumer appliances, medical services or environmental protection scarcely anyone could fail to be affected by the new products and systems which have become available.

No single firm or small country could possibly hope to make more than a small proportion of the important advances in science and technology. Even large countries find it hard to keep abreast or achieve leadership in every branch simultaneously. Yet the pressure of international competition imposes severe penalties on those who do not keep close behind the leaders. In these circumstances it is scarcely surprising that the question of "technology transfer" has assumed much greater importance in recent years.

Transfer of technology has many different dimensions. It is obviously important between countries in every field of industrial technology. The successful industrialisation of may third world countries has been based to a very large extent on imported technology. The earlier industrialisation of Japan and the Soviet Union also depended to a very large extent on this process. But the transfer of technology is vital not only for countries who were once far behind and are catching up; it is no less important between countries and firms who are among the leaders, for example in relation to nuclear power, micro-electronics and telecommunications.

The available channels for the transfer of technology have greatly increased in range and capacity in the post-war world. The spread of multi-national enterprises around the globe is now a common place. The ease and speed of travel and communications have greatly facilitated the spread of information systems of all kinds. Payments for patents, licences and know-how have increased at an extraordinarily rapid rate for 30 years. International consultancy is a booming industry.

Yet despite this vast increase in technology transfer activities, very little was known until recently about the relative importance of the various different mechanisms, and still less about their relative efficiency. Cooper's study for the UN was one of the very few which attempted this elementary analysis and assessment.

This book is one indication of the increasing recognition by academics, industrialists and governments that the subject deserves a great deal more attention, discussion and research. The seminar was an extremely lively one, but the editors have resisted the temptation simply to produce a verbatim transcript of the proceedings. Although quick and easy to produce, such a report is always far more boring to the reader than to the actual participants in the seminar. There is an unbridgable gap between oral and written communication. The editors have done something far more useful: in presenting carefully selected excerpts from the various papers, they have produced a new analysis of the whole field which will be helpful to all students of this topic.

As both the analysis and the papers make clear, international technology transfer is only one dimension of a much more complex set of activities, which include internal transfers within laboratories, firms and industries, the web of relationships between scientists and technologists, and the complex interchange between government, universities and industries. We are still only at the beginning of undertaking this complex network, but Professor Bradbury and Stirling University are to be congratulated for organising this genuinely seminal meeting and still more for producing this carefully edited book as an invaluable starting point for much future work.

Prof. Christopher Freeman,
Science Policy Research Unit,
University of Sussex

TABLE OF CONTENTS

PREFACE

This book is about a group of activities usually referred to as "technology transfer" and much of the material it contains was first presented at a meeting held at the University of Stirling in July 1974 which brought people together to discuss "Technology Transfer — Research and Implementation". What happened at that meeting, and in subsequent discussions convinced the four authors that they needed to put a new label on the technology transfer bottle. The objective of the meeting, or more correctly the objective we ascribed to the meeting in the preliminary publicity, was stated thus:

To exchange ideas on concepts of technology transfer and the ways in which research and analysis can make an effective contribution to improving technology transfer performance. It is hoped to provide a forum for discussion for all those concerned with technology transfer, whether they be producers or receivers, policy makers or "catalysts", or researchers.

The composition of the audience attracted to the meeting is an indication of the interests and expectations that such a description aroused. Government, represented by Departments, Laboratories and other institutions, provided 11 people, industry and professional bodies 9, research associations and the National Research Development Corporation 4 and universities 19.

The occasion turned out to be one of more than usual significance because of timeliness of the discussions concerning the scope of the subject. The structure of the meeting was to group papers into sessions and for each session chairman to draw on these to emphasise the points he perceived to be important. The format afterwards adopted for extracting the learning that had occurred was the basis for this book. Some of the presented papers (but not all) are printed in Part II; Part I is an extended introduction and analysis of the papers and their discussion. We have not attempted to report the very lively exchanges of the meeting in verbatim terms.

Instead we have made free use of the medley of ideas and comments to form the basis of the opening six chapters. Whilst the authors take full responsibility for the views expressed they are grateful to all participants for their contribution. At the possible cost of distorting the views of speakers we have gained freedom to put together what was said in our own way alongside and interwoven with our own ideas; and, whilst we paid great attention to the transcripts of what was said, we avoided the interminable task of trimming, elaborating and updating the material to meet the current views of individual contributors.

How far the objectives stated above were achieved may be assessed by the readers. The authors feel that progress was enough to make an analysis of the main ideas and a presentation of a selection of the papers worthwhile. The book is the result of many months of drafting during which time ideas have developed and understanding increased.* The subject of transfer processes in technological change is and will remain in a very immature state in these early years. It is for this reason the proceedings and commentary are presented here with minimum of structuring. We hope that those interested may glean a useful idea or two to assimilate into their own thinking and understanding of what is indisputably a contemporary issue of major importance.

We wish especially to thank Dr. E.J.P. Clarke (Atomic Energy Research Establishment, Harwell) and Mr. Keith Pavitt (University of Sussex) for the valuable assistance they gave in chairing sessions.

Manchester, Oxford, Stirling
January, 1978

---

* The authors are glad to observe that this is now clearly happening in the area of U.K. technology policy and industrial strategy, outdating some of our comments, especially in Chapter 3. However, the debate on technology transfer, its analytical, methodological and prescriptive problems, continues to grow so that what was written here becomes more, not less, significant with the passage of trial. (August 1975.)

X

PART I

ANALYSIS AND
GENERAL DISCUSSION

Chapter 1

INTRODUCTION

The Concept of Technology Transfer

1.1 The current interest in the concept of technology transfer reflects its perceived relevance to a range of different interests. In government, there is concern over the level of return on large investments of public money in research and development (hereafter R & D) and high technology, associated with the belief by some that there has been too much concentration on the production of knowledge and too little on its utilisation. Trade in technology is another important issue, both as an export because of its immediate contribution to the balance of payments and its possible long-term economic disbenefits, and as an import as an alternative strategy to R & D — led technological development. For nations of the Third World, the transfer of technology is seen as a vital aid to development and there is concern over the role of multinational enterprises in assisting or hindering the achievement of this goal. There are many signs of increasing public concern with the type of technological development that has occurred over the past two or three decades. It is now suspected that the type of technological novelty which has traditionally been sought may be inappropriate for the resolution of the pressing social issues of today, and consequently that mechanisms need to be devised to direct resources to a new range of problems such as those raised in the provision of adequate housing, transport and health care. This concern is demonstrated by the popularity of the writings of authors such as Schumacher [1] and Pirsig [2].

Definitions

1.2 In order to sharpen our understanding of the concepts associated with the movement of technology and its related science and engineering we must undertake some definitions.

Definitions, in so far as they attempt to describe a complex

3

system in a sentence, are heroic things at best and utterly confusing at worst. No clearer exemplification of this could be found than in the literature and at meetings about technology transfer. One common definition is "the process by which a technology is applied to a purpose other than the one for which it was originally intended" or, in other words, "Technology transfer is putting technology into a different context". This view reflects the origins of the term "technology transfer" in the United States where since 1940 the federal government has been responsible for the direction of a steadily increasing share of national R & D resources, primarily for achieving military, space and atomic energy goals. This progressive concentration of R & D resources has raised warnings of consequent damage to the economy and to the achievement of broad social goals. The standard defence has been that this federal expenditure has created a vast technology that has been or could be transferred to the civilian economy, thereby maintaining economic growth as well as supplying funds to achieve other national goals. Hence evidence which suggests that "spin-offs" are both infrequent and suffer from long time-lags [3] [4] has induced a search for policies to ensure the maximum transfer of information and technology resulting from federally financed R & D. In this situation, "technology transfer" could be interpreted as a political response to maintain the hegemony of the defence, aerospace and atomic energy agencies over federally funded research.

1.3 Brooks has offered a wider definition of technology transfer [5]

> "Technology transfer is the process by which science and technology are diffused throughout human activity. Wherever systematic rational knowledge developed by one group or institution is embodied in a way of doing things by other institutions or groups we have technology transfer. This can be either transfer from more basic scientific knowledge into technology, or adaptation of an existing technology to a new use. Technology transfer differs from ordinary scientific information transfer in the fact that to be really transferred it must be embodied in an actual operation of some kind."

Brooks extends this discussion to recognise two types of transfer, which he designates as "vertical" and "horizontal". Vertical transfer is the process by which technology is transferred from the more general to the more specific, for instance by the incorporation of new scientific knowledge into technology and by the embodiment of a "state of the art" into a system. Horizontal transfer

4

involves the adaptation of a technology from one application to another, as in the adaptation of a laboratory analytical instrument for on-line process control, and hence corresponds to the more restricted notion of technology transfer first introduced.

This suggests that it is not satisfactory merely to think of technology transfer as one single type of process, and the distinction that Brooks draws between technology transfer and scientific information transfer is a sharp reminder that no definition can be considered adequate unless it encompasses the thing that is being transferred, as well as its source and destination. We will return to the Brooks' definition later in the chapter.

1.4 A survey of research on the subject of technology transfer reveals that the term has been adopted over a wide range of fields, sometimes in order, one suspects, to give a new look to some well worn ideas. Areas to which the concept has been applied include the examples already given, transfer from industrialised nations to less developed countries, from the western industrialised countries to those in the Communist bloc, transfer between companies, and transfer problems that occur between departments or groups within a single organisation. It is also used to describe the professional activities of those engaged in licensing. The phrase "technology transfer" is applied so universally that in fact it becomes a featureless and all enveloping cloak which disguises the characteristics of those who wear it.

Resolving the problem of definition is important, because it identifies the problem to which the researcher or decision maker intends to address himself. Grouping phenomena ranging from invention, innovation and diffusion to international trade, licensing and the activities of international firms produces such a complex and variegated system that analysis becomes almost impossible; by selecting a definition we are defining for study a sub-set of the system of problems (a phrase coined by R.L. Ackoff [6]). We need to find a way of describing the diverse activities previously called Technology Transfer so that a' clearer picture of the scope and boundaries of the area emerges. The definition must be flexible without being indiscriminate and selective without being over-narrow.

What is Technology?

1.5 As we recognised above, the definition of both "technology" and "transfer" must be agreed before technology transfer can be analysed. What then is technology? If we start with Donald Schon's wide definition of technology [7] as "any tool or technique, any product or process, any physical equipment or method of doing or making, by which human capability is extended"

and if we ask what is this something which extends human capability we are likely to come to the view that technology is the body of practical knowledge techniques and equipment which people use to enlarge their work power, their ability to overcome constraints, their dominance over natural forces. The paper by Bell and Hill (Chapter 18) develops this view of technology in some detail.

1.6 If we move on to ask what is technology made of, the answer is simply technology. We have a nest of dolls situation; as you take apart any technology, you find many more technologies inside and many more inside each of these. Think of a process plant for making the weedkiller paraquat — a piece of innovation in which one of the authors was intimately concerned. Sodium is reacted with pyridine to make an intermediate which is further processed through a number of stages to produce the weedkiller. The paraquat manufacturing technology not only contains some important parts of sodium handling technology, it also depends completely on the existence and functioning of that technology for a vital material supply; likewise for pyridine and all other chemical materials used. Furthermore, every vessel, pipe and instrument on the process plants embodies other technologies. Of course, the paraquat plant is more than its component technologies just as any system is more than its parts.

Staying with this weedkiller it is easy to see how, in extending the capability of the farmer in matters of weeding and ploughing and seeding, the paraquat technology becomes embodied with, and in, a whole array of farming technologies. For example, it changes farming practice, maybe radically, by replacing the plough by a chemical, and it may demand parallel creation of enabling technologies such as special equipment for its application. Nonetheless, the net effect is simply to add one more piece of technology to an existing array; technology is absorbed into other technology, very probably displacing some existing technologies in the process.

But if we accept a definition as broad as Schon's, then almost anything which might be the subject of a transfer process could be called "technology". And if we allow this we run the risk of covering up differences once again. For instance many authors have found it necessary to distinguish "science" from "technology", and Brooks has postulated boundaries for technology and

6

argued from this that many things lie outside the definition of technology

"technology is essentially a specifiable and reproducable way of doing things ... the term technology does not span the whole domain of human action but only that part which can be specified in a replicable way. Thus it excludes many human skills and arts which, at least at the present time, cannot be codified, but must be learned from experience and by doing."

We do not accept the limitation that Brooks imposes on the concept of technology; much of human capability lies in the exercise of craft skills which can certainly not be codified but which nevertheless can be transferred. *Bricolage* is a term used by Levi-Strauss to denote a non-professional and instinctive craftsmanship. On this Sypher writes [8]. "A great deal of Leonardo da Vinci's work in both art and science was *bricolage*; the charge has been made again and again that Leonardo was a failed scientist because he never sustained his inventiveness by theories, which is only one way of saying he was not academic." *Bricoleur* Leonardo may have been but there is no denying his claim to being a technologist of the greatest eminence. The implication of these various views about the definition of technology is that there is no easy way of defining the word so that it will help us put boundaries around the phenomena we are seeking to understand. A broad definition encompasses everything, without illuminating it, while a narrow definition excludes many types of activity which people clearly feel the need to discuss at meetings on "technology transfer". If we have to argue that a person's experience or problems are not relevant because he is discussing not "technology" but "science" or "information" then, while we may take our own semantic problems easier, we serve very little purpose.

1.7 With so much variation between the various definitions of technology it is hardly surprising that a variety of different views have been advanced about the activity of transfer. For instance Price, [9] having distinguished between science and technology discussed at length the way that each develops and evolves, building on previous knowledge within its own field, with relatively little cross-fertilization between science and technology. Similarly Gibbons and Johnston [10] have shown that the ways organisations interact with and use sources of technological information differ from the way they interact with scientific sources, and we have seen above that Brooks differentiates sharply between technology transfer and scientific information transfer. If we return to our example of the development and adoption of paraquat technology and examine the process from the developers' viewpoint rather than the users' we can see differences in the various transfer processes involved. These are differences of degree rather than kind, but significant ones nevertheless. In the early stages of innovation, invention and development, technologies and science and engineering are deeply implicated, being absorbed in the emerging new system or innovation. The inventor is aware of existing weed control technologies, he is aware of existing chemical technologies, of chemistry, of physics, of engineering, all of which he draws upon to extend his capability as an inventor. The designer calls on the technologies of computing, of drawing, of testing and so on, and the plant constructor has access to an array of construction and fabrication skills and techniques. The whole operation of innovation viewed as the progress from "invention" to "technology in the hands of the user" is characterised by identification, selection and absorption of relevant technologies, science, know-hows and skills. It is not surprising, therefore, that delegates at technology transfer symposia will insist on discussing innovation processes at their meetings. Our discussion of paraquat technology suggests that conceptual models of innovation should be surrounded by arrows indicating the input of existing technologies (and science) into the process. This idea is shown at least in part, in one of the earliest and most widely quoted models of innovation, by Myers and Marquis, (Figure 2.1) [11] and perhaps more explicitly in a recent one by Jervis (Figure 1.1).

1.8   We accept that there is as yet no completely satisfactory way to codify and describe some parts of our broad category of technology, especially those components which are bricolage. Because of this their transfer can only be achieved, as Brooks' states, by experience and by action. We will return later to the technology transfer learning process but before leaving the Brooks' definition, we must observe that it is precisely the view that a technology can be specified in a replicable way that leads to an underestimation of the problems of transferring it to less developed countries, (LDCs) a case strongly argued in Bell & Hill's paper and discussed further in Chapter 2. But the major consequence of our discussion is that, however we operate on the words "technology" and "transfer" we make little progress towards a clearer view of the field of play.

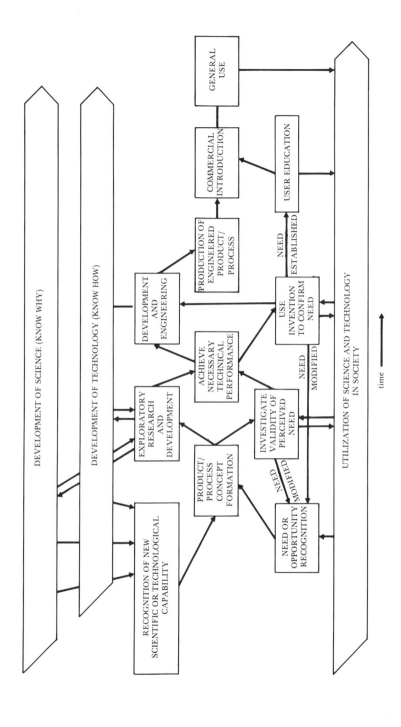

Figure 1.1 *The Process of Technological Innovation (after Jervis)*

9

The Importance of Context

1.9   If we sidestep the problem of defining technology for a moment, and accept Schon's definition as being sufficiently broad that all the movements usually discussed under the title of technology transfer are encompassed, then one particular virtue can be seen in the definitions which describe it as a shift of technology from one context to another. It is the emphasis on the need for the matching of technology to its environment. This need emerges from many of the recent studies of innovation and technology transfer [12], and was frequently stressed in discussions at the Stirling meeting. We believe that this stress on matching technology to environment is an important new emphasis which may be the key to many of the present problems of innovation and technical change. Where the sources of energy and materials are limited, where environmental impact is becoming a critical issue, securing a good fit of technology to the technical, social and economic context in which it is to be used becomes of overriding importance. It is argued by some that the era of the "heroic" innovation, which had such technical virtuosity that it could sweep aside all but the most severe economic and social barriers, is on the wane; Concorde may be the last and most spectacular of the genre. This is not to say that Concorde, or DDT, or PVC failed to fit their contexts. At the time of their emergence and often for many years afterwards they were perceived so to do so and hence their existence. The passage of time, the learning process and increased social awareness have changed the assessments to potential misfits. Today innovations fight every inch of the way by repeated and substantial modification to secure the acceptable fit to user context which is necessary for their survival.

1.10   The problem of context and of fitting technology to context is of general importance for those engaged in bringing about technological change today. The debate over the various definitions of technology transfer can be viewed in retrospect as an iterative approach to the heart of the system of problems facing us. Starting with the problem selected by space agencies and others of how to move some at least of their technology into the private and industrial sector, there emerged the shift of context type of definition. The attempt of innovators and R & D workers in general to adapt this definition to their work brought the whole of this context issue into a wider field and reveals it to be of critical significance for the successful prosecution of R & D now and in the future. Screening, testing, evaluation, should all be concerned with the securing of an acceptable fit of new technology or existing technology to the context in which it has to be used, recognising that the fit may result, in part at least, from modification of the context.

Repeatedly, in explaining their view of what they described as technology transfer, participants at the Stirling conference produced evidence of the importance of this contextual fit for technology. The importance shown in the SAPPHO work [13] of recognition of user need as a contributory factor to success in innovation may be seen as an expression of the contextual fit concept. We believe that any further progress in understanding the process of technological change, in all its guises, depends on recognising this contexted nature of technology. But, more than this, many of the contributions at Stirling led us to the inescapable conclusion that the transfer processes themselves are contexted, just as much as the technology.

What are the features which form this context? There are many, and most of them will be discussed, in some form, later. They comprise things as diverse as the experience and characteristics of people involved; the nature and size of organisations participating, and their objectives; the nature of the thing that is being transferred, be it technology or science or information; the stock of technical knowledge available to receivers or transferred technology; and the economic, social and cultural values of the societies between which the transfer happens.

Transfer Processes in Technical Change

1.11   As we have come to appreciate the unsatisfactoriness of existing definitions, and of the importance of the contexted nature both of technology and of the way in which it is transferred, so it becomes both inescapable and logical to choose as our central concept not technology transfer but transfer processes in technical change. In doing this the message we seek to convey, and the insight which we believe is new, is that there are a multitude of transfer processes which are occurring now, and which must continue to happen, which are as yet insufficiently understood. The key to further understanding of these processes lies in seeking to delineate and understand the context in which they happen, a context which is determined in part, but only in part, by technology. The change of nomenclature from technology transfer to transfer processes in technical change describes, we believe, as well as four words can, the plethora of circumstances and events usually discussed under the former appellation. In particular we believe that the concept of transfer processes in technical change gives us a better way of structuring and describing much of the existing information, and also makes it possible to represent, in a more systematic way than hitherto, the interests and requirements of those concerned with "technology transfer".

1.12 Going back to the Brooks' definition on p. 4 it may now be seen that it is unnecessarily confusing to sweep "vertical transfer", the incorporation of new scientific knowledge into technology, and "horizontal transfer", the adaptation of a technology from one application to another, into the same net under the overall label of "technology transfer". We would call them both transfer processes in technical change but only the second "technology transfer".

In the remainder of this book we try to present the material discussed at Stirling and analyse it in terms of transfer processes in technical change. We do not see our task as the establishment of a comprehensive taxonomy of transfer processes. Such a task is beyond the present state of our understanding — and, we suspect, of anyone else's. But we hope that the ideas and suggestions we put forward here may provide some building blocks which may prove to be useful later.

The focus of attention we urge with this shift is upon the *transfer* processes in various kinds of technical change. By adopting this more general concept, we can examine the similarities and the differences between the transfer of various kinds of knowledge, in various forms, by various mechanisms and across various interfaces. Technology transfer is returned to its original and significant meaning of the application of embodied technology to a use different from the one for which it was originally conceived.

1.13 In innovation the transfer processes differ in degree, if not in kind, as one moves back from the lateral shift of fully developed technology from one user context to another towards the early stages of innovation in which existing technologies are being brought to bear in creating a new technology. The key to the difference lies in the loss of degrees of freedom which accompany the incorporation of detail and the meeting of user specification. The early stages of the innovation process are characterised by a search, test and reject operation which is rapid and relatively inexpensive in resources; the later stages in which the emerging technology has assumed the detailed shape and design required for its incorporation into an end-user's system of work cannot be changed in any major way except by the very costly and slow process of going back to the drawing board. Hence, questions of contextual fit loom large in transfer of technology from one user context to another and agencies who seek to exploit spin-off from existing technology to other spheres of use through technology transfer have a bigger problem than may at first appear likely. Welles [4] demonstrated the difficulty of achieving transfer of well developed technology by his finding that the main point of entry from spin-offs from NASA technology was not in end-use packages but in earlier stages of engineering design studies.

1.14   From what we have already said it will be apparent to the reader that the transfer of scientific knowledge, techniques and hardware, as well as the more general issue of information flow, can also be included under the rubric of transfer processes in technical change. There are complex institutional and disciplinary barriers to such transfers as Burns recognised [14] and as Johnston describes in his paper (Chapter 9).

Despite these barriers the transfer of science and engineering into industry is a less intense problem than that of transferring technology precisely because science and engineering are inherently more transferable than technology. With science and engineering we are dealing with knowledge, methods and practice, all of which are embodied in hireable people trained to retrieve information from the literature. The universality of science and its firm commitment to publication greatly eases the associated transfer processes. But with technology we are dealing with applied knowledge, usually embodied in usable products and components or processes, and by comparison with science, the transfer of technology is greatly hindered. The free market competitive economy rests on the erection and maintenance of barriers to transfer of technology. These arise from competition and commercial confidentiality; patents; a fragmented and inadequate literature which is poorly structured and not easily searched for retrieval. There may also be legislation against technology transfer. Not only are there barriers to technology transfer, but there are also formidable obstacles to the transfer of information relating to all aspects of innovation, including transfer processes, as academics who have attempted research in this area of industrial activity will know only too well.

1.15   When people examine transfer processes in technical change they do so for a variety of reasons. If a major part of the innovation process consists of transfers of one sort or another perhaps it would help to look at the total activity to seek the objectives, and to suggest modifications to practice which we expect to aid in the securing of those objectives. If we accept the ethical basis of welfare economics as being linked with the criterion of partial or pseudo Pareto optimality, meaning that we are prepared to implement change which gives a net benefit to society even though some may be worse off as a result of the change, the question arises as described below. However, it must be noted that, in many quarters the partial Pareto ethic is strongly challenged. Society may not subscribe openly to the proposition that the good of the many may be accepted at the cost of loss to a few; improved crop yields at the cost of loss of wild life for example. Nonetheless society does implicitly accept such trade-offs — people motor and thereby accept the cost of road accidents, or consume the products of a factory despite accidents which could be completely eliminated only if the factory were to be closed.

In trying to secure the best net benefits to human capability our present and emerging technologies permit, where should we seek to apply the priorities — in creating new technologies or transferring existing ones? The question is not crisp because the two categories are not mutually exclusive, as our discussion of transfer processes in technical change reveals. As we have seen in earlier sections the essence of new technology is the absorption of and development of existing technology.

Perhaps the difficulty lies in the objectives. If we genuinely wish to use our technology-building talents to extend human capability in the most effective way, we may have to give less emphasis to the objective of using R & D to secure market domination and control. The urge to temporary monopoly creation through patentable innovation puts an exaggerated premium on novelty. (It also substantially hinders transfer — at least in the short term). The patent system, geared to the encouragement of innovation by protection of inventions, throws the emphasis of business in developed countries on the creation of new technology in the sense of patentable products and processes. True these continue to extend human capability but maybe not in the most effective way for mankind as a whole. The criterion of benefit to mankind as a whole takes cost-benefit beyond its conventional national boundaries. There are no rules against this but global cost-benefit analysis, to be meaningful, needs global authority for its implementation. The World Health Organisation evidently has aspirations in this direction, as its sponsoring of a code of practice for technology transfer reveals [15]. But the response to this document from industry and from OECD [16] shows very clearly that the world is not yet ready for decisions based on global cost-benefit analysis.

14

But, such is the pace of change in this area, as we go to press in 1978 the world seems a good deal readier to consider transfer processes from an international standpoint than it was in 1974.

1.16 It is arguable that the needs of developing countries, the social and economic problems of poverty and disease, the political overtones and outcomes of these problems, the problems of the conservation of the environment and the prevention of the exhaustion of raw material and energy supplies, are now priority tasks for those who would extend human capability in the most effective way for the closing decades of the twentieth century. Should these be our objectives, the emphasis of technology builders and those who deploy them might arguably be away from patentable technological novelty and towards the extension and modification of existing technology into forms appropriate to solving the new problems. As indicated above, this formulation presents great political issues, including the possible demise of the free market economy as we know it, the complete abandonment of belief in the guiding functions of Adam Smith's "invisible hand" in the direction of public good, and effective world government!

1.17 In considering the function of transfer processes we can also remark that organisations, and especially small and medium sized high-technology firms, increasingly look to technology transfer as an alternative to *ab initio* research and development for much of their new business. This view arises in part from the daunting and increasing costliness of full-scale research and development today and in part to the movement of such firms into diverse fields of often unfamiliar technology in their attempts to seek new and more profitable business areas [17]. So we find, for example, speciality chemical manufacturers becoming interested in building materials and in engineering and communication systems. Movement away from the familiar well-understood technological base can rarely be by means other than the assimilation of substantial amounts of existing or partly developed technology from outwith the firm.

1.18 Doubts can, and have, been raised about the desirability of technology transfer, and it is now many years since Schumpeter [18] uncompromisingly equated innovation with progress. Nevertheless, accepting Schon's definition of technology as being that which extends man's capability (and recognising that man is capable of evil as well as of good) we argue that the transfer of technology must be still equated with progress in this and immediately following decades, with the important following provisos.

In Schumpeter's day the future (from an American viewing

point) could be seen as more of the present. In this light extending man's capability by more and more innovation was clearly progress. Technology was a dominant force for change which swept aside constraints, human and physical, with a ruthless and crude arrogance. Today other forces are dominant and are shaping the future; technology steps down from being a pace-maker. One would like to think that sociology now calls the step — but this is academic naivety; sociology like economics and psychology follows the social and political movements, maybe shining a torch from the rear.

The other critical proviso is that on a world view, new technology which merely extends the capability of industrialised or post-industrial society is certainly not to be equated with progress. This simply exacerbates the imbalance between nations and increases political instability. This raises ethical and political issues which were touched on at the Stirling meeting only in the opening paper. An interesting analysis of the opposing tensions of national states and international technology, which underlies much of the political debate concerning the role of multinational enterprises in technology transfer is to be found in the work of Lindbeck [19].

The Case for the Study of Transfer Processes in Technical Change

1.19   Students of technology transfer, or as we now prefer to say, transfer processes in technical change, are concerned with ways in which research and analysis can make an effective contribution to understanding the way transfers happen. We believe that the improved understanding gained in this way can make a valuable contribution to improving the effectiveness of transfer processes.

Throughout this book, and especially in the section on methodology, we discuss the contribution research and analysis of transfer processes in technical change can make to improving transfer performance. The conference revealed that not only is the study of transfer processes in technical change in a very immature state but that there is a good deal of scepticism on the part of practitioners concerning the usefulness of academic work on the subject. The writers of this book do not share the view of the sceptical practitioners, but are keenly aware of the need to improve the effectiveness of research and analysis as a prerequisite to its acceptance by practitioners and to its ultimate usefulness. There is, of course, no lack of problems to study. One of the most pressing is the location of existing technology relevant to a specified problem area. Current awareness of technologies and technology information retrieval systems are greatly needed. In this respect, as noted above, technology information flow is much less well developed than corresponding science awareness and retrieval systems. The work of Allen and his concept of "gatekeepers" is, of course, relevant here (20).

1.20 It is pertinent to ask to what degree those studying technological transfer topics are able to do useful work to further the aims outlined above from an academic base in an industrialised economy. At the best, we suggest, they may help the technology builders by an improved analysis of the transfer processes in technical change, while remaining aware that the models and methodologies of transfer in the industrialised economy context are not directly relevant in all their aspects to the new problems. The building of the technology relevant to the new problems, such as the development of the productive capacity of a developing country, must rest with those whose base is in the developing economy. The researcher in U.S., U.K. and Europe can aspire no higher than to be consultants to such builders, and to their own governments, on matters of transfer. This topic is developed at length by Bell & Hill (Paper 12).

1.21 In the industrialised countries the study of transfer processes in technical change may be expected to be beneficial if one makes the assumption that whatever the political and economic diagnosis of the current ailments may reveal, the improved hygiene of more effective movement of technologies (and science) among innovators and across departmental, establishment, firm and industry barriers can be beneficial. In this context our existing models may not be fundamentally unsound (as Bell & Hill argue that they are for the developing country situation) and their updating and improvement is relevant, with emphasis on the transfer processes in technical change aspects rather than the technology transfer one.

It should also be noted that the developing country technology transfer and transfer processes in technical change models are not without relevance to substantial parts of the industrial scene in developed countries and that much might be done to improve the economic health of so-called developed countries by improved understanding of transfer processes and especially how the body of knowledge and know-how may best be brought to bear on the problems of small and medium sized firms and establishments. It has indeed been claimed by some that the promoters of intermediate technology have so far found more interest coming from the developed countries than the less developed ones.

1.22 We may however conclude this introductory section by observing that there is, in our opinion, a long-term need — implicit in much of the current writing on technology transfer — to shift the emphasis of study from technology transfer depicting solely bonus spin-off benefits from existing research and development programmes to transfer processes aimed more directly at meeting human needs. We have to look towards a new context, starting from an assessment of needs, identifying the contributions that technologies may make to extending social capability in these areas and seeking to facilitate the transfer processes appropriate to establishing these technologies in their new contexts. It is, of course, naive to assume that students, or practitioners, of transfer processes in technical change can have any direct effects on these essentially political issues. But the associated political and economic issues are important ones for man's future, and those engaged in the field of transfer processes in technical change must be keenly aware of this background to their work. This holds equally for the practitioners of transfer in industry and elsewhere. Whilst in those industrialised countries with a free market economy the assault on satisfaction of needs is likely to remain indirect and mediated by market forces the awareness of need and of contextual fit as a prerequisite for successful innovation is now a dominant factor in research and development work and project management. Moreover, as indicated earlier, research and development are likely to become more dependent upon transfer processes than they have been hitherto.

We believe that the researcher and academic has a role to play in the reorientation that there must be if these new challenges are to be met and the new goals achieved. A better understanding of the mechanisms underlying transfer processes in technical change, if itself effectively transferred from the scholars to the doers, can play its part in improving transfer performance. That is the justification for meetings such as the one we write about, and for publication of this book. We are aware in saying this that we create the yardstick by which we may be judged.

References

[1] Schumacher, E. F., *Small is Beautiful: A Study of Economics as if People Mattered*, Blond & Briggs, London, 1973.
[2] Pirsig, R.M., *Zen and The Art of Motor Cycle Maintenance*, Corgi Books, London, 1976.

[3] Doctors, S., *The Role of Federal Agencies in Technology Transfer*, M.I.T. Press, Cambridge, Mass., 1969.

[4] Welles, J.G. in *Technology Transfer* by Davidson, H.F., Cetron, M.J. and Coldhar, J. D., Editors, Noordhoff, Leiden, 1974.

[5] Brooks, H., "National Science Policy and Technology Transfer" in *Proceedings of a Conference on Technology Transfer and Innovation*, N.S.F., 67-5, Washington, D.C., 1966.

[6] Ackoff, R.L., *Redesigning the Future*, Wiley, N.Y. 1974.

[7] Schon, D., *Technology and Change*, Pergamon, London, 1967.

[8] Sypher, W., *Literature and Technology*, Vintage Books, N.Y., 1971.

[9] Price, J. de S., "The Structures of Publication in Science and Technology" in *Factors in the transfer of Technology*, Gruber & Marquis, Editors, M.I.T. Press, Cambridge, Mass., 1969.

[10] Gibbons, M. & Johnston, R., "The Roles of Science in Technological Innovation" *Research Policy* 1974 (3).

[11] Myers, S. & Marquis, D.G., *Successful Industrial Innovations*, N.S.F. 69-17, 1969.

[12] *R & D Management* "Technology Transfer", Special Issue, 1976.

[13] Achilledellis, B. *et al.*, *Success and Failure in Industrial Innovation: Report of Project SAPPHO*, Centre for Industrial Innovation, London, 1972.

[14] Burns, T., "Models, Images & Myths" in Gruber & Marquis, *Factors in the Transfer of Technology*, M.I.T. Press, Cambridge, Mass., 1969.

[15] *Draft Outline of an International Code of Conduct on Transfer of Technology*, UNCTAD, Geneva, May 1975.

[16] *OECD Declaration on International Investment and Multinational Enterprises*, Paris, June 1976.

[17] Wilmot, P. "Technology Transfer in a Multinational Firm" in Cetron, M., Davidson, H. (eds) *Industrial Technology Transfer*, Noordhoff, Leiden, 1977.

[18] Schumpeter, J., "The Instability of Capitalism" in *The Economics of TechnologicalChange* by Rosenberg, Editor, Penguin Books, London, 1971.

[19] Lindbeck, A., *Kyklos*, 20 (1975) 23.

[20] Allen, T.J., "Managing the Flow of Technology" M.I.T. Press, Cambridge, Mass., 1977.

Chapter 2

MODELS OF TRANSFER PROCESSES IN TECHNICAL CHANGE

2.1 Having decided to examine the problems of technology transfer within a framework of transfer processes in technical change, we can draw on studies of all the phenomena which fall within this broad rubric, including innovation, diffusion and information flow, for general models of the transfer process.

The vital role of models in the theoretical explanations developed by the natural sciences has been increasingly recognised of late [1, 2] In particular the imaginative manipulation allowed by the essentially qualitative nature of models directs the attention of the scientist to new areas, new questions and new possibilities. The more precise mathematical models also have the same power to generate new perceptions.

2.2 In an immature and underdeveloped field such as we are discussing here, it is important to recognise that much can be learnt from the wisdom-based contributions of practitioners. These may lack rigour or objectivity but nevertheless they do reflect a perceived interrelationship between activities and events. At a meeting such as the one at Stirling any participant who makes a contribution of the sort "In my organisation we do it this way ..." or "we have found that it is important to ensure that ..." is implying an operational model, for all the faults it may possess. Most importantly, these perceptions can offer valuable insights which can contribute towards the development of more general models.

2.3 Rather than starting with a discussion of some of the models of "technology transfer" which have been advanced, it may be more helpful to examine those which reflect the wider process of technical change, and in particular models of innovation and diffusion. In that we are concerned with transfer processes in technical change we should expect to be able to place models of these transfer processes within those which describe the broader scene.

Models of Innovation

2.4   Models of innovation have customarily been represented graphically by boxes interconnected by arrows. This is, of course, partly a device used because it is convenient for the draughtsman. However this representation is itself a model, commonly used in such diverse fields as cybernetics, communication theory and organisational design, which has its origins in electrical circuit diagrams. Adoption of this model entails the assumption that phenomena can be divided up into events or processes which can conveniently be considered as relatively self contained activities (the boxes), receiving inputs or stimuli, operating on them, and providing outputs directed towards other boxes. The inputs and outputs are the arrows.

Boxes can be of a number of types. They may denote events, such as "need or opportunity recognition" or "idea formulation", and they may refer to activities, like "research" or "development".

The compartmentalisation into boxes provides a convenient way to describe the system which is being investigated, the boxes representing a division of the system into what appears to be its component parts. Of course it is always possible to take the components apart and go to a lower level of aggregation. Just as we had a nest of dolls situation with technology so we have with components of a system. In today's television sets electronic components are mounted on panels or circuit boards. The service engineer repairing a set takes it apart for repair, but replaces a panel, discarding good components with the faulty, rather than replacing the one or two elements in the panel which have failed. The engineer stops disassembling at the panel stage, because it is the most suitable way for him to operate. Similarly the modeller describing a system splits it into components and stops when he has gone far enough for his purpose; that is it is the purpose of the modeller which determines the appropriate level of disaggregation.

2.5   The description of a system by reference to its component parts is an easy one for us to accept, because it fits with our everyday experience. The developed, industrialised economy is marked by increasing specialisation and institutionalisation of skills. But the division into boxes causes problems, in two ways. Firstly, the activity based division may not reflect the organisational or skill-based compartmentalisation which occurs in real life. Thus in the process of technological innovation the activity called "research" may, and in fact usually does, involve scientists and technologists in universities, others in the research organisations established and maintained by industry, and yet more in the production and engineering departments. Secondly the box arrangement assumes that the output from one box is in a form suitable for the input to the next — but this does not always happen. A parallel in domestic electronics is that one cannot use any loudspeaker with any amplifier — it is necessary to match the impedance of the speaker with the output impedance of the amplifier.

2.6   In the past most attention has been focussed on the boxes in the box and arrow models, with the assumption that if the components within a box operate properly the output will automatically be accepted by the next box. People have concentrated on the box and ignored the arrows, whereas our focus on transfer *processes* throws stress on the importance of the arrows though we do not suggest that the boxes are unimportant. Our attention on the arrows however, leads us to ask questions such as "what are they?" — in other words what medium carries the output from one box to another; is the analogue of the wire between amplifier and speaker or "ether" between speaker and ear more appropriate? What are the obstacles which may prevent the arrows reaching their targets — are there barriers of one sort or another in the way?

Thus the transfer processes with which we are concerned are activities represented in the classical schematic models of innovation, such as that of Myers and Marquis (Figure 2.1) [3], and many others by arrows leading from box to box. It is notable that most models of innovation have concentrated on the content and arrangement of the boxes. Nevertheless, to the extent that innovation depends on the processes represented by the arrows, such studies can provide useful insights into transfer mechanisms.

2.7   When institutions or departments become established their walls or boundaries can modify, moderate or even prevent transfers. The boundaries created by the institutionalisation process can become barriers, and indeed the phrase "barriers to transfer" is commonly found in the literature on technology transfer. Since boundaries present potential barriers it is tempting to suggest that the solution to many problems may lie in removing the boundaries. This may have superficial appeal, and has been the aim of some organisational changes in industry in recent years. For instance the move towards matrix organisations in industry, and the emphasis on multidisciplinary teamwork, is an attempt to reduce the problems caused by institutional or departmental separation of marketing, production, engineering and finance from R & D. For

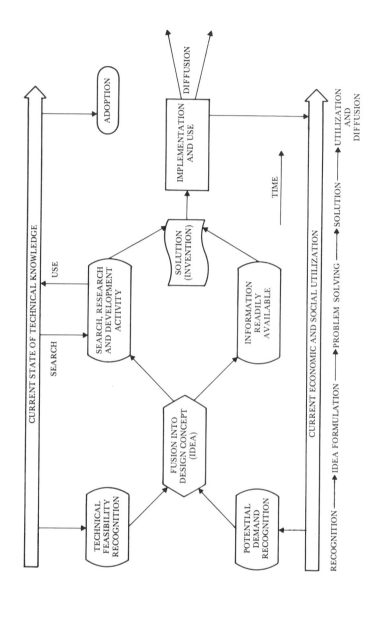

Figure 2.1 *The Process of Technical Innovation*
(Source: Myers and Marquis, [3])

24

similar reasons the idea of a separate, central, corporate R & D organisation is less popular than a few years ago.

This thinking misses the point. Not only is the existence of boundaries an inescapable part of modern society, they also have a necessary part to play and their elimination would be undesirable, a point Bradbury makes in the opening paper (Paper 1). It has been shown that institutional barriers in science and technology have their roots in the developments of the 19th century [4]. Johnston (Paper 3) demonstrates the vital role of institutionalisation and specialisation in science and technology for the build up of specialist skills and know how. McCarthy also argues (Paper 5) that the divisionalisation of company structure can be a source of strength, and we believe this to be an important point, although perhaps not commonly accepted. Subsystems can be a source of strength to the whole system, and not merely an undesirable artifice imposed to accommodate man's inability to comprehend or to manage the whole.

2.8   However recognition of the inescapability, and the desirability, of departments or institutions, does not deny that these form barriers to transfer. Such barriers are in part a consequence of the existence of departments the very separation of which, in one way or another, may inhibit information flow or communication. They may also result from the characteristics of the members of such departments in so far as they traditionally look to particular sources for their information or ideas, a difference which may be more fundamental than one purely consequent on the organisational structures of enterprises.

Models of Diffusion

2.9   In the area of technical change there is one phenomenon which has been the subject of much research, and for which many models have been proposed. It is the diffusion of innovation. Where does diffusion fit within our concept of transfer processes in technical change, and how do models of diffusion relate to descriptions of transfer processes?

We suggest that diffusion must be seen as a special case of the broad category of transfer processes in technical change. The models of Rogers [5], Mansfield [6] and others have the common feature of describing the spreading of the usage of a technology within a population of users, usually within a group characterised by some common element of productive activity such as farming or mining. The lateral shift type of technology transfer implies a shift of technology from one population or group of users to another say, from farming to mining. In so far as the contextual details of one group differ from those of another this "lateral shift" operation is likely to be harder, and to be impeded by more barriers, than movement by diffusion within a group. We think it useful to make this distinction between lateral shift and diffusion because it may improve our understanding of barriers to transfer processes. Mansfield's [7] quantitative models of diffusion of innovation may be used as starting points for the construction of models of transfer processes, recognising that the characteristics of the barriers to lateral shift transfer are likely to be more restrictive than in diffusion. Of course, it is recognised that even diffusion is rarely a simple imitative process. Bell and Hill (Paper 12) argue that adaptive innovation is frequently necessary to satisfy the needs of a non-standard market.

2.10   We would expect the horizontal transfer of technology to be followed by diffusion. Let us take an imaginary case of the innovation of a new harvester for wheat. This extends in some way the capability of wheat farmers, maybe by saving costs, time or reducing crop losses. The acceptance of this innovation by early adopters and its rate of spread through the population of wheat farmers will be determined by perceived characteristics of the innovation, of the wheat farming community, by social and psychological attributes of individuals and groups, and by pay-offs expected and costs — in ways thoroughly explored by Rogers [5], Mansfield [6], and Toulmin [8]. It may be assumed that the process is catalysed by a complex of factors including promotional and service support by those selling the new technology. This is diffusion.

2.11   If we now wish to apply this new technology to maize harvesting it is evident that we have a new type of problem of which the obvious characteristics are the requirement for substantial redesign of the harvester to meet new technical requirements of maize harvesting, and to suit it to the experience and capabilities of the new population of farmers in whom we are now interested. This is transfer and it implies a reworking of the innovation process before the shift or transfer can be achieved. Once the new design problems are solved and assuming the product has advantages over existing maize harvesters we may expect diffusion through the population of maize farmers to begin, aided as before by promotional and service activities. The rate of diffusion of the maize harvester is unlikely to be identical with or even close to that of the wheat harvester because there are now different values

26

on the critical rate-controlling variables given a new technology-use system and a different adopting community of population.

In short we see diffusion as one of the numerous transfer processes within technical change, but we distinguish it from lateral shift transfer which is another special category of transfer process in which there is a contextual shift of technology from one user to another.

Some New Models of Transfer Processes

2.12 We mentioned, in the first Chapter, the distinction made by Brooks [9] between information transfer and technology transfer. The implication of that discussion, and of our focus on context, is that we cannot discuss the various models of barriers without taking into account either what is being transferred or the objectives of the transfer process. The models discussed at Stirling fell more or less clearly into two categories, one corresponding fairly closely to what Brooks would have called technology transfer and the other being close to his concept of information transfer.

2.13 The first category of transfer processes might be called "activity transfer" and it occurs when the transfer accompanies a change of venue, or of responsibility, for the development of a piece of technology. Examples of this type of transfer are the transfer of development work on a new product from the R & D Department to Production, or from a government laboratory to a firm. Transfer of technology to less developed countries also falls into this class.

The second type of transfer process relates to the input of information experience, or skill needed by a particular group to accomplish its tasks. For example, the input of marketing information, about customer needs and attitudes, or of details about new product opportunities, to the work of a Research and Development department fall into this class. Clearly, this second type "information transfer", also accompanies "activity transfer" but the converse is not necessarily true.

2.14 Bradbury (Paper 1) puts forward a conceptual model for the activities which culminate in technology being applied for a purpose other than the one for which it was first developed. This process is the one to which Brooks [9] gave the name "horizontal transfer" and which Bradbury termed "lateral shift" (Figure 7.2). His model anticipated much of the subsequent discussion in the way that it described how technology developed and applied in one context cannot be applied in another without some adaptation or modification. To apply technology in a new context demands the reworking of at least some of the later stages of the innovation process. Descriptions of the activities of the Government Research Establishments and some of the Research Associations indicated that one of their primary difficulties was ensuring that this adaptation was done appropriately and effectively.

Jervis in particular built on this concept by suggesting that early attempts by Government laboratories at this horizontal transfer had relied on a two stage process, a transfer from the laboratory to a manufacturer or supplier who would then be responsible for all dealings with the eventual user. This approach had proved to be unsatisfactory and a three-cornered relationship with the originating laboratory, end user and manufacturer had been found necessary. In terms of our discussion of context the reason that this triangular relationship is needed is easy to see. Transfer to the user requires the adaptation of the technology, but that adaptation can only be done if the context of the technology is understood. It is much easier for the creators of a technology to adapt it to a new use than it is for an intermediary. And when the intermediary, the supplier or manufacturer, is selected both ability to handle the technology and possession of suitable links with potential users (in marketing terms things such as sales forces, distribution channels, after-sales service capability, and credibility with the potential customers) are important criteria.

2.15   The second conceptual model put forward at the meeting is contained in the paper by Morphet (Paper 10). He is concerned not with an overall model of transfer but with a description of one of the components. Morphet argues that an organisation will not be uniformly receptive to new ideas, but that receptivity will vary with time. The model he proposes is based on theory, at present without any supporting evidence, and is advanced in the context of the single-product firm. Discussion at the meeting showed that the basic concept, that there is a time when a firm's receptivity to ideas may be at a maximum (the New Idea Point) had some credibility. Mansfield [6] has shown that for a number of processes in the U.S., maximum innovation appeared to occur at about 75% capacity. At full production the surplus capacity necessary for experimentation is not available. At low production, the resources are not available for investment. The main problem with Morphet's approach lay in the difficulty of extending the model from the hypothetical single product company to the multiproduct firm found in practice, and finding a way of collecting empirical data which would verify the concept.

The concept of a New Idea Point has potential significance for those involved in generating and "marketing" innovative ideas — whether they be in external organisations in the business of selling "contract research" or "technology transfer" or in the firm itself. It would appear that the reverse of the New Idea Point, a time of minimum or at least low, receptivity, is easier to identify than the time of maximum receptivity. For instance, when a chemical firm has just made a decision to introduce a new process, and is at the expensive transition from pilot plant to full scale operation, it is unlikely to be willing to consider other new processes aimed at the same end product. The New Idea Point theory is another manifestation of the importance of context. In this case it stresses the importance for the purveyor of new ideas of trying to anticipate the reaction of potential customers, and to detect incentives and barriers to their acceptance.

2.16   It was also suggested that there might be a point of maximum transferability for a piece of technology, when barriers to transfer would be at their lowest. The participant who made this point spoke of a node in the curve relating complexity of an emerging technology against time, at which complexity would be at a minimum.

> "What I am suggesting is that maybe there is a point at which so much of the complexity (of the early prototypes) has been eliminated and at which important user interactions have been built in, so that there is a sort of complexity minimum. As soon as it gets into the hands of the design engineers and production department the complexity will increase again".

At what stage this occurs — if it occurs — must depend on the context into which it is to be moved. If the context is an end-use one then the MTP — maximum transferability point — will be near the end of the development process; but if the context is that of another technology builder a much earlier phase of development, where the transferred technology is both credible and plastic or mouldable, may turn out to be the MTP.

2.17   In terms of completeness perhaps the most comprehensive of the models advanced was the one by Bell and Hill (Paper 12), who put forward a model based on their experience of the problems of transferring technology to a developing country, Thailand. Bell and Hill comment that most models of innovation and technology transfer are inappropriate to the developing country situation, and that one of the primary reasons for this is that they ignore the need for a continuous interchange with a diversely located "technological stock", a body of knowledge and know-how

(Paper 12, Figure 1). Their argument is that all innovation and transfer processes need to draw on this stock of knowledge but in industrialised countries its existence can be, and in practice is, automatically assumed.

They argue that, in the context of transfer to less developed countries, this stock of knowledge does not exist. It is not merely that the receiving countries do not have the necessary scientific and technological infra-structure but that, if the technology being transferred has been chosen with due regard to all aspects of user needs and constraints, the necessary infra-structure may not exist even in the industrialised countries. This is because the technology appropriate to the less developed countries may have passed out of use in the industrialised countries so long ago that, to all intents and purposes, it is no longer available. In the majority of cases the developing countries need technology which is not at the leading edge of technical change but some way behind the trailing edge of practice in the industrialised countries. If it is no longer in use it is difficult to identify and retrieve information about it. It was pointed out that the stock of technical knowledge does not expand indefinitely. There comes a time when, as with memory, new inputs force existing information to be stored beyond easy recall. In Bell's phrase, where the stock of technical knowledge is concerned, "there is an awful lot which has fallen off the back and is not around any more".

2.18   The Bell and Hill model is, in fact, only another of the many contributions at Stirling which argued or indicated the need for a focus on context. It focussed attention on the specific difficulties that the needs and problems of the less developed countries pose, and by reflection onto the situation of the industrialised nations, revealed that most if not all of the models of transfer processes take important contextual features, such as the technological infrastructure, for granted; i.e. in the language of the model, critical boxes and arrows are assumed, or ignored.

2.19   Before moving on to discuss some of the concepts that these models illustrate there is a final point which should be made about the nature and limitations of models. Every model is only an appropriate description of events which occur within certain boundary conditions. Applied outside these boundaries the models are incapable of satisfactorily describing events, in the way that Newtonian mechanics can describe the vast majority of everyday situations involving force or motion, but must be replaced by quantum mechanics when the motion of small particles is being considered or by relativistic mechanics when velocities become large. Models should be extended only with care outside the context for which they were proposed. This caution is of particular relevance to policy-makers who may fail to appreciate the importance of context and appropriateness.

Models of the Context Function

2.20   Time and time again, in different ways, participants stressed that the fundamental concern in transfer processes was the understanding of the environment, attitudes, needs and skill of the receiver. The shift of context involved in transfer processes demands the adaptation and shaping of the technology to match in detail the constraints of the different system which comprises the new context. At every step in the transfer there must be dialogue between those who would transfer and those who would adopt; dialogue concerning design detail, specification detail, user need detail — contextual mapping to use the jargon of the morphological analysts. Such is the abstract nature of the language, it was argued, that any attempt to convey information about users needs or to describe systems purely by documentation cannot hope to be sufficient. It is only by the iterative process of information exchange culminating in direct verbal discussion with repeated readjustment of understanding and rephrasing of questions that a sufficient knowledge of context and specification can be achieved. The statement that an understanding of context is vital, is of course, of little use unless ways can be suggested of seeing that this happens in practice. Many of the mechanisms discussed in Chapter 3 describe attempts to ensure this.

Information inputs can be related to transfer processes in another way. The transfer of information or ideas about technology can stimulate action which leads to "activity transfer". In fact the early attempts to encourage utilisation of developed technology for new purposes, Brooks' [9] horizontal transfer, were, as can be seen from Doctors' [10] description, largely based on the assumption that dissemination of information about the technology would lead to complete transfer.

2.21   A paper given by Tressel at the 1975 NATO Advanced Study Institute on Technology Transfer [11] indicated that it may be possible to catalyse the initiation of "activity transfer" by encouraging a search procedure. It is perhaps instructive to look at Tressel's paper as an example of a screening operation and to suggest that it may offer an approach to the modelling of transfer processes.

The terminology used in this section was suggested by Baines, Bradbury and Suckling who created the terms for characterising screening parameters [12] and which are referred to by McCarthy (Paper 5). This model of the search situation describes the sequential process of screening as a method of resolving the dilemma of sampling and observational errors characteristic of such situations. They are characterised by there being a limited number of "winners" to be found in a large number of candidates; screens of increasingly sharp definition are employed sequentially to reject "losers" and retain winners, thereby coping with sampling errors and preserving the survivors of the screens for more detailed examination, thereby adjusting to problems of observational errors. The terms "mesh size" (to indicate rejection rate) "target definition" (meaning degree of specification of rejection criteria) "sufficiency" (to describe the match of the test criteria to the real-life situations they simulate) and "abstraction" (to indicate the theory-dependence of the test criteria) are used to characterise the screening operations. Tressel's problem was the matching of individual members of an array of available U.S. public sector patents (assigned to DOD, NASA, AEC, etc.) to individual users out of an array of possibly interested people or groups. Here was a double screening operation in a back-to-back situation. The patent array was subjected to a fine mesh wide target screen by a panel of experts who were instructed to reject ruthlessly on a perusal-and-judgement basis. The survivors were now brought to potential users by a coarse mesh wide target screen which selected a wide spectrum of potential users of the surviving patents.

2.22   When making available to the target population information about patents in the sample *abstraction* was high, only the very broad concepts of the technology being described. *Sufficiency* on the other hand was kept low − the aim was to get as many fish into the net as possible by reducing demands on the readers' time. Sufficiency was increased in progressive stages by allowing survivors of each round (i.e. those who remained interested) to come back and ask for more information.

Tressel's approach is interesting in terms of context. The deliberately broad and abstracted description of the patents encouraged potential users to envisage them as relevant to uses that their originators may not have anticipated; and the iterative process of collecting additional information gave the originators a way of beginning to understand the context in which the technologies might be used.

2.23   Most of the above discussion has been most relevant to "horizontal" transfer processes, but we must also consider the important activities of absorbing science and technology into new technology development. In these transfer processes it is to be expected that benefit to transferee will be the dominant driving force since in technology development — say in the R & D process — the developer or innovator is actively searching and keenly receptive to any sources which may help him and of which he is aware. Accessibility of the useful pieces of science and technology needed by the innovator is likely to be a critical parameter, and it may be that search models of operational research could form a basis for modelling transfer processes of this sort. The theory of screening has been developed more towards finding objects (submarines for example) and products (drug invention) than towards science and technology finding. The techniques of morphological analysis and of Synectics are attempts to structure the search problem and as such may offer something to the transfer process modeller.

We chose Tressel's paper to illustrate a screening model of transfer processes, which we believe to have some generality. It throws emphasis on an aspect of transfer too readily overlooked following Burn's underscoring of the role of agents, namely the key role of impersonal approaches through media (agencies) in facing up to the sampling problem of finding those who may be interested in receiving offered technology. It is only after this critical step that the quality of the transfer operation can be raised by bringing in the agents to eliminate the observational errors inherent in the work of agencies.

2.24   It is evident that in considering the absorption of science and technology as they affect the innovator we are back to the scientific and technological information retrieval problems which have for so long been the province of information scientists. Although we did not discuss this area at Stirling the science and technology seeking and absorbing function of inventors and innovators is an important aspect of transfer processes. The starting point for modelling these features is likely to be found in the work of Allen [13] and Pelz and Andrews [14].

But there are some differences which we can already notice. A feature of the technology transfer screening situation is a double sampling problem due to almost infinitely wide spectrum of users coupled with an infinitely large number of "pieces" of technology. Tressel treated the two populations sequentially. But where the innovator is seeking to transfer science or technology into his project one of the two populations, the project, is tightly defined.

Industrial information retrieval systems are designed to meet this case.

2.25 From this discussion it should become obvious that in many cases "information transfer" is a necessary and natural precursor to "activity transfer" and that one process may grow into the other. One of the most famous and most widely quoted statements about transfer is the aphorism of Burns that "technology transfer is a process of agents not agencies" [4]. This model of transfer being achieved by the movement of people has wide support, and received more at Stirling, although, as Johnston points out (Paper 3), concepts have evolved little since Burns first made his comment in 1966.

The transfer of people is a way of breaking down barriers, and is at its most effective in activity transfer. For instance, the needs and constraints of user and designer all evolve and are modified in technology transfer. To adapt the transfer process efficiently to accommodate such changes calls for the removal of unnecessary constraints on communication among participants, and therein lies the strength of Burn's aphorism. One comes back here to the familiar cyclic model of problem solving in which recognition, analysis, selection, implementation, control follow each other, leading to the recognition and recycle of a modified problem situation. When agents communicate they have the opportunity of rapidly and repeatedly traversing the problem analysis cycle and a corresponding better chance of success in the transfer process.

2.26 We mentioned earlier in this chapter the need for a three-cornered relationship between originator, manufacturer and user. Bringing the consumer of technology into a three-cornered examination of the transfer process with transferor and the transferee is a natural extension of the emphasis several recent studies have placed on the importance of the innovator understanding user need if he is to be successful. This point is especially important for government establishments that aspire to transfer technology to industry. Consulting the user prior to or during the transfer process and giving him the opportunity to influence product and process shaping, may be expected to make the final output of the transfer process more easily accepted by the user. In the transfer processes early in the development of a technology all parties will probably be at some remove from the ultimate user.

Important as it is, the use of agents is only one way to identify and remove barriers to transfer. Increasingly organisations are using more formal techniques to avoid or surmount such barriers. For example, Synectics, or for that matter any one of the array of

34

methods of encouraging lateral thinking or brainstorming, contributes to barrier penetration by presenting a person-to-person guided search and review process which can lead to the transfer of information needed for problem solving in technology development. The question and answer seeking and exchanging of such sessions may be seen as a highly effective screening operation in which problems and possible solutions are rapidly traversed in dialogue mode. Indeed it may be said that the whole force of that aphorism of Burns derives from the power of *people* to make institutional barriers sufficiently permeable for an effective transfer of information to take place through them. At the same time it is important to recognise that it is people, through the operation of factors like the NIH (not invented here) syndrome, that can prevent transfer processes.

2.27 We discussed earlier the concept that transfer will only be effective if what is transferred manages to achieve a satisfactory "fit" with the context into which it is being placed. But all transfer processes in technical change, including transfer from one user context to another, share the objective of changing the system into which the transfer occurs. In the case of technology development the transfer of science, other technology, or inventive ideas has the objective of changing the shape of the emerging system to make it more nearly conform with a desired specification. In the case of transfer of technology into a productive system — be this an industrial plant or a whole economic system of production — the objective is to change it towards greater productivity or improved quality or some other desired goal. In so far as change is the objective of transfer, a degree of *misfit* is an essential requirement for what is transferred; that technology which fits its context like a hand in a glove is not likely to achieve the purpose of changing beneficially the way of life of the transferee; at best, such hand-in-glove transfer confers simply the benefits of service to the transferee, perhaps by make-good work, restoring him to his pre-breakdown state of capability. In other words, effective transfer implies some disturbance of the system entered into; if there is no perturbation of the system on entry the transfer is likely to be of minimal impact.

2.28 "Fit" is determined by many factors and systems can tolerate a high degree of mismatch in some — but probably not all — aspects. This is demonstrated by the innovations which appear not as incremental changes to existing technology or logical extensions of trends but radical interventions such as the incursion of chemical technology into the textile industry or of electronics into the watch making industry.

The radical change is the hardest to achieve, and yet is the most significant. Firms (and industries) can disappear almost overnight if they do not see the challenges and adopt the new technology, and in fact one of the key features is knowing the right answer to the corporate strategist's standard question "what business are you in?". That firms survive such incursions of new technology demonstrates the robustness of organisations to change, yet in these extreme cases the need to understand context, and to appreciate where fit is needed, and where mismatch can be tolerated, is at its most urgent.

Implications for Future Modelling

2.29   We cannot conclude this section with any single model which encompasses all transfer processes in technical change. By its very nature the concept defies reduction to a single description. Any satisfactory representation would be composed of elements of the form of Figure 2.2, which is the basic component of all pictorial descriptions of innovation and transfer models. But each element would be capable of further sub-division, as in Figure 2.3 so that it could be represented as a network of interacting components, growing in complexity as the finer detail of "within box" activities is added [15]. In this way we can get a hierarchy of boxes and arrows which at the lowest level describe the point at which arrows represent exchanges between individual persons.

However we represent it diagrammatically, the emphasis in any model of transfer processes in technical change must be on movement or transfer and the constraints on such movements. No quantitative models of such movements were put forward at the Stirling meeting; indeed the subject area at its present state of development is poor in quantitative relationships, perhaps because of its immature state of development – a theme we will return to later. All that can be said here to conclude this section on models is that the emphasis placed on transfer processes and mechanisms makes it more than ever desirable to conduct further research into modelling of transfer processes. The fundamental need is the construction of models of barrier structure and penetration (perhaps based on analogies with biological membrane structures) and the identification experimentally of the parameters which control barrier penetration.

2.30   In attempting this the quantitative diffusion models of Mansfield [7] and others may be some guide, but no more than this. In the diffusion models imitation is a key parameter as well as

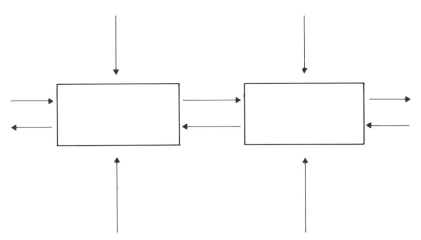

Figure 2.2

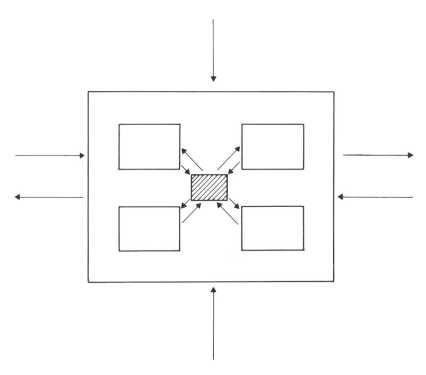

Figure 2.3

pay-off to the adopter and the size of investment demanded of him for the adoption. Barrier-penetration models for lateral shift technology transfer would be unlikely to use the imitation parameter; moreover since in lateral transfer more is demanded of the transferor and receiver than in a diffusion situation (because of the reworking of the innovation spiral that lateral shift demands) one might expect to have to introduce some measure of the transferor's motivation as a driving force. This question of incentive of the transferor in technology transfer is an important one; it is also bound up with other factors. In diffusion situations there is the strongest motivation on the part of the supplier who will encourage the diffusion process by all the resources of his sales and marketing organisation. In technology transfer situations, especially those in which production capability is being transferred to other producers, the transferor's incentives are dulled. It is often the case that he himself is being cajoled into the transfer by would-be receivers or pushed by his government — or indeed restrained by his government as in USA today [16]. The diffusion model might, on the other hand, be expected to run parallel to the lateral shift model in so far as the motivation of the receiver would be a factor likely to affect the ease of surmounting barriers to the transfer.

2.31 A further factor one would expect to have to take into account in modelling transfer processes is the role of technological infra-structure in the receiver's environment. Bell and Hill (Paper 12) argue that this factor is crucial in transfer to developing countries. This is a plausible argument and to model it quantitatively one needs a measure of the dependency of the transferred technology on an existing technological infra-structure. This dependency is itself a matter of contextual fit.

In the first instance we need models of barrier penetration and contextual fit which can be used for descriptive purposes. Although the physical scientist leans towards models which are sufficiently robust to permit their use in prescribing effective courses of action the student of transfer processes in technical change must be less ambitious. His models, even if quantitative, will do well if they are good descriptors of the problem area.

References

[1] Black, M., *Models and Metaphors*, Cornell University Press, Ithaca, New York, 1962.

[2] Hesse, M., *Models and Analogies in Science*, University of Notre Dame Press, Notre Dame, Indiana, 1960.

[3] Myers, S. and Marquis, D.G. *Successful Industrial Innovations*, NSF 69-17, 1969.

[4] Burns, T., "Models, Images and Myths" in W.H. Gruber and D.G. Marquis (eds) *Factors in the Transfer of Technology*, M.I.T. Press, Cambridge, Mass, 1969.

[5] Rogers, E.M., *The Diffusion of Innovations*, Free Press, Glencoe, Illinois, 1962.

[6] Mansfield, E., "Technical Change and the Rate of Imitation" in N. Rosenberg (ed) *The Economics of Technological Change*, Penguin, Harmondsworth, 1971.

[7] Mansfield, E., *Industrial Research and Technological Innovation*, Norton, New York, 1968.

[8] Toulmin, S., "Innovation and the Problem of Utilisation" in Gruber and Marquis (eds), 1969, *op. cit.*

[9] Brooks, H., "National Science Policy and Technology Transfer" in *Proceedings of a Conference on Technology Transfer and Innovation*, NSF 67-5, Washington D.C., 1966.

[10] Doctors, S., *The Role of Federal Agencies in Technology Transfer*, M.I.T. Press, Cambridge, Mass, 1969.

[11] Tressel, G.W., "The Critical Role of Communication in Technology Transfer" in M. Cetron and H. Davidson (eds), *Industrial Technology Transfer*, Noordhoff, Leiden, 1977.

[12] Baines, A., Bradbury, F.R. and Suckling, C.W., *Research in the Chemical Industry*, Applied Science Publishers, London, 1969.

[13] Allen, T.J., "The Differential Performance of Information Channels in the Transfer of Technology" in Gruber and Marquis (eds), 1969, *op. cit.*

[14] Pelz, D.C. and Andrews, F.M., *Scientists in Organisations*, John Wiley, London, 1966.

[15] Bradbury, F.R., "Aspects of Process Development in the Fine Chemicals Industry", *Chemistry & Industry*, 1974, p. 392.

[16] Pickarz, R., "Assessing Effects of International Technology Transfer on the U.S. recovery" in M. Cetron and H. Davidson (eds), 1977 *op. cit.*

Chapter 3

OBJECTIVES

3.1 So far we have discussed the overall concept of transfer processes in technical change and described some models which may be useful in describing aspects of this concept. We now want to concentrate, in this chapter and the next, on more specific examples of transfer, to discuss what we know about them, and to suggest ways in which our understanding needs to be extended. So interrelated are all the topics which we discuss that any framework or sequence must, to a large extent, be arbitrary, and some subjects would be equally at home in almost any chapter. This is particularly true of the issues we discuss under "Objectives" and "Mechanisms", We start with a discussion of objectives since in most cases the mechanism of a transfer process will be influenced, consciously or sub-consciously, by the objectives it is designed to achieve.

Much of the discussion at Stirling, and particularly the contributions of the industrial and government participants, concerned objectives and mechanisms, and we should perhaps emphasise here that by mechanisms we mean the ways in which things happen, or appear to happen, in real life. We include within this descriptions of the methods people have developed to stimulate and encourage transfer. We reserve the term "methodology" for the academic activities involved in studying and researching the phenomena of, and within, technical change, and for the building of models which attempt to describe the system of activities studied.

3.2 Since we start in these chapters to draw more extensively upon the contributions of the participants at the Stirling meeting it is appropriate to mention here the basis on which these contributions are founded. A frequent observation is that the contributions found in the literature, and comments made elsewhere, about innovation and technical change are of three kinds. These three categories, "wisdom", "case study" and "experimental" (or sometimes "empirical") have been defined elsewhere [1], and are discussed further in Chapter 5.

The normal direction for a discussion of these categories to take is to note, almost with regret, the dominance of contributions of the first and second types and to deplore the lack of experimental studies. Bradbury (Paper 1) chose to emphasise a different aspect when he made the point that experimental investigation, in this subject at least, often indicates that intuition and wisdom have been right. In other words the wisdom contributions often lead the experimental ones in providing significant insights into the phenomena being studied. In this, we suggest, lies the main value of the experience-based contributions of "practitioners" which we sought and obtained at Stirling.

However, in the light of our previous discussion it becomes important to recognise the context within which these wisdom contributions are made. They will reflect experiences and observations drawn from a particular context, and they can only be considered as appropriate within certain limits. No automatic generalisation from such observations can be made. It is important to recognise this concept of appropriateness, and always to examine wisdom-based models and hypotheses in relation to their context, a context which will be made up of the many features we mentioned earlier; at the same time they can contain useful insights which can provide the basis for developing more general conceptual models.

3.3   In this chapter our primary concern will be with the types of institutions which are involved in transfer processes in technical change, and with their objectives. In this context we must consider not only the objectives of the organisations, but of the people within them. In the next chapter we will look in more detail at the mechanisms for transfer which are employed in various circumstances.

Issues about the type of organisations involved in transfer processes, their objectives, the criteria by which their performance can be judged, and the alternative approaches possible, were raised in a number of papers and were frequently introduced in the discussions. The main foci of attention were the universities, government research establishments (GREs), research associations (RAs) and certain areas of industry and the professional intermediaries, whether they be government supported like the National Research Development Corporation (NRDC) or the various types of licensing brokers.

Universities

3.4   The role of universities in processes of innovation, technical change and economic growth has been of interest for some time. Thus during the 1960s there was a considerable debate, highlighted by research such as that on Project Hindsight [2], the TRACES project [3], the study of the Queen's Awards to Industry [4], the SAPPHO project [5] and the work of Gibbons and Johnston [6], all of which examined, inter alia, the contribution of basic research to industrial innovation. Other, less studied, aspects include the roles of the scientifically qualified manpower produced by universities, and of the body of expertise and experience concentrated in these institutions. A detailed survey of the resources of universities available for transfer and the conditions of their development is to be found in Johnston [7].

3.5   Langrish [8] has argued that many of the activities on which universities are engaged are irrelevant to practical situations, not only in the short term but also, with some important exceptions such as scientific instruments and techniques, in the longer term. Using data on the origin of ideas used in British innovations, he has suggested that university science tends to be more useful in the early stages of development of a discipline, citing as examples astronomy in the Renaissance period and its importance for navigation, high energy physics at the turn of the century, and chemical research at about the same time.

Langrish suggested that the reason for the shift of weight of contributions from university to industry over a long period is that industries and universities have different objectives, and do different things. He claimed that university scientists want to understand why things are happening and to publish papers whereas industrial scientists want to make things work and to make profits. But he also commented that things may change in the future.

"This does not mean that university research is a waste of money; the situation may be changing. Concern about such matters as resource depletion, ecology, pollution, fire risk, health hazards, quality of working life etc. coupled with the increasing scale of industrial operations may mean that industry will have to pay more attention to understanding what it is doing. It could be that in the future, many sections of industry are going to require an increasing reliance upon theoretical research aimed at understanding as the empirical approach, which has been so successful, joins the quest for economic growth as a thing of the past."

3.6 There has been considerable disagreement with the arguments of Langrish. The work of Gibbons and Johnston [9] has demonstrated a larger and more significant role for university research in the process of industrial innovation, and at Stirling, Pavitt suggested that the contribution of the university system to industrial growth was broadly consonant with its proportion of the total national R & D budget (which is of the order of 10% in the U.K.)

Rather more fundamental questions, which focus attention on the objectives of the universities and the objectives which, implicitly, people might ascribe to them were raised in reference to the work of Johnston [10], who has questioned whether university research should be described in economic terms as an investment good, to be evaluated in cost-benefit terms, or a consumption good – a necessary element of high civilisation. On this basis, Pavitt suggested that the present division of labour might not be so inadequate or harmful as suggested.

3.7 A different viewpoint on the objectives of university research and of individual researchers is provided by the paper by Norris. (Chapter 14) This raised a number of important issues concerning both methodology and mechanisms for transferring university research to industry which will be examined in later sections. However, the finding that a significant amount of university research could be of direct and fairly immediate relevance to certain sectors of industry is important in this discussion of objectives.

Not surprisingly Norris found that some people produced more innovative ideas than others. His conclusion that those most involved tended to be from the engineering end of the spectrum of university activities, and that the degree of utilisation appeared to be influenced by the amount of prior (and continuing) contact between the industry and university participants, is similar to Roberts' [11] finding that technical entrepreneurs tended to be development oriented rather than research oriented in their previous laboratory work and Peters' [12] comment that people in universities producing commercial ideas were more likely to have spent some time acting as consultants.

In discussing Norris' results, as with many other similar studies, it is essential to consider the objectives and motivations of the people involved, as well as those of the organisations to which they belong. Nowhere is this more important than in the universities where the traditions of academic freedom and individual initiative have persisted for so long. While one university scientist may be perfectly happy to dissociate himself from the exploitation of any of the results of his research, preferring instead to move on to further academic challenges, others may gain their satisfaction by entrepreneurial behaviour and close involvement in the exploitation process. McClelland [13, 14] has shown, for instance, that achievement motivation is associated with entrepreneurship or exploitive behaviour but that outstanding scientists do not necessarily have this characteristic.

3.8 A focus on objectives can, for instance, introduce a different element into the debate about the role of universities. One of the reasons that "university scientists want to understand why things happen and to publish papers" is that success in this constitutes one of the major criteria against which they are assessed and promoted. These criteria have traditionally been used because they appear appropriate to the primary objectives of the university. But they may actively discourage involvement in transfer activities. The way that organisations change, or do not change, their objectives and assessment criteria to meet changing needs can be one of the most crucial factors in determining their success or failure. This point is relevant to many of the organisations involved in transfer processes in technical change.

As far as the objectives of universities are concerned, in the UK there is still strong opposition to any kind of external direction of research. This was manifest in widespread and spirited defence of the right to pursue "curiosity-oriented research" at the time of the enunciation of the Rothschild "customer/contractor" principles of funding some university research [15], and there are many who are utterly opposed to any demand for "relevance" in university research. Nevertheless a number of universities now have significant "contract research" type activities or are in the process of developing this type of operation, prompted by many different pressures. Primarily, one suspects, it is a reaction brought about by a tightening financial situation, resulting in a shortage of research and other funds, and the belief that the situation may intensify if no attempt is made to encourage support from other sources and to accept and demonstrate relevance. However it is also recognised that there can be advantages to university staff and students in a closer involvement with potential user organisations.

Given that there is an established and growing interest in actively promoting rather than passively permitting closer university-industry co-operation there remains the problem of deciding the most appropriate form of any linkages and of how they might be set up. We will return to this subject in the chapter on Mechanisms.

Government Research Establishments

3.9 The role of government research establishments in technology transfer has been one of the major topics for research and debate. Some of the earliest transfer programmes involved the American mission-oriented laboratories of the Department of Defence, NASA and the Atomic Energy Commission, and much of the early "technology transfer" research examined such programmes [16]. In the United Kingdom the label denotes the Laboratories controlled by the various government departments. In terms of industrially oriented research the most significant of these are the Industrial Research Establishments of the Department of Industry, of which the National Physical Laboratory (NPL), the National Engineering Laboratory (NEL) and the Warren Spring Laboratory (WSL) are the largest, and perhaps the best known. Other Departments or Ministries with research laboratories include the Ministry of Agriculture, Fisheries and Food (MAFF), the Ministry of Defence (MoD), The Department of Energy (DEn) and of the Environment (DoE), the Department of Health and Social Security (DHSS) and the Home Office. In total there are more than 80 laboratories or research establishments controlled by Government Departments.

Strictly speaking the Research Laboratories of the United Kingdom Atomic Energy Authority (UKAEA) are not Government Research Establishments, since the UKAEA is a statutory body which receives its funding by Parliamentary vote, and whose chairman reports to Parliament through the Secretary of State for Energy. The Research Group of the UKAEA, and particularly the Atomic Energy Research Establishment at Harwell, have developed a considerable expertise in technology transfer to industry, and many of the contributions at Stirling drew on this experience. Since there are many similarities between the position of the UKAEA laboratories and the GREs both will be discussed under the latter heading.

All the laboratories included in the general category of GREs rely on government (or, in the case of the UKAEA, Parliament) for a major part of their financial support. So too do the Research Associations (RAs) although in recent years to a diminishing extent. The RAs have several differences from GREs and are discussed separately in the next section.

3.10 The GREs are by no means a homogeneous set. Some have much more clearly defined objectives than others, some relate specifically to one area of activity or one industrial sector while others have remits of much wider scope. The GREs have evolved over a fairly long period of time (the NPL, for example, was established in 1900) and many are considered as centres of expertise which should be maintained as such through government support. But in recent years there has been a growing pressure for the laboratories to recover a proportion of their costs by direct charges made to their "customers". The effects of this pressure have already proved significant for the management and staff of GREs, and there can be little doubt that in the long term it will influence the whole pattern and organisation of research in the GREs. As the Stirling meeting showed, not everyone views the possible consequences of this move towards revenue earning with equanimity. Reservations are expressed, and they relate to an underlying debate about the objectives of GREs, the mechanism employed to attempt to achieve those objectives, and the criteria which should be used to assess the extent to which objectives have been fulfilled.

There is a complex interaction between objectives, mechanisms and criteria, and this affects all the organisations involved in transfer processes. We can illustrate the general problem by reference to the specific case of the GREs. We can first note that there has been a consistent and growing emphasis in government policy, throughout the past decade, aimed at bringing the personnel working in GREs into closer contact with industry. This need was recognised in the Zuckerman report of 1968, [17] which included as one of its recommendation,

"the encouragement of GREs to act on a commercial basis as agencies for private manufacturing industry not only in the R & D phase, but also in the later stages of the innovative chain".

Some two years later the Ministry of Technology (now the Department of Industry) suggested the merging of the GREs, NRDC and the UKAEA into a British Research and Development Corporation which would have as one of its aims,

"to encourage and support the development and application of innovation and technological improvement in industry for the benefit of the U.K. economy, and to carry out research and development for this purpose, both itself and in collaboration with industry and on repayment". [18]

A change of government prevented this amalgamation of research establishments, and the new government embarked on the implementation of the customer/contractor principle as defined by Rothschild. The principle states that, for all applied research, there should be a customer and a contractor. "The customer says what he wants; the contractor does it (if he can); and the customer pays." [19] There are two situations in which this principle is applied by government. The first is where a government department will actually use, or specify the use of, the end product of the applied research. Weapons system development, for instance, falls in this category. The second is where government will not itself use the results, but provides funding because the research is considered important and no one else is likely to provide support for it, at least in the early stages.

In this second situation government is acting as a "proxy customer", and it is this manifestation of the customer/contractor principle which is perhaps the more controversial. The Department of Industry established a series of Requirements Boards to act as proxy customers for all industrially-oriented applied research funded by the Department, and other government departments have established similar mechanisms. Much of the funding of industrial applied research in the GREs now comes from the Requirements Boards, and the implications of this new mechanism were often introduced into the discussion at Stirling. What is of interest here is the effect the mechanism for implementing the customer/contractor principle has on the objectives of the GREs.
3.11   The Rothschild report is concerned with mechanisms more than objectives, as indeed were most of the preceding government papers mentioned above. Objectives for government funded applied research are implicit rather than explicit in most of the documents, but the underlying theme in all is the need to make research more effective in stimulating national industrial and economic performance. The pressure for revenue earning by GREs comes because it is believed that if "market forces" are allowed to influence research programmes they will become more relevant to real needs. The Rothschild proposals do not challenge the preceding thinking, they extend it and suggest a new mechanism for ensuring industrial involvement and the relevance of research.

It is often rather cynically stated that the only real objective for any organisation is survival, and certainly if a GRE knows that its performance will be assessed by its ability to earn industrial receipts then generating such income will become one of its objectives. But, as was quite apparent from the contributions at Stirling, this gives rise to worries about the impact this will have on the type of research undertaken. For government, revenue earning by the GREs is a proxy objective, and it is believed that increasing income will be indicative of increasing relevance and utility of research. But for the GRE revenue earning may become the over-riding objective, being the one that ensures survival, and the content of the GREs work programme may alter significantly to meet this expedient.

Evidence indicates that most firms use external "contract research" organisations to provide skills or equipment unavailable internally, or in cases of short-term overload. The contractor is usually seen as a minor auxiliary rather than a full partner in industrial research. An evident concern was that if the GREs concentrate too much on generating income to justify their continuing existence they may well be drawn into areas of research which are of less significance to the national economy than other less immediately profitable ones might be. Indeed, given a free hand, it is not difficult to see that gaps in technological capability could very soon arise as a consequence of GREs moving to areas where support is more readily forthcoming and the demands for technology transfer are easier to satisfy. This seems to be an important policy issue requiring attention. As one participant developed the point:

"If you make a research organisation, which happens to be a national laboratory, maximise its income this may not be the same as maximising information transfer into industry. For example, many of the research activities of the national laboratories produce design data and improved design methods. It can be argued that the best way to ensure that these are used, and thus to achieve national objectives, is to run seminars, to publish openly in appropriate journals, and to get to people who need it quite free, without any cash flow. But if on the other hand the same group in a laboratory is charged with increasing its income then it keeps that new design data and those new design methods to itself and goes out to certain firms and says 'look how we can help you to get the edge on the competition'. We are trying to see which is the optimum viewpoint, to maximise your income in a truly commercial, entrepreneural way or to spread the knowledge freely to U.K. industry, and inevitably in so doing to world industry".

These are only some illustrations of the interrelation of objectives, mechanisms and criteria mentioned earlier, and also an example of the hierarchical nature of systems of objectives. A criterion introduced by government (revenue earning) as a proxy measure of achievement of its objective (industrial relevance and economic benefit) becomes an objective, at a lower level in the decision-making hierarchy, of the GREs, and this in turn affects the nature of the research they undertake, and hence their ability to meet government's original objectives.

3.12   There are other concerns about the customer/contractor principle, which in the formulation made by Rothschild is a gross distortion of the reality of mission-oriented research and development. It is not a matter of the customer "saying what he wants", because in practice the customer may not know. And at the outset the customer may be wrong. Rothschild quotes the military field as an example of how the customer/contractor relationships should work, but in that very area the "customers" initially rejected many of the most significant innovations such as the tank and the aircraft carrier. As our earlier discussions show the innovation process consists of an iteration between needs and capabilities and thus needs a dialogue between customer and contractor.

This gives the key to the importance of the Requirements Boards in their proxy customer role. Their job must be to ensure that the contractors they support identify suitable potential users with whom to establish such a dialogue, and from whom they can develop a proper appreciation of context and identify the appropriate parameters of fit. The Requirements Boards themselves have industrial members who may be able to do this, but failing this they must help ensure that links are made to people who can.

3.13   This discussion has been confined to the particular institutional organisations and relationships within the U.K. However more general implications can be drawn, as all governments are concerned to develop industrial policies appropriate to promote technological progress and economic growth, and one of the instruments which is available, though to a varying extent, is research establishments under the direct government control. In fact, the U.K. concentrates rather more of its R & D in government research establishments than do the other OECD countries (Fabian et al [20]) and hence has a special need to ensure effective transfer from these laboratories. At the same time, this particular concentration has meant, that, in a climate of cost-effectiveness, a considerable degree of experience of promoting transfer has been gained. Hence issues of the appropriate function for GREs, the validity of payment as a criterion for adequate performance and the "proxy customer" role, as well as the development of attitudes and mechanisms to encourage transfer, which are dealt with in the next section, seem of general relevance. Recent pronouncements by the Chief Scientist and Engineer of the UK Department of Industry foreshadow an increased emphasis by government on transfer processes (27).

50

Research Associations

3.14 Many of the arguments about trends in the GREs also arise in the case of the Research Associations, where there is a similar movement towards contract work. In the past they have tended to serve an industry (as in the case of HATRA, the Research Centre for Knitting, Dyeing and Making-up of Knitted Textiles, which was formerly known as the Hosiery and Allied Trades Research Association) or a function or technology (such as PERA, the Production Engineering Research Association or the Welding Institute, formerly the British Welding Research Association). Initially the RAs were funded by a levy system which produced size-dependent subscriptions from all firms in an industry, with government providing a one-for-one contribution to enable an adequate level of expertise to be developed and maintained, with output being available to all member firms. In recent years the automatic government contribution has been greatly reduced. RAs have been undertaking an increasing amount of contract work for individual firms, or small groups of subscribers. Some have even completely renounced their research association status and become independent contract research organisations (such as the SIRA Institute, formerly the Scientific Instrument Research Association, and ERA, the Electrical Research Association). Now all Government funding to the Research Associations is channelled through the appropriate Requirements Boards of the Department of Industry.

There have been many studies of the RAs, the most recent being the Bessborough Report [21] which is a valuable review of the work and government/industry relationships of the British Research Associations. It emphasises that the RAs have closer ties with industry than GREs, and argues that GREs should not compete with RAs in the matter of repayment work for industry. In 1970/71 the Report shows that the RAs between them devoted some two-thirds of their effort to co-operative work for member firms, and twenty-nine per cent was devoted to contract work for government or for industry or other bodies. Co-operative work was then the most important single type of RA work and through this co-operative function RAs "represent a focus for industrial technology and by their very existence help to stimulate technical communication between firms in an industry". The analysis offered by the Bessborough Report indicated that the British RAs have been an important agency for stimulating transfer processes in technological change and that there is much to be learned by an analysis of their experience.

3.15 Each RA has its own objectives. Nutting suggests in his paper (Paper 9) that the objectives of importance to HATRA are as follows:

(i) to transfer information resulting from their own research to members of the RA;

(ii) to encourage the use of that information;

(iii) to obtain feedback from the industrial members on current or potential future research;

(iv) to provide a source of, and encourage the use of, information not originating in the RA.

The structure and funding of RAs predispose them to objectives sharply localised to their own parishioners, with an emphasis on information dissemination.

The task faced in realising this set of objectives can be very formidable. For example, HATRA has 935 establishments as members. Other RAs may have fewer but they all cover a wide variety of companies, not always with many common interests. The RAs support to their particular industrial members and their contacts in their own industry should therefore be good, but despite this there have been some criticisms. Some sectors of industry complain that their RAs have paid too little attention to "real" problems. They have been accused of being too academic and of lack of communication with industry leading to failure to identify changing needs. The case history reported by Catling (Chapter 12) illustrates some of the problems which have occurred.

Some of the criticisms made of RAs could have been more fairly directed at industry for seeing them as university-type establishments with which they were not willing to share information about possible developments in their own situations — a not unnatural reluctance perhaps, but one which has encouraged RAs to do more specifically oriented, and often confidential, work for particular firms.

3.16 There have been substantial changes in the organisation of RAs in recent years and many have reduced their staff and are now more streamlined. Some have set up specific marketing groups along the lines Nutting described in the case of HATRA (Paper 9). The changes have been designed to try and match the skills of the establishment more closely to user needs, or to identify new markets which more closely match their skills. The movement towards improving contextual fit has therefore been done from both ends, technology and market, with the clear objective of more effective promotion of technology transfer, which must be the main function of the RAs. They do not have a high level of direct support which guarantees their survival, as do the universities and GREs, nor do they have any significant production capacity. They are developers and sellers of skills and know-how, and their success at doing this is the key determinant of their future progress. The only problem from a national policy point of view is again whether the movement towards contract work will leave gaps which will not readily be filled by other bodies and which might have long-term effects on the economy as a whole. The Bessborough Report quoted above, is reassuring on this, but does call for individual RAs to make a fundamental review of their objectives. The recommendation reads:

"We believe that it is critical to full RA success that each association defines explicit objectives and plans its medium-term future in a detailed fashion. RAs individually should now undertake a fundamental review of their objectives. Some may need to review or restate their functions and redefine their markets. A clearer expression of their own objectives as institutions is essential to the effective framing of future policies, particularly towards submissions to government for financial support. It is also essential to ensure that RAs reflect changing industrial structure and demand".[22]

3.17   The three types of institution discussed so far, universities, GREs and RAs, could all be considered as part of a framework established primarily to serve the national interest. It can be argued that their objectives are set in terms of direct national benefit, and that they serve private interests indirectly, in the process of meeting these objectives. We have pointed out that recent policies may have had the effect of changing this emphasis, although it is by no means clear that national objectives have changed. The three types of institution together provide the means for developing the basic skills on which technology depends for its development and operation, for fundamental research, for nurturing technology in centres of excellence, and for active transfer of technology to satisfy the needs of industry. But until recently there has been little co-ordination of the efforts and contributions of the institutions concerned.

Government Objectives

3.18   This lack of co-ordination is, in fact, part of a wider problem in that, in the U.K. there is no clear national technology policy. It is a *sine qua non* of planning, at whatever level, that there exists a statement of objectives and strategy. In the areas of research and development, and technology, any objectives must be derived from, and consistent with, national industrial, economic and social policies. Too often in the U.K. science and technology policies have been considered in isolation, as ends in their own right, rather than as inputs to a larger process designed to achieve wider national goals.

Recently an attempt has been made in the U.K. to launch a national industrial planning process which will involve government, unions, and industry. Although far from a satisfactory statement of objectives — indeed the mechanism for reaching consensus on any such objectives is far from perfect — some of the guidelines for industrial policy clearly have implications for technology policy. Commitment to a high output, high wage economy, and the apparent intention to concentrate government attention and national resources on the regeneration of British manufacturing industry forms part of the boundary constraints for a national technology policy. Other boundary constraints appear as, for instance, national energy and resources policies become established, and their consequent R & D strategies become apparent.

3.19 Maddock, the former Chief Scientist of the Department of Industry, has repeatedly drawn attention to what he considers a maldistribution of the UKs R & D resources. He has commented that most of the UK R & D effort is devoted to industries or technologies which do not contribute significantly to GNP or export performance, whereas in Japan, for example, the opposite is true. [23] Maddock has stressed the importance of using "best practice" technology in those sectors of manufacturing industry which contribute significantly to national economic performance, and stated that the Department of Industry now considers "technology transfer" to be one of its major priorities. Other evidence makes it clear that what "technology transfer" means in this case is the wider utilisation of existing technology which is available "off-the-shelf". Thus technology transfer is seen as the alternative to technology development.

3.20 Nothing short of an overall technology policy, consistent with wider economic and social policies, will resolve the problems raised by the sort of analyses described above. The indications are that the need for more co-ordination and rationalisation of R & D policy is at last being realised. The recent changes in the system of providing government funding of research and development go some way towards providing a mechanism, but as yet relatively little progress has been made toward objectives.

3.21   Although there were several industrial managers at the Stirling meeting not much was said concerning the objectives of industry either in seeking technology inputs or in promoting the outward movement of technology to other users. In part this was because there were no representatives present who were directly concerned with technology transfer to and technology development of less developed countries. Moreover, the whole subject of the objectives of industry with regard to transfer processes, and particularly the outward movement of technology to LDCs, is in the process of substantial review and reformulation.

There is no general consensus among industrial owners of technology that this outward movement of technology to developing countries is desirable, as the Les Arcs meeting showed. [24] At the Stirling meeting no explicit case illustrating the disadvantages of such transfer was presented, but the conflict of objectives between the developing country which desires to build up appropriate industries, its infrastructure of crafts and skills, and its innovative capacity, on the one hand and the MNE operating branch establishments in the country on the other was discussed. The common complaint about the MNEs having a natural tendancy to ship problems requiring technical expertise back to the home base was expressed, and a delegate commented that cost effectiveness arguments operate against R & D establishments in LDCs since it will usually be quicker and cheaper to send the problem back to the centre.

Also political intervention by governments to control the flow of imports of goods and equipment and the flow of profits from branch to parent may strongly influence the technology transfer practices of multinational companies and a delegate instanced India where the effect of legislation was to encourage foreign companies to carry out R & D programmes in India, often very effectively.

We see in this type of discussion the conflict of objectives appropriate to investment appraisal decisions by private companies, for which profitability is crucially important, and those appropriate to cost benefit decisions by governments, for which social welfare is crucially important. There is no reason why these objectives should coincide and failure to recognise this is a source of much confusion, as Johnson makes abundantly clear in his recent book [25].

3.22   There was some discussion of the objectives of receivers of transferred science and technology in industrial R & D departments. It was recognised that in industrialised countries there is widespread acceptance of the beneficial effects of firm-to-firm movement of technology within industries. Here the objectives of the receivers are fairly obvious. They are to obtain sooner and by less costly means than inhouse R & D solutions to problems of innovation, diversification and expansion. The only alternative to do-it-yourself open to industry with technological problems is the buying of appropriate technology. Solving of technical development problems *ab initio* is expensive and lengthy, with costs escalating, and, as Altenpohl has described [26], firms are increasingly looking to technology acquisition as an alternative to in-house R & D as a way of achieving corporate objectives. A great deal of the licensing activity is devoted to this type of transfer, and is discussed later.

Professional Bodies

3.23 Finally, brief mention must be made of the objectives of the professional bodies such as the National Research Development Corporation and various firms of licensing brokers. These are neither users nor sources of technology but intermediaries in transfer processes. Although there are many differences, all these organisations exist to facilitate transfer, and to do so profitably. NRDC is now involving itself more in the support of actual development work, but in the early stages of negotiations with inventors it must pay particular attention to the characteristics and uniqueness of the technology proposed, and to the type and level of future activity which is likely to be required in order to realise its benefits, whether these be narrowly measured in terms of direct and possibly short term profit or in terms of longer term and wider, perhaps national, objectives. The interesting point raised here is the apparent conflict, already mentioned in the case of GREs, between the short-term private and public interests, objectives in both cases being to be self-supporting in the longer term. A related conflict of interests is faced by the licensing agent in so far as he has to satisfy the demands of the buyer of technology for a profitable investment whilst protecting the global interests of the seller and his markets. [27]

3.24 It is evident from what we have said in this chapter that conflict and uncertainty characterise the objectives, which in many cases are insufficiently explicit, of the organisations discussed in this chapter. While they all have a major contribution to make to transfer processes in technical change, the clear formulation of objectives, stated or as perceived, is a prerequisite to the formulation of their policies, and hence to the design of mechanisms to achieve their objectives.

References

[1] Douds, C.F. "The State of the Art in the Study of Technology Transfer — a Brief Survey", *R & D Management*, 1 (1971) 3.

[2] Sherwin, C. and Isenson, R.S. "Project Hindsight", *Science* Vol. 156, (1967) 1571-1577.

[3] *Technology in Retrospect and Critical Events in Science*, Illinois Institute of Technology Research Institute 1968.

[4] Langrish, J. *et al.*, *Wealth from Knowledge*, Macmillan, London, 1972.

[5] Achilladellis, B., Jervis, P. and Robertson, A., *Project SAPPHO: A Study of Success and Failure in Innovation*, Science Policy Research Unit, Brighton 1971.

[6] Johnston, R. & Gibbons, M., "Characteristics of Information Usage in Technological Innovation", *IEEE Transactions on Engineering Management* Vol. Em-22, No. 1, 1975.

[7] Johnston, R.D., *Transfer of Technology in the U.K.* Special Report for the Science Sub-Committee of the Parliamentary Select Committee on Science and Technology, 1976.

[8] Langrish, J., "University Chemistry Research: Any Use to Industry?", *Chemistry in Britain* 8 (1972) 330.

[9] Johnston, R. and Gibbons, M., *op. cit.*

[10] Johnson, H.G., *Technology and Economic Independence*, Macmillan Press Ltd., London, 1975.

[11] Roberts, E.B., "Entrepreneurship and Technology" in *Factors in the Transfer of Technology*, Gruber W.H. and Marquis D.G., editors, M.I.T. Press 1969.

[12] Peters, D.H., *Commercial Innovations from University Faculties: A Study of the Invention and Exploitation of Ideas*, M.I.T. Sloan School of Management, Working paper 406-69, July 1969.

[13] McClelland, D.C., *The Achieving Society* New York, Van Nostrand 1969.

[14] McClelland, D.C., "On the Psychodynamics of Creative Physical Scientists" in *Comtemporary Approaches to Creative Thinking* editors Gruber W.H., Terrell G. and Wertheimer M., New York, Atherton Press 1962, pp. 141-175.

[15] A Framework for Government Research and Development, Cmnd 4814, HMSO, London, 1971.

[16] Doctors, S.I., *The Role of Federal Agencies in Technology Transfer* M.I.T. Press, Cambridge, Mass, 1969.

[17] *Technological Innovation in Britain*, HMSO, London, 1968.

[18] *Industrial Research and Development in Government Laboratories*, Ministry of Technology, HMSO, London 1970.

[19] "A Framework for Government Research and Development", Cmnd 4814, HMSO, London, 1971.

[20] Fabian, Y., Young, A. *et al, Pattern of Resources devoted to Research and Experimental Development in the OECD Area, 1963-71*, OECD, Paris, 1975.

[21] *Industrial Research and Development*, The Report of the Committee of Enquiry into the Research Associations. Chairman: The Earl of Bessborough, Conference of Industrial Research Associations, London 1973.

[22] *Industrial Research and Development, op. cit.*, p. 172.

[23] Maddock, I., "Science, Technology and Industry", Seventh Royal Society Technology Lecture, *Proceedings of the Royal Society, A*, 345 (1975) 295.

[24] Cetron, M. and Davidson, H. F., *Industrial Technology Transfer*, Noordhoff, Leiden 1977.

[25] Johnson, H.G., *op. cit.*

[26] Altenpohl, D., "Acquisition of Technology as one specific way to achieve Technology Transfer", in Davidson, H.F., Cetron, M. and Goldhar, J.D., *Technology Transfer*, Noordhoff, Leiden, 1974, p. 595.

[27] Davies, D.S., "The Resurgence of the Engineer", *Chemistry & Industry*, 1978 p. 375.

58

Chapter 4

MECHANISMS

4.1 Transfer processes in technical change include a wide range of phenomena. Given this range, and the diverse objectives of those institutions and individuals associated with transfer processes, it is obvious that there is no single best method of transfer. What we have to do is to examine the way in which a variety of factors affect the choice, operation and effectiveness of mechanisms for transfer. These factors have been grouped together into three categories which reflect behavioural, intra-organisational, and inter-organisational aspects.

Behavioural Aspects

4.2 Under this category we deal with those factors operating primarily at the level of the behaviour of the individual and their relation with mechanisms of transfer. The importance of these considerations can be captured in the bald statement that "technology does not move of its own accord, people move it." The importance of people in transfer processes has been repeatedly stressed in these chapters and elsewhere.

It has now to be asked in what ways people crucially affect the transfer processes we are investigating. There are a number of elements in an adequate explanation. The first of these rests on the fact, emphasised by Johnston (Paper 3) that technology is not a "black box" which can be shifted at will from one situation to another. One of the important results to emerge from the conference was that technology and its context of people, equipment, materials, social and economic forces, cannot be divorced. The lateral shift view of technology transfer from one context to another (Paper 1) argued that to be successful, such a shift demands a degree of reworking of the technology to secure an acceptable fit to its new environment — which itself will be changed to some degree too. Recognition of the contexted nature of technology also provides some insight into the key role of people. For much of the context is, by its very nature, not explicit, nor can it be made so. Polanyi's concept of tacit knowledge or Ravetz's notion of craft skills, developed in the analysis of scientific knowledge, provide an admirable model for the elucidation of the contexted nature of technology which, as noted by Bell & Hill (Paper 12), means that learning can only effectively occur by doing; that is to say that the translation of tacit components essential for the effective transfer of technology can by its very nature only occur at the inter-personal level. This concept has also been expressed (Paper 1) in stating that person-to-person contact permits a cyclic exchange of statements, questions and answers which can speedily reveal the nature and extent of the mismatches between a technology and its proposed new situation.

4.3   Another feature which imposes the demand for interpersonal contact for effective transfer, especially where the information to be transferred can be loosely described as crossing the science/technology interface, is related to the progressive institutionalisation and specialisation of knowledge which has occurred particularly in the last 30 years. Johnston (Paper 3) has shown how the barriers around knowledge areas are necessary for their rapid development, but that transfer of information across these barriers is consequently hindered. Effective transmission will occur through personal contact where, once again, the transferor with his contexted knowledge and the receiver can affect the exchanges necessary to translate the information or process transferred into the receiver's work conditions. Allen's well-known work [1], which is itself based on earlier work in the field of psychology, has developed the understanding of the interaction of people (technological gatekeepers) with agencies (the literature sources) as well as with other agents.

4.4   There is, therefore, an impressive array of information which demonstrates the crucial influence which individuals have in transfer processes. But we must also recognise that individuals can fulfil both formal and informal roles. By formal agents we mean people such as liaison or transfer officers whose major function is to promote transfer and who operate at the interface between their own organisation or department or that of a contractor, and the potential receiver organisations. This category would also include the research scientist who after developing a product has his responsibility extended to transferring it out of the laboratory and possibly further, out of the innovating organisation. A much wider range of actors can be grouped under the heading of informal agents. They include the university inventor or scientist in a gov-

60

ernment laboratory who feels motivated to ensure that industry takes up his ideas, and devotes time and energy to championing his product although this does not form part of his official duties. Schon [2] has commented that such "product champions" also occur in industry, and can have a powerful effect in lowering or removing barriers to innovations. Other examples of informal agents include technical sales service personnel who may act as transfer agents in serving small customer companies; or staff who move from one department to another or one organisation to another. When discussing transfer processes in technical change we recognise that there are two classes — those that will happen, in any case, and others which people actively seek to promote. We might refer to these as unplanned and planned transfer processes. Most of the discussion of technology transfer relates to ways of stimulating and enhancing the success rate of planned transfers. Clearly, plans to induce transfer can include the setting up of formal agents for the processes; informal transfer, by its nature, cannot be set up but may be occurring and be playing an important part in information flow. Comments made during the discussions at Stirling showed that many organisations are trying to embody the lessons from unplanned transfers in their planning, and one aspect of this involves formalising the roles of agents.

4.5   The employment of formal liaison or transfer agents is considered to have been started within the U.S. Agricultural Extension Service, which is a late 19th century conception. The role of this Service in the promotion and diffusion of agricultural innovations has been widely studied (see for example the writings of Rogers [3]). The use of formal agents has usually been patterned directly on the model successfully established in the agricultural field, with the agent developing close and regular contacts with a limited number of potential customers and having a strong back-up providing information about new developments and technical support. The allocation of potential customers to agents was done on a geographical basis, each agent having a "parish" within which to work. Just as the Extension Service located its agents in agricultural colleges, so the geographical allocation of resources located at teaching or research organisations has been adopted in many later transfer programmes. In the 1960s an attempt was made in the United States to apply this approach to technology transfer to a wider context when Hollomon established the Office of State Technical Services. In essence the Office's aim was to use the universities as a means of bringing technology to industry by a variety of methods one of which was liaison in the form of Extension Agents who were placed in the field. Few of these ventures turned out to be successful, the failure being attributed to negative attitudes in the Universities. Where success was achieved, it was correlated with some form of institutional separation from the university, the existence of facilities and communications networks to back up the agents, and strong ties, approaching the level of identification, with the particular industry. Currently a project known as the City Technological Extension Scheme is being operated to allow a more rigorous investigation and evaluation of the applicability of the agricultural extension agent concept to the adaptation and utilisation of existing technology for the resolution of urban problems in US cities. Agents have been appointed in 27 cities; the experiment is being monitored closely, and results compared with other similar cities in which no agents are working.

4.6   In the U.K. one of the approaches which bears the closest similarity to the extension model would appear to be the use of formal transfer agents by many of the Research Associations. These institutions were developed in the U.K. in the 1920s to serve the needs of particular industries, such as the paper and pulp, or wool industries, or of a technology, for example, welding. A good deal of information about the rise of formal agents in the Research Associations' work was provided at the conference, including the paper by Nutting (Paper 9). The need to develop relatively permanent relationships as a necessary basis for the confidence needed to open the way to transfer disposes the Research Associations towards the use of formal agents. In particular their concern is not merely to deliver technology to the industrial site but to ensure effective transfer by integrating the new technology into the existing system. This can only be achieved by people whose major orientation is to a particular section of industry, who have a detailed knowledge of that industry, and who are able to spend most of their time in it. Referring to the Hosiery and Allied Trades Research Association (HATRA) Nutting (Paper 9) explained the reasons for this emphasis:

> "We have liaison officers rather then sending research people out to give the good word. We do this partly because the liaison officers identify themselves with their firms. It is they who have this relationship with their firms and they want to get the thing done for their firms. There is a tendency for research people to get things done for their projects."

We should, however, emphasise that not all British Research Associations, or other government-supported establishments, are alike in this respect. As the case study presented by Catling (Paper

62

6) showed, familiarity with an industry does not always guarantee correct selection of projects or effective technology transfer to industry. The value that industry, and especially the larger firms, have found in the co-operatively sponsored work of the Research Associations has sometimes been questioned, and, as we noted earlier, many Research Associations have increased the amount of contract work they do for individual customers. To this extent there is a move away from the identity with specific industry groups with which the work of the Associations has traditionally been associated.

4.7   It was suggested by some that since both technology and the needs of customers change over time, relationships with customer groups should be transient. An example of this was given by the Warren Spring Laboratory in describing the way in which "clubs" of customers were formed:

> "A club differs from a Research Association by being a temporary thing. It lasts until the technology has been transferred after which people move on to other things. Although the research workers are not part of an industry, over five or ten years they get to know their customers extremely well, they have regular meetings, they oversee work, and they run related research programmes. Some of the questions for study may appear to have obvious answers but this is not so, there are all sorts of little things that have to be done ..."

4.8   Another attempt to use formal agents in the U.K. involved the establishment by the Department of Industry of a regional network of Industrial Liaison Officers. These agents were located in colleges of technology or polytechnics around the country and were involved with the technological needs of small and medium sized firms. The agents were intended to visit all such firms in their area at regular intervals. The scheme was not particularly successful and was abandoned in the early 70's, although some of the Liaison Officers were retained by the colleges or polytechnics where they were based, who took over the financing of their activities. The Department of Industry does still maintain regional officers who help and advise local industry, but this new liaison scheme is less formalised and much smaller in scale than the earlier one.

4.9   Licensing organisations and intermediary bodies such as the National Research Development Corporation (a U.K. government agency for promoting the exploitation of inventions) have very little choice other than to act as liaison agents between interested organisations. Usually they have technology, often in an embryonic form, to exploit and they must search until they can identify a suitable receiver for it. Once a possible receiver has been found the skill of the liaison agent is to stand aside from the essential interchange of information about needs and opportunities, while remaining sufficiently involved to see that overall progress with the collaboration is made at an adequate rate. Sometimes, it appears the liaison agents may have a retarding effect on collaboration. A study commissioned of the activities of the National Research Development Corporation [4], while producing overall a favourable view of its activities, did indicate that there were cases where this negative effect was found:

> "it was frequently said (by university inventors) that the inventor was not kept properly in touch with the development by NRDC and that his technical abilities to help in the development were not properly used ... The major criticism (by private inventors) was that after having been requested to assign the rights to NRDC the inventor was unable to influence or effectively participate in the development and exploitation of his invention ... The dislike on the part of certain Industrial Research Establishments of having exploitation carried out at second hand arises partly from ... technical arguments resting on the desirability of maintaining the closest links between inventor, the development team and exploitation."

4.10   One of the considerations which will affect the choice of mechanism will be the attitudes and motivations of the people involved.

We discuss motivation later, but we should notice here that some organisations, largely for motivational reasons, have decided to encourage their technologists to act as transfer agents for their own projects. Marshall [5] when describing early years of the diversification programme at the United Kingdom Atomic Energy Research Establishment at Harwell, commented

> "One obvious decision was that we needed a larger commercial office to negotiate and draw up agreements with our industrial partners ... However, it was more difficult to decide exactly how much responsibility this central office should carry: should they provide the main drive for commercial business or should this be left to the scientists themselves? We decided to place the full responsibility for projects directly and unambiguously on the individual scientists leading the projects. We think this was the correct decision because it means that each scientist is directly concerned with the mar-

ket and final application of his work: this gets him thoroughly involved, committed and enthusiastic to make his work a success."

Thus the Harwell scientists were given responsibility for the technical and commercial success of their projects, and this implied that where appropriate they must supervise the transfer of results to their customers. They became transfer agents. The Harwell example can be considered to be at an extreme of a spectrum of involvement by scientists and technologists in transfer programmes. By placing the responsibility for commercial success of their projects with the scientists concerned, management turns them into formal transfer agents.

However, other organisations, while encouraging communication and involvement with potential users, still use the technologists as informal agents for transfer.

4.11 We conclude, therefore, that formal agents can be used as a mechanism to encourage and facilitate transfer processes, but that the success they will have will depend on their ability to act as an interface between sources of technical assistance and possible customers. A liaison agent can act as a catalyst for information flow, but wrongly chosen, or operating in an inappropriate way, he may become a barrier to the dialogue which is needed if the contextual mapping of technology on to use-system is to be achieved. The choice of mechanism for communicating between the source of the technology and the potential user is one of the main decision points for those involved in managing transfer programmes. As with other aspects of the subject there is no one "right" answer, and the choice made will, in each case, be constrained by different concepts of appropriateness.

4.12 In cases where the technology to be transferred is so complex, or novel, that only the innovator fully understands it and its potential, agents who lack close knowledge of the technology may not be aware of the possibilities for transfer, or the difficulties in achieving a contextual fit in a new environment. It therefore becomes necessary to involve research staff in transfer activities. Involving such staff in the transfer processes has added benefit in that a learning process may well occur whereby the scientist becomes more fully aware of the needs of a potential customer and of the impact of his research ideas in the market place. A disadvantage of over-reliance on the scientist as transfer agent may arise because his primary orientation is not to the transfer process. The phenomenon of the scientists whose major concern is to produce research which meets the standards of the scientific community, thereby achieving the reward of peer approbation, is well known. Such an orientation may be reinforced if it is perceived as linked to career advancement. Another problem of a scientist in the role of transfer agent is that, even if enthusiastic, he may lack the necessary skills to promote transfer. One comment pertinent to this was:

> "We seem to spend a lot of time teaching people various branches of science and sending them out with disciplines which are supposed to be effective. And they are effective up to the point at which they get to the stage of transferring the work that they have done to somebody else, or putting it into some different context — and then the whole thing seems to come apart at the seams."

4.13 Despite these potential difficulties it has been established by sociological research that the commitment of the scientist to science is neither as complete nor as unchangeable as some had suggested [6, 7]. If the scientist's reputation and career depend at least partly on successful transfer of the results of his research into user organisations as in the case of Harwell, cited above, he may not wish to entrust this to a formal agent but rather be concerned to have some control over it himself. In this context it is interesting to refer again to Norris's paper (Paper 8) which illustrates the difficulty of drawing conclusions from observations of situations in which many influences may be operating. Norris indicated that one particular mechanism — namely the establishment of links with the user prior to the execution of the research — gave a higher probability of utilisation. But the formation of those contacts will be influenced by each individual scientist's willingness to act as an informal agent — by his attitudes and interests. Thus some scientists may be highly committed to making utilisation occur and thus likely to seek industrial contacts, while others may be content to move on to new research leaving the exploitation of results to bodies like the National Research Development Corporation. Thus one must at least suggest that difference in motivation to achieve transfer, which will affect the probability of successful transfer, may also influence the choice of mechanism for exploitation of results.

4.14 We have considered formal agents with jobs specified as transfer roles, technologists whose remits have been enlarged to include some transfer activities, and the multitude of informal channels, involving very many members of an organisation, operating spasmodically and with a degree of serendipity through chance encounters and personal acquaintance. The problem in practical terms becomes one of blending and balancing the skills and attributes of this variety of actors in the transfer processes. In certain situations, where it is necessary to draw from a multiplicity of technologies and the skills of many experts, some formal agent or agency appears to be an inescapable and necessary part of the transfer process. Of course, within and around such a formal medium there must also be a variety of informal backups and ancillary mechanisms. For large, prestigious or difficult transfers, especially where there is a one-to-one relationship between a technology, an expert, and a customer the technologist/transfer agent will be indispensable. What emerges from this discussion is that it is not possible to provide a simple heuristic for selecting the most effective mechanism for transferring a technology or piece of information. Each technology has associated with it a particular context and needs to be translated into a new one for effective transfer. It requires the judgement of those involved with each transfer operation as to the most effective combination of agents, formal and informal, and agencies, given the constraints and opportunities present in each case.

It does, however, seem probable that a certain level of continuous activity by some formal transfer agents, such as in the example given by Nutting (Paper 9) is a necessary basis for effective regular transfer operations. Whatever the media of transfer, the agent's role must be to gain the confidence of the receivers, to understand their needs and constraints, to demonstrate the relevance of what is offered and to establish and maintain effective communications.

4.15   The vital importance of personal contact in transfer processes results from the fact that certain types of information can be communicated only in this way. Thus face-to-face communication is necessary for the penetration of the interfaces between increasing specialised and differentiated areas of knowledge and expertise. We need to examine how different forms of communication contribute to various mechanisms of transfer. The failure of many transfer programmes can be attributed to the confusion of dissemination of information with communication. A good example of this is an incident which occurred at the Hosiery and Allied Trades Research Association (HATRA). In response to customer demand they had developed in 1956 an instrument to measure the speed of yarn going to knitting machines, and had widely advertised its existence through all their channels of publicity. Yet in 1974 they were contacted by a small company which had been a member since 1949, requesting HATRA to "invent an instrument to measure the speed of yarn going to knitting machines". While the distribution of documentation may ensure a minimal level of awareness, it is the synergistic combination of documentation and personal interaction which enables the level of communication necessary for effective transfer to be achieved. (Chapter 15). This case also demonstrates Morphet's thesis, (Chapter 16) since the firm's need occurred in 1974 and was not apparent in 1956. Thus their receptivity to the information was probably low when it was first disseminated. Indeed, it may be argued that in 1956 the small firm did not need the speed-measuring instrument and that no amount of persuasion would have affected this. In 1974 what the firm needed was what it got, an effective information retrieval through its Research Association, which is a much better approach than the alternative of attempting to store information which may prove useful 18 years hence!

4.16 Even when face-to-face contact is established there are many further barriers to effective communication. One of these is that the transmitter and receiver may not be "speaking the same language" (see Pearson and Rickards [8]). If the transferor does not know the language and terms of the industry with which he is dealing he will have great difficulty in translating and communicating concepts derived from his own experience. Nutting (Paper 9) spells this out for the Research Association transfers, in his statement that:

> "All printed information to the reader is generalised information. The reader wants to know what is in it for him and, as a consequence,
> Information needs to be presented to different levels in an organisation in a way that is relevant and meaningful to that level."

A further impediment to transfer is imposed when there are personal differences in educational background or even class. The added impediment on transfer imposed by different nationality and language can be substantial. In this connection Black's report on technology transfer in Thailand [9] is illuminating. Black's mission identified needs in the technology transfer area virtually the same as those identified by numerous previous missions, and it is probable that the success of this mission was in setting up a successful conference at which similar conclusions were reached *in the Thai language*. Given the need for effective communication, recognition of the effect of context on the language and perceptions of individuals indicates the necessity of "personalising" information. Information, whether transmitted by document or personally, needs to be oriented as much as possible to the specific interests of the audience being aimed at, and expressed in suitable language. Not only is a different language needed for the managing director from that necessary for the machine operator, but they will also have different interests. For instance cost effectiveness may be meaningful to the director, but the operative may find ease of task and job security more relevant.

Moreover the style of communication will necessarily have to be tailored to the type of information to be transferred; very little technical information can be communicated by handwaving. An examination of the mechanisms of transfer employed for in-house flows by international firms [10] reveals how much attention and effort is applied to detailed and speedy communication, making use of all forms, from letters to dialogue with and between computers.

4.17 A further dimension of the need to personalise information will be added by the characteristics of the receiver organisation. A different base of information and language of presentation will be appropriate for knowledge-based compared with experience-based or craft industries; the latter in particular operate with a much shorter time horizon and hence the need for demonstration of relevance will be much more immediate. Personalising information is referred to in Nutting's paper (Paper 9) and involving all participants in the transfer process is a key feature of "contingency planning" as described by Woods & Davies of Unilever [11]. This point is also demonstrated by the brief case described in paragraph 4.18 below. There is no reason, of course, to assume that any of the barriers referred to in the preceding paragraphs are insurmountable. They may call for a substantially increased effort to overcome them where they exist, but the dialogue method of barrier penetration discussion above is a powerful one and from it arises the widely acknowledged supremacy of agents. Agents need to recognise that effective communication is a key to successful transfer and that the form, style and content of communication needs to be specifically designed to aid the translation of the technology into the context of the potential recipient.

4.18 Motivation is one of the most important behavioural factors in any organisation, and structuring the work situation so as to encourage and reward appropriate motivation is perhaps the most important management task. Within both technology transmitting and receiving organisations there are often many conflicting motivations. One particular barrier to transfer lies in the degree of "ownership" of particular technologies. A researcher may make such a commitment to a "pet project" that he is loath to relinquish his hold on it, while at the other extreme there is the "not-invented-here" syndrome, where the lack of any feeling of ownership provides the basis for rejecting technology developed elsewhere. Some of the many problems of motivation and ownership can perhaps be best illustrated by an extended account related during the conference by a representative of a large chemical company.

"In the early sixties many chemical companies throughout the world were undergoing major changes of scale on their major processes. These changes sometimes involved use of different feedstocks or changes in the chemistry of the processes, but more often resulted from practical engineering developments which made a much bigger scale of operation possible. In the particular case I am talking about these developments necessitated virtually the complete replacement of existing plant plus a very large increase in total capacity over a relatively short time scale. We had a very competent and quite large engineering department which had been used to handling all the contracts, doing a lot of fairly detailed designs, certainly all the flow sheeting, and keeping a watching brief on all the details. It would have been impractical for them to have done this for all the new plants which were needed. So the work had to be done largely by contractors. It was an era when the method of the turnkey plant was still around, so a decision was taken to leave things virtually entirely to a contractor, the flow sheeting as well as the detailed design which they always do. Much less checking would be done on the design work by our own people. That sounded like a sensible decision.

Now put it in motivational terms. What the senior management were perceived by our engineering department to be saying was 'Oh yes, you have been building similar plants for years now, but you are really not competent to handle this. Go away. Stand clear. Don't interfere. These contractors know all about it, in fact they know much more than you.' Now that was not what was intended by the senior management and in fact it was not true. The decision was sensible — indeed the only possible one — but it was interpreted by the engineers in a way which made it hard for them to take any interest in, or feel any ownership for the plants. 'Well, if they don't need us, let them get on with it — it isn't our problem.'

Well, the plants were built rather shoddily, as the process construction industry was grossly overloaded at the time, there were a lot of things wrong with them and there were things wrong with the flow sheet too. Once they had been built and the initial commissioning tests had been done by the contractors a commissioning team from the engineering department was asked to go in and get them fully commissioned and the bugs ironed out. It sounds a reasonable thing to do, doesn't it? Actually, the commissioning team spent at least the first six months pointing out why the plants were absolutely no good and could never really work properly. They didn't just get down to solving the problems, they looked for problems. They found problems even where they didn't exist. What they had to prove, to themselves as much as to others, was that these outsiders who had been given 'their' job were not as competent as themselves.

To cut a long story short, a good deal of work was done and people finally began to get some sense of ownership in the plants. And then they were turned over to the works, who had had nothing to do with them previously, with the instructions 'here is a going plant, or it is going fairly well anyway, now you start to operate it'! And again you had the same sort of thing happening. You see that all of the things that were done were superficially very reasonable and done for very good reasons if you didn't look at them in human terms. But in motivational terms, and indeed even in terms of simple communication, of the hand-on of know-how gained by the commissioning team to the operating team, the whole thing was a very badly planned exercise. Fortunately this was recognised by senior managers and in subsequent plant building and commissioning deliberate steps were taken to involve fully not only the engineers but also the production people from the earliest stage. The result was plants which came on stream and up to flowsheet capacity within days, not months, of completion, with very large cost saving."

4.19   The problems described in the foregoing case will be only too familiar to those who have been involved in R & D projects. The particular example deals with transfer within a firm, but the characteristics are found in all types of transfer process. They show clearly the way in which conflicting motivations can hinder transfer. To avoid such problems all participants in the transfer process need to be effectively informed, able to contribute to its overall progress, and motivated to make such a contribution. There are, as we have indicated earlier, many factors which play a part in determining personal attitudes and objectives, and which therefore affect motivation towards specific projects. Where new ideas or new ways of doing things are involved the works of sociologists and studies of behaviour in organisation [12] can give important insights on which managements may be able to base their planning and decision making.

Positive motivation of individuals towards transfer depends, among other things, both on the rewards of personal satisfaction and the financial incentive of customer-contractor type relationships. As the case quoted shows, with a little foresight many of the potential difficulties could be anticipated and removed, but so often the seemingly obvious is ignored.

Intra-organisational Aspects

4.20 Motivation operates at the level of the individual. However, there is a corresponding factor of receptivity which operates at the organisational level and which affects the mechanism and success of transfer. Firstly, receptivity will be a function of the perceived appropriateness of a particular technology. We have already examined how technology needs to be fitted into the context of the user for effective transfer. At the level of the organisation, receptivity to a technology will depend on the way it is perceived to fit existing production, distribution, sales and service capabilities, as well as such obvious factors as estimated market size, profitability and financial return. Receptivity will also be influenced by the long term objectives and plans of the organisation.

4.21 The financial indicators and driving forces towards receptivity to new technology by a company are not well understood. Accepted wisdom has it that receptivity to new technology and to the inward flow of technology is a function of previous profit levels. However, Robbins reported at the conference work which cast doubt on this because no very significant correlation had been found between profits and R & D expenditure whilst in some cases there has been a significant correlation between sales and R & D expenditure. It was further concluded by Robbins that R & D is not a cost-driven function but one determined by expectations of future revenues. This is reflected in the way that government now tries to encourage R & D. It was stated that

> "The National Science Foundation has now shifted its entire focus on incentives to end-game incentives rather than R & D incentives. They are now concerned with how industry can be helped to perceive the future pay-off, rather than dealing directly with R & D."

72

Whatever the U.S. picture may reveal it should be remembered that a different relationship may apply in the U.K., and it will in part depend on companies' attitudes to profit and the importance which they place on income to shareholders. It could at least be argued that in an entrepreneurial atmosphere allocations to investment programmes, including R & D investment, would be made first, with remaining profits going to the shareholders, while in a different climate the maintenance of payments to shareholders would take priority. It is noted that in both U.K. and U.S. the justification of R & D expenditure levels is now undergoing some sharp reappraisals. The effect of this may be, of course, not to reduce the frequency and significance of transfer processes but increase them (see below). The empirical analyses of Mansfield [13] have shown that levels of R & D expenditure can be related to both sales (turnover) and profitability of past innovatory projects.

Clearly, expected sales and profit, and considerations of investment needs and cash flow, are likely to be major determinants both of the level of R & D investment by industrial establishment and of the selection of specific projects. However, conditioned partly no doubt by the lessons of the 50s and 60s when it was believed that investment in R & D would automatically lead to prosperity, there is now much greater concern to relate R & D programmes more explicitly to long term strategic objectives. This is already evident at the level of individual firms, and government is attempting to adopt the same approach for the projects it supports.

4.22 Programmes aimed at receiving technology need initially to be tied closely into ongoing research activities and to the setting of new goals, which makes their most appropriate home the R & D department. In this connection there is a task for research to consider how transfer options may be more effectively incorporated into the selection and evaluation procedures for project assessment. Programmes directed to the outward movement of technology, because of their need to adapt to new markets, may best be carried out as a marketing activity with important contributions from research and production departments. The need in such cases to adapt to new needs and new contexts suggests that technology transfer mechanisms should be developed in the light of marketing theories. The Harwell Laboratory of the United Kingdom Atomic Energy Research Establishment has probably gone further than most in applying marketing concepts to the development of mechanisms for transfer. Harwell classifies its activities, or its "product range", into three types, technical services, contract research, and exploitation. The first involves the sale of time on existing equipment, or the performance by Harwell staff of routine analytical or operational procedures, while the second involves the execution of research programmes agreed with, and fully paid for by the customer. In exploitation, the smallest in terms of receipts but perhaps the most demanding in terms of management time, Harwell will develop and adapt technology to new market requirements before licensing to a customer. In this case Harwell recovers its investment through royalty payments. In this context Clarke, Harwell's Marketing Director, commented

> "... we decided that, to get innovations successfully accepted, you had to have marketing; the scientist or somebody closely associated with him who is driving the thing forward has to think marketing, has to think in a market way. He has to be product-led in this thinking and he has to assimilate market knowledge."

To summarise, the dissemination of technology can best be considered as a marketing activity, but programmes to obtain technology on the other hand clearly have to operate in complementary fashion with other technical knowledge gathering departments, and in particular the R & D departments. It is now widely accepted that R & D programmes need to be developed taking full account of existing technology, and of the possibility of acquiring technology rather than developing it internally [14]. At the same time industry is becoming more aware of the advantages of transferring out technology which they may have developed which turns out not to fit sufficiently the requirements and context of the organisation [15].

Inter-organisational Aspects

4.23 Just as behavioural features influence the mechanisms and outcomes of transfer programmes, so too do various aspects of the relationship between the technology producing and receiving organisations. There are formal aspects of this relationship, such as the contractual arrangements under which the transfer is carried out, and also contextual ones which have their origins in the nature and abilities of the partners. Throughout this discussion we have been emphasising the contexted nature of technology and the need for the transferor to be aware of the environment of the receiver.

However, it should be noted that there are dangers in the excessive domination of the transfer process by the customer; complete accord with customer wishes changes the exchange from one of technology transfer to that of a service operation. This view, strongly argued in the opening paper (Paper 9) and with origins in the writing of Ansoff [16] on synergy, cannot be said to be more than a wisdom-based hypothesis. The argument is that if a technology is genuinely to extend the capability of the receiving organisation it will necessarily produce a disturbance in the receiver's existing operations. Conceptually we can suggest that the most beneficial technology transfer occurs when the technology neither fits immediately into present patterns of the receiver, nor is so incompatible as to invite immediate rejection. We discussed in Chapter 3 some of the arguments put forward when the customer/contractor principle was proposed. They can be seen to be related to this same point about customer domination of research and development. The worry is that, in order to earn money, too much effort may be deployed on service activities which have little or no effect in extending capability because the degree of fit is too high.

4.24 A hazard of protracted transfer processes is that time may so change the characteristics of a productive process as to destroy the possibility of the useful interaction which may have been perceived at the start. Technologies which are appropriate and effective in one industry at a particular time may not be effective in another.

A long drawn-out development time may result in an attempt to transfer a technology appropriate to yesterday's context and not today's. This is well illustrated by Catling's case study (Chapter 12). The case concerned the attempt to transfer automatic control technology and automatic transfer devices to the preparation of short staple fibres for spinning. What went wrong?

There was failure to appreciate that during the ten year period 1955 to 1965 card production rates and sliver drawing rates were increased tenfold whilst at the same time producing a significantly better product. The results of these changes were to reduce the number of carding engines required, making direct transfer cheap and simple without automatic handling; likewise increased drawing speeds made the economic size of sliver package larger and less in number. Increased drawing speeds also drastically improved sliver quality, eliminating need for the proposed automatic draft control.

4.25 There are other aspects of this case which show that neither the customer nor the scientists concerned with introducing the new technology kept in touch with other parallel developments in the industry. Thus there were faults in the organisation of the project, as well as in the original decision to allocate resources to its particular objective rather than others. There are many possible ways of setting up a relationship between producer and receiver which will prevent such mistakes. One way, suitable at least for major transfers, is provided by the experience of NASA, where potential sub-contractor firms worked with the parent organisation to determine the requirements and standards before a contract was drawn up. Similar experience in the U.K. under more stringently controlled financial conditions, has occurred between government departments, their research requirements boards and contracting research organisations. The transfer of technology between firms is normally carried out under the aegis of some sort of contractual relationship. With the increasing application in the U.K. of the customer/contractor principle more work in government establishments is carried out under such conditions. We have drawn attention to the concern expressed by some that the effects of such a relationship might be to over-emphasise short term advantages to institutions contracting for work at the expense of the long term interests of national policy. There is, however, an argument that a formal contractual arrangement can bring benefits to the relationship between the parties to the contract. It was stated that

> "there is much to be said for paying because that can create a relationship which does not otherwise exist. The customer/ contractor relationship has the advantage that those who pay for the work are likely to make some demands on those who are supplying. In other words, instead of taking what is on offer, or not, the customer can demand more information on this or that aspect of the innovation, especially as regards its tailoring to his requirements."

Norris's paper (Paper 8) also indicates that the formation of contractual links may increase the chance of transfer of technology from university to industry. However, the whole question of the role of contracts in generating and transferring useful science and technology is one of great ignorance and all too little experiment.

Licensing

4.26 The licensing executives often refer to their business as "technology transfer" and such a description is clearly appropriate in the context of our previous discussions. The role of licensing is given separate consideration here although many of the individual aspects reflect subjects that have already been considered. To apply the word "technology" to the licensing activity it is important to interpret it in Schon's very wide context [2]. Much of the licensing involves products in which the technical content is straightforward and simple, and where the transfer involves virtually no adaptation. This can lead to difficulties in assessing the importance of licensing in the exchange of industrial technologies.

Millar (Paper 11) pointed out that there are many ways in which the available statistics on licensing are distorted, one being that payments in respect of franchises in such activities as snackbar and restaurant chains are included alongside payments for high technology licences. Licensing is a distinct form of transfer process in that it is based upon the abstraction of key elements of the "technology plus context" for sale as a closed package, although even here there are many ways of operating and the form which the eventual agreement takes may well be modified in the process of exchange. There are, therefore, some similarities with the mechanisms discussed earlier under the heading of formal and informal agents, and comparison can be made with the approach adopted by other types of establishment in identifying potential customers and working with them towards mutually beneficial ends. For example, the need to personalise information and to build up mutual trust are important aspects of the licensing process.

4.27   Licensing starts with information transfer, and the brokers, although institutionally agencies, must frequently play active roles as agents.

> "As an agency a licence broking organisation transfers pieces
> of paper and this is information transfer, on the basis of
> which companies decide if they want to investigate further.
> As an agent within that agency I am concerned with technology transfer — when I come face to face with a situation."

The degree of assistance and involvement of the individual broker will depend on many things, including the nature of the technology and of the partners in the transfer. The skill of the broker lies in selecting and describing the key features of a licensing venture. Licensing information is a very specialised kind of scientific and technical information, and the licensing process is essentially "a process of abstracting things from the real world of the technologist and scientist and defining it", to quote one description. The essence of licensing, it was argued, is to pick on those factors that can be abstracted, and which are the key.

4.28   When the licence broker works for a large company he augments the resources and sources of technology available to that company. In such a company his role may embrace inflowing as well as outflowing technologies. Because the R & D cost of developing new products and processes is very high there is an incentive to maintaining a flow of new ones by buying licences and know-how. In a small company the licence broker may be almost the only means for bringing in new technology and it is true that most licence offers are not large advances of technology and do not present great perceptual problems. The cases which most need personal involvement are ones in which there is a problem of contextual fit. It was pointed out, for example, that differences in environmental factors usually required a sustained effort on the transfer of attitudes and values as well as on the technological aspects; as individuals change there may be a change in the know-how required for the application, which reinforces the need for "personalisation" of communication referred to earlier.

4.29   Promotion of licensing activity, especially by large international firms, may lead to the transfer of inappropriate technology if what is offered is uncritically accepted. The mismatch of some industrialised countries' technologies with the developing countries' (LDC) contexts may then be dramatic. The argument is made that firms in developing countries have been too eager to take licences for western products, and to use western help in creating markets for these, and this encourages diversion of resources away from other activities which might be more valuable to the LDC in the longer term. It is necessary to repeat here the *caveat* made earlier in this monograph that technology transfer is not an unquestionably "good thing"; the arguments of this chapter for improved mechanisms of transfer must include the call for improved methods of assessment of the social costs and benefits of what is to be transferred, which reiterates the need to study the technology in context rather than in isolation or merely in the existing context from which it is to be transferred out. Millar (Paper 11) comments that U.S. companies appear to prefer to establish or acquire their own subsidiary companies in overseas markets and to use this method to transfer technology and know-how. This suggests that the transferring parent wishes thereby to secure better control of both the operating conditions for his technology and the markets in which its products will be sold. In other words it is by means of the branch affiliate that the international firm establishes a congenial context for its transferred technology, a context which by appropriate plant design and housing, by appropriate staffing and by effective communication links ad from the parent matches closely the environment for which the technology was originally developed.

4.30 It was noted (Paper 11) that the increasing tendency to establish foreign affiliates as the preferred means of technology transfer internalised such transfer processes and diminished the role of licensing brokers. However this may be for the movement of complex and highly differentiated technology (which is a characteristic of the international firm with worldwide branch establishments [17]), there is reason to believe that the licensed flow of technology among firms and nations must continue to increase as the demands of the third world for more and more technology go on growing. If this is so the licensing broker will be of increasing importance in transfer processes, both as agent and agency.

References

[1] Allen, T.J., "The Differential Performance of Information Channels in Transfer of Technology" in *Factors in the Transfer of Technology*, Gruber & Marquis, Editors, M.I.T. Press, Cambridge, Mass., 1969.

[2] Schon, D., *Technology & Change*, Pergamon, London, 1967.

[3] Rogers, E.M. & Schoemaker, F.F., *Communication of Innovations*, Free Press N.Y., 1971.

[4] *First Special Report from the Select Committee on Science & Technology Session 1972-73*, HC43, H.M.S.O., London, 1972.

[5] Marshall, W., "Harwell and Industrial Research", *6th Maurice Lubbock Lecture*, O.U.P., Oxford, 1969.

[6] Cotgrove, S. & Box, S., *Science Industry & Society*. Allen & Unwin, London, 1970.

[7] Sklair, L., *Organised Knowledge*, Paladin, London, 1973.

[8] Pearson, A.W. & Rickards, T., "Current Problems in Transferring Science to Technology" in *Technology Transfer* Davidson, H.F., Cetron, M.J. and Goldhar, J.D., editors, Noordhoff, Leiden, 1974, p. 67.

[9] Black, R.P., "Technical Report RSSC-TR 8318 − 17" Vol. 1 *SRI* California, 1922.

[10] Behrman, J.N. & Wallender, H.W., *Transfers of Manufacturing Technology within Multinational Enterprises*, Ballinger, Cambridge, Mass, 1976.

[11] Woods, M.F. & Davies, G.B., "Potential Problem Analysis: a systematic approach to problem recognition and contingency planning − an aid to the smooth exploitation of research", *R & D Management* 4 (1973) (1), 25.

[12] Cyert, R.M. & March, J.G. *A Behavioural Theory of the Firm*, Prentice-Hall, N.J., 1963.

[13] Mansfield, E., *Industrial Research & Technological Innovation*, W.W. Norton, N.Y., 1968.

[14] Altenpohl, D., "Acquisition of Technology as One Specific Way to

Achieve Technology Transfer" in *Technology Transfer*, Davidson, H.F., Cetron, M.J., and Goldhar, J.D., editors, Noordhoff, Leiden, 1974, p.. 595.

[15] Bendaniel, D.J., "The Technical Ventures Operation" in *Technology Transfer* Davidson, H.F., Cetron, M.J. and Goldhar, J.D., editors, Noordhoff, Leiden, 1974, p. 611.

[16] Ansoff, H.I., *Corporate Strategy*, McGraw Hill, London, 1965.

[17] Johnson, H.G., *Technology and Economic Independence*, Macmillan Press Ltd. London, 1975.

Chapter 5

METHODOLOGY

Research and Implementation

5.1 It is most common at gatherings in which technology transfer is the subject to hear two general types of criticism of research. Indeed these two types of criticism dominate all fields which choose as their subject phenomena which some people deal with on a day-to-day basis. These two criticisms may be paraphrased briefly as "What is the use of this research?", and "Why isn't this research more scientific?". It is to these two questions we now address ourselves.

5.2 The meeting at Stirling brought together those involved in the transfer of technology, to whom we have applied the description "practitioner" and those who have as one of their main activities research designed to further our understanding of transfer processes in technical change. The latter group have been labelled "academics", largely for want of a better word since other terms such as "researcher" may cause confusion between the technology and the study of the transfer process. We designate the tactics and techniques used by practitioners as "Mechanisms", and will refer to the approaches used in the study of the transfer processes as "Methodology".

The Americans have a descriptive phrase which they apply to the study of all aspects of the system within which science and technology are developed and applied. They refer to it as "Research on Research", and we discuss in this chapter the various tools and techniques at the disposal of the "Researcher on Research". Clearly, although we shall be concerned principally with research methods, some cross-referencing from methods of study to methods of doing is as desirable as it is inescapable.

5.3 The academic has a legitimate concern with the methodology of research because research is, in part, what he is paid to do. The pursuit of knowledge necessitates an attempt to discover how best research into a subject may be conducted. The research results, when obtained, are used in several ways. The most immediate effect normally lies in their use in the teaching that academics do at undergraduate and postgraduate level. But research results are also disseminated from academic institutions and may be taken up and used by others, and many of the ways in which this diffusion happens have been discussed earlier. The concept of transfer processes is as relevant to the results of research on research as it is to scientific and technological research findings. In general the *primary* objectives of academics studying transfer processes in technical change are not concerned with helping the scientist, technologist or manager to achieve their goals. However, once research has yielded results which give a deeper insight into these processes, the academic has the capability to make contributions which may improve transfer performance.

5.4 This interdependence of research and practical utility is not always recognised. The practitioner at the Stirling meeting who challenged the academics by saying (of the Requirements Boards):

> "they live in real life and have to find out how the system works. But you (academics) don't because you are not living in that world. I would just ask you, are you studying the subject or are you trying to do something?"

was creating a false dichotomy. Doing depends on understanding, at least to an appropriate level, the operation of the processes involved. It is clear however that the law of diminishing returns must apply to research on research, just as much as it will to other forms of research. There will perhaps come a time when our understanding of transfer processes in technical changes is sufficient to enable decision makers to control their rate, direction and effectiveness well enough that any further research would become Pavitt's (Chapter 3) "conspicuous intellectual consumption".

In this sense the same practitioner quoted above was on stronger ground when he reacted to Bradbury's rhetorical question "does more technology mean better?" with the question "does more study of technology transfer mean better?" Our response to Bradbury's question would be ambivalent. There are clearly areas in which more technology would not be better, whereas in other places there is a desperate need for new, appropriate technological solutions to existing problems. We discuss this point in more detail in the next chapter. Our response to the second question would be an unequivocal affirmative. At this stage our understanding of the transfer processes within technical change are not sufficient for the needs of decision-makers who wish to encourage, direct or retard such change.

5.5 This questioning of the value of research appears to be rooted in the belief that only a practitioner, actually engaged, on a regular basis, in doing something can know anything about it. Thus in our context only those involved in transferring technology can provide insights into how it can be done. The favourite analogy for those who advocate the primacy of the "learning by doing" process appears to be sex, which "you learn by doing, not by abstract theorisation". This is a dangerous and somewhat unsatisfactory analogy because it can also be used to illustrate a need for technology transfer. In sex it is true that, in most cases, an adequate level of performance can be achieved through learning by doing, but the existence of a flourishing market for technical aids, both software and hardware, is some indication that other forms of learning can contribute to the improvement of performance.

The ultimate resolution of the theory versus practice argument lies in the realm of much discussed philosophical and ethical questions of the relationship between knowledge and action. We believe that learning by doing is an important process, and it is, traditionally, the way of transferring many craft-based skills and techniques. As we said earlier in discussing Brook's definition of technology (Chapter 1) much has still to be conveyed by involvement in doing. But we also believe in the process of learning from the analysis of doing, whether this analysis is based on "scientific" methodology or on wisdom-based reflections.

We accept, of course, the need for relevance in research, and do not mean to say that *any* research into the phenomena within technical change is automatically justified. But we believe the law of diminishing returns has not yet set in, and that more research, in certain specific areas which we will discuss later, could mean better transfer. But how should that work be conducted? What methods can we use to further our understanding of transfer processes? These questions form the basis of the running debate about methodology in which many of the academics are involved, and which surfaced from time to time at the Stirling meeting, to the annoyance, we suspect, of many of the practitioners.

The Justification for Research into Transfer Processes

5.6 Having said that we believe more research can be beneficial we should first say why we hold this belief. The first reason is that, as Bell and Hill argue (Paper 12), abstract models do form the basis of policies, designed and implemented by practitioners (sometimes in consultation with academics). The ramifications of policies based on some perceived model are potentially wide-spread, and it therefore seems sensible to devote some effort to attempts to discover if the models afford a sufficiently accurate description of reality for the purposes of policy making.

5.7   The second point, closely related to the first, is that the effectiveness of policies, or of changes in policy, should be subject to evaluation. As has frequently been demonstrated, for instance by Forrester [1], complex social systems may not behave as intu-ition suggests, and thus policy changes may not achieve the desired results. Research can be used to provide a way of assessing the impact of changes in policies or mechanisms. However, this can only be done if the research is implemented alongside the change in mechanism.

An example of this interrelationship emerged during a discus-sion of the customer-contractor relationship when Jervis asked whether the capability existed to conduct an examination, perhaps three or four years after their establishment, of the activities of the Requirements Boards to evaluate whether the new way of funding research has led to more, or better, technology transfer than that occurring under the old system.

A representative of the Department of Industry responded to the question thus:

"Very briefly I would like to comment on how can one judge the effectiveness of Requirements Boards in the longer term and how far the mechanism for evaluation exists. I think it is useful to see how far the current Research Requirements Boards are very similar to what has happened in the past, and where they vary. It is nothing new that industrialists and academics are advising on the programmes of research which are undertaken in the government laboratories. But the great difference of the present system is that where the Research Advisory Committees made confidential reports to the Se-cretary of State, the reports of the Research Requirements Boards, as far as our own department is concerned, will be freely published every year. Equally every year now the De-partment is publishing precisely how the resources are divided into the different programmes — detail which has never pre-viously been provided. Equally the boards are clear as to what their long-term strategy is. I think it will be possible for all universities and anyone who is interested to look at these annual reports, look at their strategy papers, and look actually at what happens from when they come into the pic-ture to when they finish".

5.8   In terms of open government and the exposure of decision making to comment and criticism this is a welcome advance. But, as it was argued, it still may not allow proper evaluation of the mechanism:

"Retrospective studies are incredibly difficult to do because you have to get rid of all the mythology and so on. And so I think one has to try and build in to the operation of the policy, in real time, some measures to help with the evaluation. I think I would find it difficult to assess the Requirements Boards retrospectively in, say, five years time. Industry is going through a very difficult time at the moment and its R & D budgets are being squeezed, so there may well be pressure to look for other sources of technology. We may see in hindsight, in five years time, a lot more technology being transferred out of places like Harwell and the GREs. But I think it would be very difficult to say whether this was due to something that happened because industry was under pressure or because government picked a new way of funding R & D. It is this sort of thing which you may be able to find ways of looking at in real time which would be very difficult to sort out in hindsight".

5.9   The paper by Douds and Rubenstein (Chapter 8) also contains an argument for more real-time rather than retrospective studies, and many of the R & D incentives programmes in the US, such as the City Technological Extension Scheme described in Chapter 4, are being evaluated in real time by controlled experiments. There is, by contrast, very little conscious adoption of such an experimental approach in Britain. Of course we recognise that real-time studies are difficult, time-consuming, and constitute no panacea for the problems of research on transfer processes. Nevertheless their incorporation into major government programmes would appear worthwhile.

5.10   These then are some of the justifications for extending and strengthening the research-based understanding of transfer processes in technical change. But there remains some disagreement about the best way of conducting research in this area, and it is on the consideration of merits and demerits of alternative methodologies that we concentrate in the remainder of this chapter.

Problems with Existing Methodologies

5.11   We have already discussed the categorisation of the literature on technology transfer into "wisdom", "case study" and "experimental" classes. This tendency was separately commented on by Bradbury (Paper 1) and Douds (Paper 2). The analyses we make of this categorisation are somewhat different from the more traditional arguments of management scientists such as are presented in Paper 2 and such as in reviews by Douds [2] and others of the "Northwestern school" [3]. The argument is that too many studies in this field are ill-conceived and poorly planned by researchers with little long-term commitment, and that it is time a halt was called to studies labelled "exploratory" when "the *researcher* is not familiar with what is known about the phenomena" [2].

This categorisation of technology transfer would appear to have been drawn from that developed by Folger and Gordon [4] who argue that fields develop in three stages, from speculative impressionistic treatments through reports of a specific universe or case to "studies generalising from a representative sample to the total universe". As we noted earlier, in technology transfer the state of the art appears to be such that the field is still heavily dominated by the discussive or wisdom approach. This, of course, is the level at which most practitioners with their wide range of anecdotal evidence, tend to contribute. Most "formal" research has been of the case study variety and the "highest" level that has been achieved is the comparative multi-case study. Remarkably similar conclusions have been arrived at by Gayer [5] in his review of progress in studies of innovation — a topic which, as we have already indicated, is very closely related to transfer processes in technical change.

5.12   Rubenstein and his colleagues at Northwestern University have been particularly vocal about the inadequacies of the state of research and argued for more explicit research design, hypotheses and methodology in general. The reason that we are anxious that the value of anecdotes and case studies be recognised is that, at a fairly simple level, it can be argued that it is precisely this anecdotal evidence which enables the researcher to arrive at "reasonable", as opposed to purely speculative, hypotheses. After all, intuition has all too frequently been shown to be based on some special insight into a phenomenon. Bradbury (Paper 1) goes further in arguing that as one of the goals of research into technology transfer is to assist the practitioner, a rough cost-benefit analysis may show that, at least at this stage, "experience, reinforced, broadened and extended by case work" may most rapidly provide an effective guide to action.

5.13   While some of Doud's criticisms were accepted there was little agreement about the validity of the expressed desire for a more "scientific" approach to research. Jervis questioned the appropriateness of methodologies based on the natural sciences for topics which may be of an inherently different nature, and Bell introduced a time dimension to the debate by commenting that "*the* scientific method", namely testing of propositions, may not be applicable in the early stages of research in a given field. He suggested that such methods become appropriate only at a comparatively late stage, and that prior to this a much more loosely structured approach is appropriate. In Bell's words "one is looking at things, scratching one's head, going backwards and forwards and asking many questions. And then at some stage one moves towards a more formalised structuring and a rigorous testing of propositions". The consensus was that at certain times and circumstances it may be inappropriate to pursue too hard, or to be too concerned about, imitating "the scientific method" of the natural sciences, which might tend to constrain the growth of concepts and models if applied mechanically at a stage when the subject is still immature.

5.14 Discussion of alternative methodological approaches to technology transfer research should be seen as a subject of a wider debate on research method and practice. The short discussion which follows is based largely on the work of Ravetz [6]. We believe that a brief consideration of the social basis of scientific practice and its development will give coherence and theoretical justification to many of the opinions on methodology expressed at the Stirling meeting.

The Development of Research Standards

5.15 Recent findings within the sociology of science, in which research has been directed at determining the mechanisms by which science progresses, offer some useful insights in the context of technology transfer research. The first, and most immediately relevant, is that, despite popular notions, there is no scientific method universally applicable to all fields. Thus the demands of many for "more scientific studies" rests on the misconception that there is a standard method ready-made and available for adoption at any time.

Kuhn's analysis [7] has been particularly influential in demonstrating that the scientist develops theories and carries out experiments not according to demands set by nature but by those set by the community of scientists of which he is a member. Kuhn has shown that the progressive nature of science rests on the consensus achieved and maintained with respect to a ruling paradigm, but that this is not a static consensus. Ravetz [6], in particular, has shown that the standards by which research is judged to be adequate and of value are themselves dynamic, developing in response to the progress in theories, concepts and techniques within the field. This may perhaps best be understood as a dialectical "lifting by the bootstraps" operation. The important consequence for our purposes is that there is no externally validated research methodology or set of standards which can be applied to any new field. The success of any field depends on the gradual mutual development of theories, concepts, and techniques together with standards for their assessment which have some stability, and explanatory power, and which are not in sharp disaccord with the concepts and standards of neighbouring fields. It is only when this development has occurred successfully and a field settles down to relatively stable development that standards and methodologies become so well recognised and unquestioned that they may appear to have an existence independent of the particular field in which they were developed. Attempts to improve a field by a mechanical imitation of the methods of a mature and successful discipline may not only be inappropriate but do much harm.

5.16   Ravetz's analysis of immature fields of inquiry appears particularly apposite for those concerned with the methodology of research into technology transfer. An immature field may be characterised as one in which a stable body of "facts" does not exist and is not being produced. In other words, the evidence, information and data being collected, and the conclusions of arguments based on them, are not widely recognised by members of the research community as being particularly significant. Ravetz argues:

> "The failure of nearly all of these (facts) to survive even in the short run, is an indication that most of the work of investigating problems is vitiated by pitfalls, encountered sooner or later in the work. The results of research are generally weak, or even vacuous. This condition prevails even in fields where the leaders and their associates spare nothing in their endeavours; but the absence of a body of appropriate methods of inquiry nullifies their efforts. For it is through such methods, ranging from the techniques of production of data to the judgements of adequacy on an argument that pitfalls are identified, and ways around them are charted. Because of the subtlety and sophistication of scientific inqui-

ry, these methods are a craft knowledge, built up by successful experience; and so the improvement of its methods is
not a straightforward operation.

The weaknesses in the social aspects of inquiry also contribute to the self-perpetuating condition of ineffectiveness.
The mechanisms for the processing of results, and for the
exercise of quality control, cannot be stronger than the materials on which they operate. For social reasons it is necessary
to give the formal authenticity of publication to masses of
results which are very weak; and so the effective standards of
quality cannot meet those of a matured field. Because of the
rapid succession of separate schools, each with its own objects of inquiry and principles of method, there is little opportunity for results of potentially high quality to survive
and become established as facts. And in this unstable and
frequently false social situation, the mechanisms for the control of quality and the maintenance of scientific integrity at
the highest levels do not exist".

5.17   These problems are well illustrated by the discussion concerning the interpretation of data of Langrish (Paper 7) which
was described in Chapter 3. With regard to the empirical evidence
itself, there was considerable argument over the adequacy of sampling and unique features associated with the particular sample chosen. Doubt was expressed over the validity of the type of data, in
this case citations, as an indicator of the relevance of knowledge.
At an even more general level, the underlying model of the way in
which knowledge contributes to the innovation process was questioned.

5.18   Under these conditions it is obvious that there are many
difficulties associated with working in an immature field where the
pitfalls are still unidentified. However the situation is made even
more difficult by the need to disguise this immaturity in order to
attract funds and new recruits to the field and to convince those
concerned with the practical problem which first gave rise to the
new field that a solution will be forthcoming. Ravetz again states
the problems clearly:

"The pretence of maturity throws up a host of practical
problems which aggravate the already severe difficulties of
scientific inquiry in such conditions. Recruits are generally
given no warning that their research work is likely to be very
hazardous, and after some years of producing results which
inexplicably fail to consolidate into facts, they become de-
moralized; the real state of their field becomes a shameful

secret. Nor do they have the security of knowing that their years of specialized training in the subject gives them a monopoly of practice in it, as in a learned profession or a matured science. For the founders of the field, on whose insights all subsequent work is directly based (without the enrichment that occurs in matured fields) are likely to have been philosophers, polymaths, or amateurs, rather than certified experts; and even at the present it is possible for an amateur to crash into the field, or to analyse the practical problems of its concern with more success than its practitioners. Moreover since the social mechanisms for quality control and direction in the field cannot function properly, the safeguards against the abuses of prestige are weakened, and the assessments of a lay audience, based on popularizations, can be of more practical importance in the politics of the field than those of the community of experts. Under such conditions the pretence of maintaining the social mechanisms appropriate to a matured discipline, and even more the task of improving their real condition, are rendered yet more difficult".

Thus, the arguments of Douds and Rubenstein can be seen to be concerned with methodological standards only to the extent that they represent a form of control over entry to, and quality of, the field.

5.19 How then can an immature field avoid these various pitfalls and set itself on the road to maturity? Within technology transfer attempts have been made by the amassing of empirical data and the development of sophisticated mathematical and computational tools to extract significant information, by the construction of elaborate systems to enable representative symbols to be manipulated in formal arguments and by attempts to develop appropriate methodologies. In each case, the attempt is to reproduce what is felt to be the crucial feature of an established mathematical-experimental science, without any recognition of the historical means by which such approaches developed. Alternatives are suggested by Ravetz:

"Where the objects of inquiry have but a tenuous relation to the real things and events they purport to describe, and are themselves ill-formed and unstable, an isolated investigation devoted to a supposedly 'empirical' test of some hypothesis about their relations, is highly unlikely to yield worthwhile results. As an alternative to such 'research', we can imagine a sort of 'history' conducted in a disciplined fashion and using all appropriate tools; whose objects of inquiry are those of a trained common sense, and which has a less formalized, and correspondingly more extensive and perhaps deeper, contact with its sources. The discipline which we now call history works in this fashion on the traces of human activity in the past; and it can offer tested methods, including criteria of adequacy, to this sort of work. At the other extreme, 'theory' could be recognised as a sort of 'philosophy', and could be governed to some extent by the methods of that discipline. It would then not be a cause of surprise or shame that effective new insights come only very rarely, and that they are only slightly developed by the subsequent efforts of lesser men; and it could be recognised that an essential part of a genuine education in the discipline is a dialogue with its great masters. Finally, the successful 'arts' could be recognised as the most genuine tested experience of the field, and studied and developed as such. Each of these three sorts of inquiry could eventually yield knowledge of its characteristic sort, and, in their interaction, offer mutual criticism and support."

5.20   Thus it is not necessary for a field to imitate physics in order for it to make a contribution to the advancement of knowledge which is enshrined not in laws, as in physics, but according to Ravetz in aphorisms; "an expression of a deep personal understanding of its objects, in a condensed and communicable form". There may be limitations in the universality of knowledge in this form, but such development is far more likely to open the way to maturity than the forcing of research into the mould of physics.

The Benefits of Immaturity

5.21   We have already defined the state of technology transfer research as immature, using the concepts advanced by Ravetz, and it is this fact which accounts for the predominance of wisdom literature. It also justifies some, but not all, of the criticisms of current research made by Douds. However we must stress that we do not necessarily ascribe only negative features to immature fields. Immaturity has benefits which we would not wish to see sacrificed as the state of the art matures.

5.22   The first of these benefits is that in an immature field the processes of institutionalisation and specialisation discussed by Johnston (Paper 3) have not reached advanced stages and the barriers to communication and information transfer may be relatively low. Practitioners and researchers can engage in a dialogue from which, potentially, both sides can emerge with benefit — as, we believe, the Stirling meeting showed.

Another advantage of immaturity is that it is a state in which some forms of the wisdom approach can survive and make a valuable contribution. Recently it has been suggested that more established branches of the social sciences can become sterile if they become too institutionalised and constrained within mechanistic paradigms. [8]

5.23 Bennis [9] has argued the need to reestablish reflection as a legitimate process of enquiry for the social sciences, and writes of the need to find an alternative, experiential, approach to organisational analysis. He comments that most social science written today appears lifeless in comparison with the work of the "new journalists" such as Wolfe, Capote and Mailer in traditional social science areas. The problem in this is that good journalism is often bad social science, but social scientists have, by default, turned large areas of contemporary experience over to amateurs.

Bennis argues for the integration of raw experience with analysis, involving the social scientist in a role which combines action and analysis. In this role he says:

> "the scientist is more akin to the 'new journalist', with his personal voice and cold, impersonal eye, than to most of the current writers in social science. Instead of the more traditional 'participant-observer' familiar to the anthropologist, the field sociologist and the psychologist, the social scientist in this mode becomes an 'observant participant'. This approach allows for both personal and theoretical insights. Both are in gear, but one, the personal, is the major stem-winder".

It is asking a lot to find many participants with the ability, as well as the time and motivation, to observe, and similarly there are many difficulties in the way of the researcher/observer who wants to participate. But in an immature field, because it is still relatively easy to bring forward the wisdom-based insights of participants for discussion and analysis in the presence of researchers, the effect sought by Bennis can be achieved. This is one of the strengths of immaturity and one which we would seek to maintain.

5.24 We mentioned earlier the two generic criticisms of technology transfer research, and from the subsequent analysis it may be apparent that the frustrations with research on the part of the practitioners of technology transfer and the demands of the academics represent the opposite sides of the same coin. For it is precisely the same reasons that lead the one group to see little value in research on technology transfer and the other to demands of higher standards of research patterned on the positivist model of physics. And what should also be evident is that exhortations from either side are in themselves not going to lead to change.

Priorities for the Development of Methodologies

5.25 What are the major tasks facing technology transfer researchers in the area of methodology? Clearly one concerns the development of methodologies appropriate to the topic of study. These methodologies will not be carbon copies of those developed in other fields, either of the physical sciences or the social sciences. But this does not mean that ideas or practices cannot be borrowed from other areas and adapted. There is clearly a need for the development of measures which can be used to determine the effectiveness or efficiency of various transfer processes, and this would then open the way to comparative studies of transfer processes. A possible model for such analyses is found in the innovation field in Project SAPPHO [10] itself borrowing techniques first used in biology.

5.26 Researchers need to take into account, when constructing models of transfer processes, organisational and psychological factors, as well as the influence of general technical capability of the technology receiver and his stock of knowledge and know-how. In addition future studies ought to pay more attention to mechanisms for the identification of needs, in order to throw light on what several speakers describe as the appropriateness of the technology — the goodness of fit of technology to user context. The parameters which will determine contextual fit, and in particular ways of measuring them ex-ante rather than ex-post, are clearly of great interest to practitioners and policy-makers, and should thus receive urgent attention from the academics.

5.27 Another major area of concern for those engaged in research is that involving standardisation. Definitions constrain and direct the utility of the entire body of research and knowledge. As we have pointed out, there are different meanings ascribed to the word technology, and also many transfer processes which are available for study. While we do not argue for total conformity, either in definition or methodology, there is clearly a need for comparability and communicability both between academics, and from academics to practitioners and policy makers. Just as, in the area of R & D statistics, internationally agreed definitions of the standard terms such as basic research, applied research, and development, were adopted to aid data collection and comparison, so in the area of technical change agreed definitions of words like "technology", "innovation", "transfer", "diffusion", "product champion", "inventor", "entrepreneur", "agent", "agency" and so on could speed up the development of knowledge within the field.

In this sense we support Douds (Paper 2). The study of transfer processes in technical change is never likely to lend itself to the same high degree of experimental replicability of the natural sciences, but we fully agree that academics should attempt, wherever possible, to standardise both definitions and instruments of methodology, and in all cases to describe fully their research method in addition to their results.

Douds also argues the case for more real-time experimental studies of technology transfer. From our preceding comments it will be clear that we must have reservations about the universal applicability of an experimental methodology at least to the extent that the adjective implies the approach of the physicist. But about the benefits of the real-time study there can be no doubt. Typically the real-time approach will need the full cooperation of practitioners as well as observers, and it can be conducted either by the "participant-observer" or, in the mode favoured by Bennis, by the "observant participant". As we have already said, the present immaturity of the field may be an advantage in achieving the required cooperation, provided the academic/practitioner mistrust which at present exists can be removed.

5.28 Practitioners and policy makers should also recognise the need we described earlier for the incorporation within their systems and activities ways of monitoring and evaluating the effectiveness of changes to policies or practices. We believe this to be especially important. Our belief is that the economic and social needs of the coming decades are going to place demands and constraints on technology which cannot be met simply by "fine tuning" or altering at the margin existing technology policies. More radical approaches may be needed, and these will need careful assessment. This is a subject to which we return in the next chapter.

References

[1] Forrester, J.W., "Counterintuitive Nature of Social Systems", *Technology Review*, 73 (1971) 53.
[2] Douds, C.F., "The State of the Art in the Study of Technology Transfer — A Brief Survey", *R & D Management*, 1 (1971) 103.

[3] Chakrabarti, A.K., "Some Concepts of Technology Transfer: Adoption of Innovations in Organizational Content", *R & D Management*, 3 (1973) 111.

[4] Folger, A. and Gordon, G., "Scientific Accomplishment and Social Organisation: A Review of the Literature", *The American Behavioural Scientist*, 6 (1962) 51.

[5] Gayer, G.K., *A Bibliography of Case Studies of Innovation*, Program of Policy Studies in Science and Technology, The George Washington University, Washington, D.C., 20006.

[6] Ravetz, J.R., *Scientific Knowledge and its Social Problems*, Clarendon Press, Oxford, 1971.

[7] Kuhn, T.S., *The Structure of Scientific Revolutions*, Chicago University Press, Chicago, 1969.

[8] Gouldner, T.S., *The Coming Crisis in Western Sociology*, Heinemann, 1971.

[9] Bennis, W., "The Leaning Ivory Tower", Jossey-Bass, London, 1973.

[10] Achilledellis, L. *et al.*, *Success and Failure in Industrial Innovation: Report of Project SAPPHO*, Centre for the Study of Industrial Innovation, London, 1972.

Chapter 6

ENDS AND MEANS

6.1 In the preceding chapters we have tried to describe the situation facing academics and practitioners concerned with transfer processes in technical change. We have discussed the material presented and reviewed the contributions made during debate in the context of both the existing body of knowledge about "technology transfer" and the expressed needs and concerns of practitioners. This process of synthesis and analysis has provided us with what we believe is a novel and useful way of structuring the existing knowledge in the field, of identifying gaps where new knowledge is needed, and also of indicating areas in which more use of transfer processes should be made.

6.2 The conclusions we have drawn can be summarised in seven statements:

— both technology and the processes by which it can be transferred are functions of their environments or contexts;

— there is no single best way to transfer technology. A multiplicity of transfer processes is available, only a few of which will be appropriate for a given situation;

— a major determinant of success in transfer will be the degree to which the technology establishes a contextual fit in its new environment. Many factors will influence this goodness of fit;

— if transfer is to be encouraged then care must be taken to ensure that both the technology and the mechanism to be employed for transfer are appropriate within the contexts of provider and receiver. In addition sufficient modification of the technology to fit the receiver's context must be ensured;

— existing methodologies for studying transfer processes are inadequate and definitional problems inhibit the development of a relevant body of knowledge. New methodologies are needed, designed for the task in hand and departing as necessary from those appropriate to physical science;

— the study of technical change should now progress by the examination of these transfer processes, rather than by the investigation of those parts of the activity which can conveniently be compartmentalised within institutional or disciplinary boundaries;

— in studying transfer processes more stress must be placed than hitherto on concepts such as ownership and motivation. A greater focus on behavioural aspects of the process is needed.

6.3   Over the period covered by four technology transfer symposia (Paris 1973, Stirling 1974, Les Arcs 1975 and Stirling 1976), ideas have evolved and changed. The phrase "technology transfer" now begs many questions; what does it mean; for what purpose is it proposed; in what context is it being used? By failing to answer these questions explicitly, or by assuming there could be no ambiguity in the answers to them, the earlier discussions avoided the main issues.

Thus, the 1973 meeting appeared to discuss technology transfer as if it were an end in its own right, and in common with many other debates, tended to concentrate too much on the input side of the process with little attention being paid to output. It must be emphasised that transfer is not an end in itself, and that for success transfer processes must be driven by the logic of the objectives that they serve.

6.4   If we now review the themes discussed at the earliest meeting, several features stand out. Firstly, it is now apparent that the horizontal shift concept was dominating the perception of technology transfer, and that most of the discussion concerned the establishment of new uses for recently developed technology.

We would now strongly emphasise the importance of those transfer processes involved in change and innovation. In addition the importance of the objectives of a transfer process, and the realisation that technology transfer is not an end in its own right but merely one means of contributing to the achievement of such objectives, are now seen as fundamental. To these must be added expanded ideas about context, appropriateness and fit.

Consideration of the operations of international firms and of licensing agents makes it evident that entrepreneurs and business corporations are well able to distinguish ends from means and are therefore somewhat impatient with those who fail to make clear this distinction. Thus it becomes important to challenge the relevance of policies for technology transfer *per se*, particularly when advocated as options for government.

6.5   From the viewpoint we describe here a statement such as the one made recently in the U.K. to the effect that technology transfer was now one of the Department of Industry's major objectives is confusing. Are we to assume that previously technology transfer was not an important consideration in the Department's support of applied research? Presumably the answer is no, although impressions have sometimes contradicted this. Is the Department saying that technology transfer is an end in itself? Again the answer is presumably negative since other statements show that the need to bring best practice technology into use in British industry is clearly recognised as of vital importance. What is at last being recognised is that the transfer activity is vital to the success of research programmes associated with economic or social goals, and that this is true within the normal processes of development and application of technology, not just when additional spin-off benefits are being sought. It is important to ensure that the transfer activity is seen as an integral part of the research programme, and that the resource allocations recognise this, and that transfer is not seen merely as a late addition grafted on as an afterthought. Other issues are secondary to this. Objectives can be changed, governments can seek to promote the use of technology available "off-the-shelf" rather than the development of new technology, traditional manufacturing industries can be favoured for government attention over newer, advanced technology based ones, but if insufficient attention is paid to the transfer processes and their associated incentives and barriers, the objectives will not be achieved.

6.6   In developing the concept of transfer processes in technical change we want to establish the central nature of these processes as determinants of the success of any technology policy. Dominating all the discussions we have reported here is the realisation that if effective transfer is needed before the objectives of any programme can be achieved then that transfer must be planned, and resources must be allocated to its achievement. Occasionally transfer will happen of its own accord, but these chance events cannot be relied upon for the achievement of programme goals. There is no way round this fact. The reliance on transfer cannot be avoided by changing objectives, nor can choice of mechanisms be made in isolation from considerations of purpose, context and appropriateness. If there are to be technology transfer programmes they must be seen as an integral component of a wider technology policy, and this is true whether that policy is for a national economy, an industry sector, or an individual company. Johnston [1] has elaborated on the importance of transfer processes to technology policy and we have gone to great lengths to remove the connotation of technology transfer as something relevant only to spin-off of "bonus" benefits from technological resource allocation decisions. We have referred earlier to the comments made by Doctors and others about the political or public relations nature of many of the early technology transfer programmes, and we repeat here that no amount of spin-off can justify an initially inappropriate allocation of resources. Attempts to justify programmes on the spin-off they may bring, along with arguments that programmes must go on because of the money which has already been spent, are two of the most frequently used defences of technologists protecting *folies de grandeur*. "Technology transfer" is not some magic wand which, if waved over the sacred cows of modern technology, will turn them into industrious work-horses, but transfer processes are an integral and essential part of all technology development.

6.7   Turning to future developments we can claim in the language of the corporate planner to have performed a "position audit" on technology transfer and to have identified some of the strengths and weaknesses of our current understanding of the phenomena involved. But this is only a beginning: what comes next? It is not unnatural to feel tempted to make some more prescriptive or normative comments on the process.

Some of these ideas relate more to the research and educational aspects of transfer processes, with the practical aspects of their operation being left for the practitioners' attention. We commented in paragraphs 1.39 and 2.38 that there appeared to be difficulty in locating existing technology relevant to a specific problem area. We note in passing that the trend in management information systems is towards more flexibility, with less reporting of historic data to a prestructured format and more ability to respond to specific requests or questions.

Additionally, in areas traditionally associated with the impersonal manipulation of information, such as accountancy, recent theories place much more emphasis on the behavioural aspects of information collection and interpretation. The parallels with scientific and technical information systems and the way in which they are used seem worthy of investigation, and we therefore suggest that further research on the scientific and technical information-seeking and adopting activities of organisations and individuals would be appropriate.

6.8   For understanding the various transfer processes we suggested earlier that models of barrier structure and penetration might be used as analogies. We also recognise that much needs to be done before we can understand more fully how the concepts of appropriateness and fit can be applied in real time to help transfer processes succeed. What are the dimensions of appropriateness which should be considered, and how do they vary from one situation to another? How much misfit can a given receiver tolerate and still achieve a successful transfer? Once the dimensions of fit are identified can they be estimated in any quantitative or semi-quantitative sense? All these are questions to which, we suggest, researchers could usefully address themselves.

6.9 We see another strand of our transfer process concept involving the subject of management. The relationship between management and technology is a complex one, but we would argue that if Schon's definition of technology is adopted then much that is encompassed by the term management becomes a part of technology.

There are many techniques, practices and concepts developed by management scientists, operational researchers, behavioural scientists and organisation theorists which can be thought of as forming a subset of technology. Familiarity with these tools and a knowledge of when and how to apply them extends the managers' capability. There is interest in, and a body of knowledge about, the ways in which management techniques and practices either do or do not become accepted and used. Our analysis indicates that there must be transfer processes operating in this sphere, and that concepts of context, appropriateness and fit will affect them just as they do the "normal" type of technology. We can suggest therefore that researchers in the management area might be able to increase their understanding of the development and application of management theories by trying to identify and characterise the transfer processes involved. There might also be benefits in terms of enhanced application of management techniques if people are able to identify barriers to transfer and incentives by which these can be overcome. Some material is, of course, available about this but much of it is, as with information relating to other types of technology transfer, of a wisdom or case study nature, and we suggest that the models described here might form the basis for useful research in this field.

6.10 There is another link between management and technology which might be of use in the education of scientists and technologists. In the U.K. as we write there is a continuing debate about the problems of attracting sufficient students into scientific and engineering subjects, and of persuading the graduates in such fields to enter industry. At the same time industry is critical of the quality of those graduates that it does get. This has led to proposals for various educational innovations to remedy the problem of

101

quantity and quality, such as the establishment of "teaching companies", links between companies and university departments which could enable engineers to be trained in the same way that doctors are trained in teaching hospitals [2]. Educational innovation in this field should be concerned with giving scientists and engineers sufficient grounding in social and behavioural subjects for an appreciation of arguments about appropriateness, context and fit. Having stressed the importance of learning by doing earlier we naturally see experiments such as the teaching company scheme as of potentially great importance. In the spirit of our earlier remarks we would also comment that such an innovation should be monitored in real time so that some measure of its effectiveness can be attempted.

6.11 Our final remarks are about policy implications for governments. The transfer process approach provides a different way of considering government policies which are directed partly or wholly at causing or affecting technical change. Policies can, broadly speaking, be of two types, direct and indirect. The former imply a direct involvement in the science and technology development processes, and involve direct intervention in the resource (financial and manpower) allocation decisions. Examples of indirect policies would be those concerned with changing the climate surrounding the development of technology, for example by fiscal incentives which may affect investment, legislation which may stimulate development of new technologies or restrict the use of existing ones, or educational policies which may change the supply or characteristics of scientists or engineers. We can now suggest that direct policies have often tended to be associated with the boxes in our models of technical change, and have had the effect of altering their number or size, while indirect policies have tried to affect, in the main, barriers to the transfer processes and thus to affect the arrows in our models. We can thus see that policies such as those represented by the American National Science Foundation's R & D Incentives Program, and the move towards end-game incentives described in Chapter 4, are a tacit recognition of the importance of transfer processes.

We can also remark that critiques of British policy such as that made by Pavitt & Walker [3], in which they advocate less government involvement in applied research and development and a restriction of government's role to the support of basic research, are only tackling one part of the problem — the boxes rather than the arrows. We have no prescriptive remedies for problems with technology policies, but suggest that the transfer process framework may generate questions about the options facing policymakers which may stimulate an appraisal which will lead to improved practice.

6.12 We also recognise that many more factors must now be taken into account when the introduction of new technology is being considered. For example, legal, social, political and environmental pressures are increasing and more people are taking an active interest in the debate about the effects of innovations. Critical issues such as those concerning nuclear waste, and the development of fast-breeder reactors, genetic engineering and the manufacture of toxic chemicals all raise fundamental questions about the technological decision-making process in society. The inherent conflicts will be of great significance to all those involved in the practice or analysis of technical change, and the many issues involved have only been touched on here.

This can be seen as a threat or a barrier to technology transfer, but it can equally be seen as a potential opportunity because these factors form part of the new "market" which is providing the pull for innovations which have acceptable characteristics. It has frequently been pointed out that in the past emphasis has been focussed on the characteristics of radical or "break-through" innovations. This is particularly true of academic studies. However, the majority of innovation takes place in the form of evolutionary changes to existing products, process or equipment and we would agree with those who argue that this should receive more attention. The more priority that is given to improvement of current practice in existing industries the more significant the transfer aspects of such change become.

6.13 The international aspects of technology transfer have in recent years assumed great significance in world politics. Whilst it is clearly sensed by all that the application of suitable technology is a key to improved welfare in developing countries, it is not so well understood that imported technology from the industrialised world cannot itself satisfy the aspirations of such countries — for a number of reasons. The first is appropriateness. It is scarcely to be expected that technology developed for the needs of industrialised society will match the needs of LDCs without substantial adaptation. The second reason is that concentration on the mechanics of transfer to the neglect of the social and economic objectives the movement is aimed to satisfy may produce costly failures. A third reason is, by contrast, the simple failure to appreciate the nature of technology and expect it to arrive in a package ready to work in any setting — failure to appreciate the importance of context. A

103

fourth is to use wrong transfer methods — failure to understand the crucial effect of context on transfer method.

Many of these issues can be deduced from the substantial Bell & Hill paper in Part II (Paper 12). They emerge very sharply when the transfer processes used by international firms are examined against the background of LDC demands. An OECD sponsored technology transfer forum at Stirling in December 1976 [4] strongly underlined these aspects and encouraged the authors of this volume to have confidence in the value of some of the models of transfer processes in technical change developed here.

References

[1] Johnston, R., "Government Policy for Technology Transfer: an Instrument for Industrial Progress", *R & D Management* 6, (1976) 159-164.
[2] *The Teaching Company*, Science Research Council, State House, High Holborn, London, December 1975.
[3] Pavitt, K. and Walker, W., "Government Policies Towards Industrial Innovation, a Review", *Research Policy* 5 (1976) 11.
[4] Bradbury, F.R. *et al.*, *Technology Transfer Practice of International Firms*, Sijthoff & Noordhoff, Alphen aan den Rijn, 1978.

PART II

SELECTED PAPERS

TECHNOLOGY TRANSFER

by *F. R. Bradbury* *

Introduction

The initiators of this meeting from the Universities of Manchester, and Stirling, and from Oxford felt the lack, expressed by Rubenstein at an earlier conference [1], of consensus about fundamental definitions and resolved to meet to exchange ideas on concepts of technology transfer and the ways in which research and analysis can make an effective contribution to improving technology transfer performance. We hope at this meeting to provide a forum for discussion for all those concerned with technology transfer, whether they be producers or receivers, policy makers or "catalysts", or researchers. The universities are aware of the futility of discussing technology transfer in the absence of practitioners and we are happy to have here producers and users of technology — generators and transferors — as well as those whose role it is to study the process — the academics.

Let me give my impression of the state of the art and of our understanding of the process of technology transfer.

What is technology transfer?

It is when we come to ask what technology transfer *is* that we get our first salutory shock on the state of the art: no-one knows, or rather, everyone knows best. The *New Scientist* reported these definitions of technology transfer, culled from the 1973 Paris Conference [2]:
— the multi-lateral flow of information and techniques across the boundaries of science, technology, and the practical world;
— transferring research results to operators;

* Technological Economics Research Unit University of Stirling, Scotland, U.K.

— accelerating the application of research and exploratory development results to industrial application;
— science and technology transfer to the would-be user at the earliest practicable date and in a language he can understand;
— the process of matching solutions in the form of existing science and engineering knowledge to problems in commerce or public programmes;
— getting knowledge out of the academic area and into the hands of those who apply it.

These definitions describe innovation if they describe anything, and I believe miss the essence of technology transfer. A preferred view was aptly put at Paris [3] by Susan Doscher of the Congressional Research Service as "the process by which a technology is applied to a purpose other than the one for which it was originally intended." Bar Zakay said much the same thing [3]: "Technology transfer is putting technology into a different context."

The distinction is important. Doscher and Bar-Zakay, and at least some of those present today, see technology transfer as being more than innovation and diffusion of innovation in that it implies a transverse shift, from the original trajectory of the innovation to another, aimed at another target.

(In these figures the innovation process is shown as a spiral to emphasise the cycling pattern by which problems are overcome by an iterative procedure: the diffusion is represented as the familiar

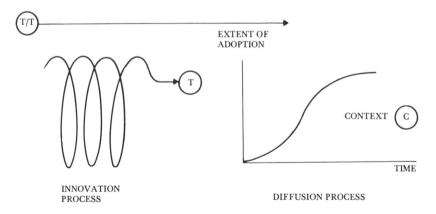

Fig. 1. *Linear development/diffusion model of T/T*

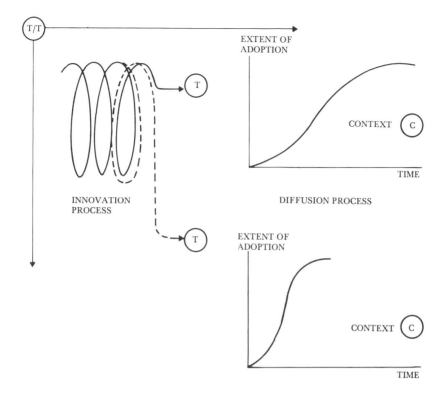

Fig. 2. *Transverse-shift model of T/T*

logistic curve relating number of adopters to the passage of time. I refer again later to the cyclic phenomenon.)

The distinction implied in the two models is important because it is precisely the transverse shift of technology which is the essential problem of technology transfer and one which is consistently and persistently underestimated.

I propose to accept the Doscher/Bar-Zakay definition of technology transfer in my subsequent remarks, but I will not be surprised if some of those present challenge my conceptual model of the process.

Some problems of technology transfer

It is convenient to start from a discussion of the innovation-diffusion process and later to assess the additional problems imposed by the transverse shift view of technology transfer.

The innovation-diffusion process is one which rests on a substantial base of R & D work, in laboratory, drawing board and computer. Indeed it is one of the major factors for success in innovation identified in the Sussex SAPPHO study [4] that development work should be thorough. How thorough and effective this development work is depends substantially on the degree to which the real world situation that the innovation will have to face can be reduced to laboratory drawing board and computer without loss of critical factors and relationships. My own contribution at Paris [5] was concerned with the important but elusive connection between abstraction and sufficiency; abstraction being the inescapable reduction in detail that laboratory work on projects dictates, and sufficiency the degree to which the abstracted test and design procedures retain their links with the real world.

A good deal of the writing on technology transfer is concerned with methods by which the R & D resources devoted to an innovation may be most effectively used to overcome this abstraction/sufficiency dilemma. The Paris papers of Gellman, Goldhar [3] and Rubenstein [1] were directed at the problems of effective and efficient control of the innovation process. One got the impression from these and other presentations at Paris that so many algorithms and heuristics have now been enunciated that there remains little more to be added to the theory of optimal resource allocation in the conduct of the innovation process. However, and this is one of the propositions I would like to see this symposium discuss, it may be argued that such a plethora of maxims indicates a still primitive state of understanding of the innovation process; it has not yet reached a degree of abstraction necessary for usefulness as a guide to action. It is to me a self-evident proposition that theory, like screening, must be gauged as to its power and usefulness by the degree of abstraction it attains, whilst retaining a high degree of sufficiency; if we have to describe the world to construct a theory we have produced a useless tool. The illuminating essays of Stafford Beer on the subject of models isomorphic and homomorphic [6] have put this point succinctly and there is no need to restate the argument.

It is a virtue of SAPPHO that it has put before us a limited number of maxims for success in innovation. The five principal rules: study user needs, pay attention to promotion and marketing, do thorough development, use relevant extra-mural information and have authoritative leadership, may be seen as aids to realism or sufficiency in the development stage of innovation. In particular the importance of studying user needs is something which bears much weight in the technology transfer problem analysis.

There is virtue in the linear view of technology transfer, presented by Figure 1, insofar as it links diffusion with innovation. For the success of any innovation, be it measured in terms of profit to the innovator or benefit to the wider community, turns on its adoption by many users and on the rate of such adoption. The numbers who adopt an innovation and the rate at which they do so has been the subject of research by sociologists and econometricians; the work of Rogers & Shoemaker, and of Mansfield, has exposed some parameters determining the rate of diffusion which the innovator should look to during project development. I have in mind those key attributes of innovations — relative advantage, complexity, compatibility, trialability and observability (Rogers & Shoemaker) [7] and profitability to the adopter and size of adopters, required investment (Mansfield) [8]; attributes which the innovator can shape-up and adjust in the project development stage if he is aware of their importance and if he can devise appropriate proxy variables for testing them.

If we take a broad view of screening, one which includes selection for technical, social and economic attributes, and one which also includes the concept of *shaping* — the process of amendment and modification of misfits so that they may pass the screens — then the whole innovation process is a screening process. The screens are effective insofar as they correctly anticipate the specification required by a successful innovation; they are efficient insofar as they achieve this effectiveness by abstraction to the degree that they may be operated at acceptable cost and over a wide range of attributes.

In other words, we may equate efficient effectiveness in innovation with abstract sufficiency in screening.

It need hardly be said that abstract sufficiency in screening is hard to achieve. Whilst the polymer scientist may have little difficulty in devising tests of a physico-chemical nature (highly abstract) which will provide very useful information about the effectiveness of a polymer composition as a pipe-lining material for use in conveying corrosive fluids (highly sufficient) it is another matter for the aeroframe designer to devise an abstract and sufficient test for the aerodynamic behaviour of an airbus. The approach to sufficiency in such a case is tortuous and attenuated. At the end of it all, however, the innovation, if it is successful, emerges to satisfy user needs and the economic-social criteria specified.

If we adopt the transverse shift model of technology transfer

111

(Figure 2) we see the extra dimension of the transfer problem. It is to secure the fit of the new technology, which is the innovation, to a new context.

Donald Schon [9] has warned against the lock and key concept of innovation and I think most of us would agree in rejecting a model of innovation which implies a straight trajectory from drawing board to a precisely located place in the market. On the other hand, I think that the technology transfer symposium at Paris revealed again and again that a fit of technology with its total context is necessary for success and that the problems of innovation and technology transfer are thereby defined. Whether the technology is changed, by iterative shaping and screening, or the context is manipulated by promotion or education or simply by passage of time, a fit must be arrived at to ensure adoption and continued use of the innovation. Looking now at the transverse step model of technology transfer we see that the innovation which has been evolved for one context has, in technology transfer, to be adapted to fit another. The problem now can be seen as moving back down the innovation spiral to repeat much of the screening process, this time to meet tests which are sufficient to the new context. Some of the difficulty of technology transfer arises from the false expectation that the transverse shift can be achieved simply by lifting the innovation from one context into another; this is rarely, if ever, possible.

Communication, Sufficiency and the Cyclic Nature of Technology Transfer

Burns' technology transfer "by agents not agencies" [10] has become a cliché of the subject area. But this must not be allowed to detract from its significance. Communication is vital for the innovator; how much more so for the technology transferor! The shift of context involved in technology transfer demands the shaping of the technology to fit the detail of the different system which comprises the new context. At every step in the operation of technology transfer there must be dialogue between those who would transfer and those who would adopt; dialogue concerning design detail, specification detail, user need detail — contextual mapping to use the jargon of the morphological analysts. Such is the abstract nature of language that direct single step transfer of system description or user need by documentation must fail lamentably on sufficiency. It is only by the iterative process of verbal exchange with repeated readjustment of understanding and rephrasing of questions that the required degree of sufficiency of knowledge of context and specification can be achieved. Such is the state of the art of technology transfer that scenarios and case studies must long remain the key to learning, be it of innovation or technology transfer; the theory and abstraction are not at the level at which numbers and mathematical models can be anything more than useful auxiliary aids to understanding.

User's needs, designer's needs and constraints, all shift in technology transfer. To make such shifts effective and efficient calls for removal of unnecessary constraints on communications among participants, and therein lies the strength of Burns' aphorism. One comes back here to the familiar cyclic model of problem solving in which recognition, analysis, selection, implementation, control follow each other, leading to the recognition and recycle of a modified problem situation (Figure 3). When agents communicate they have the opportunity of rapidly and repeatedly traversing the problem analysis cycle and a correspondingly better chance of success in the transfer process.

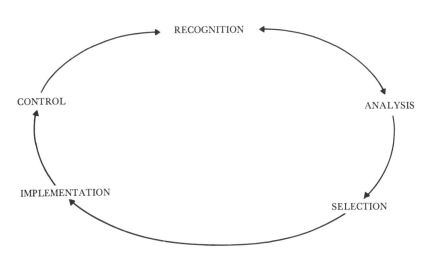

Fig. 3. *Cyclic Model of Problem Analysis* [11]

The cyclic model is not restricted to describing the communication aspect of technology transfer of course. It is a useful conceptual tool for the whole of the screening operations of innovation and technology transfer in which the "implementation and control" phases represent the test of design by experiment and observation.

In representing the innovation process as a spiral in Figures 1 and 2 I have in mind the cyclic process which I perceive to be the basic method of progressing both innovation and technology transfer; there is no straight path from drawing board to market. In his fascinating Karl Taylor Compton lecture "The Sciences of the Artificial" Herbert Simon describes the progress of an ant over a wind and wave-moulded beach — it moves ahead, angles its way up a dunelet, detours round a pebble, halts, moves on again and so arrives eventually at the target. Simon concludes that "an ant, viewed as a behaving system, is quite simple. The apparent complexity of its behaviour over time is largely a reflection of the complexity of the environment in which it finds itself." [12] This analogy describes well, I believe, the progression of innovation and technology transfer operations.

Methodology in Research on Technology Transfer

I now turn to the area this symposium has singled out for discussion: methodology.

I detect three approaches, which I may categorise as theorising on the basis of experience, case work, and experimenting.

Theorising on the basis of experience, as I am doing now, is rife and, in the eyes of the experimentalist, deplorable. Mensch at Paris [2] spoke of "dubious results from esoteric thinking" and there were frequent expressions of scorn for intuitive thinking from the floor of the auditorium.

Case work is an expression of humility in the face of overwhelming complexity and associated dearth of theoretical pathways. It is widely practised and is the essence of most teaching programmes on innovation, technology transfer and related topics.

Experimental work, reaching out towards the methods of natural science, is something all workers seem to yearn for. The great impact made by the SAPPHO study is a compound of the perceived usefulness of its findings and the scientific "soundness" of its method. Such studies are rare indeed. Bar-Zakay offered some experimentally rigorous work at Paris [2] and was, like many others, scornful of intuition, reiterating the demand for "proof".

114

We have at this symposium, of course, practitioners and champions of all three approaches. The point I would like you to consider is whether our hunger for the experimental method and proof is justifiable given the nature of the subject of technology transfer. Experimental "proof", with remarkable frequency, shows intuition and wisdom to have been right — which is reassuring since a vast number of decisions will have been based on wisdom before any "proof" is available. Of course it is dangerous and perfidious to attack "scientific method" approaches simply because they follow experience and confirm it. The reward of scientific studies of complex systems is an increase in understanding of them and the hope that in time science of technology transfer will guide practice rather than follow it. What I think we have to avoid, however, is too slavish a devotion to methods of experimental science. Experience reinforced, broadened and extended by case work is a very effective guide to practice. This we do know not by "proof" in the experimental sense, but by acceptance. The live situation facing the leader of any seminar on technology transfer is the examination and dissection of experience and cases to provide learning material. Acceptance by peers has always been the criterion for the establishment of hypothesis and theory. The crucial issue is, then, which peer group? If academics seek acceptance for their writings on technology transfer by an academic peer group, "proof" will be the order of the day. But if the peer group comprises able innovators and technology transferors then the test of propositions by discussion and debate by this peer group and the acceptance by it of the findings of experience and case studies will be the criterion of worth.

There are, of course, grave dangers in any relaxation of the standards of academic work and this is not what I am advocating; those whose business it is to make the abstractions from the real complex world, abstractions which we may grace with a variety of titles ranging from theory to heuristics, will make no contribution to solving real world problems such as technology transfer if their abstractions are unsound and unreliable guides to action. There is no reason whatever why academic standards should be lowered in "wisdom" and case study contributions to knowledge providing that they are subjected to public scrutiny and critical debate, for which purpose practitioners of technology transfer may be no less well equipped than Fellows of the Royal Society.

I believe that most of us accept the legitimacy of this approach. But it needs to be stated and defended if scholarship and research and learning in this area are to move forward within reasonable time to the construction of a body of reliable algorithms and heuristics, theory even, which is sufficiently robust and abstract to be a reliable and useful guide to action in technology transfer.

The brochure announcing this meeting states under "Aim" that the seminar will study ways in which research and analysis can make an effective contribution to improving technology transfer performance. This prompts the question what *is* the problem that draws our attention to technology transfer? Is there a problem to be solved or is technology transfer simply an interesting phenomenon for study by academics — like the chemical structure of the colouring matter of aphids for example?

I believe technology transfer to have immense present and future significance for world-wide economic and social development and that technology transfer problems overshadow in significance those of the well-worked fields of invention and innovation.

I wish to put three questions:
(1) How much technology (in the broad sense used by Schon [8] to indicate anything which may extend human capability) is in existence but awaits the removal or penetration of barriers to its application to human problems?
(2) Given that simple lateral shifts of technology contexts do not occur and that successful transfer demands a substantial degree of reworking of the innovation spiral, how sensible is it to continue to concentrate on creating more technology whilst the vast potential of existing technology awaits transfer to those who would benefit from it?
(3) How much of the talent and skill now devoted to new technology (and science) could be effectively used in achieving the transfer of existing technology? In other words what is the opportunity cost of new science and technology?

If these are sensible questions (and some may argue that they are not since all new technology may be envisaged as the old transferred to a new context — suitably shaped and adapted of course), if such questioning is sensible then one sees that those I designate as "technology brokers" — members of the Licensing Executives Society for example — are in a key position to provide some of the answers. Theirs is a catalytic activity of great significance today and in the foreseeable future. Again one might ask is sufficient of our national and international resource devoted to this brokerage? If the universal increase in human capability is the yardstick, rather than papers and patents, then the answer must be in the negative.

I hope that we shall learn more about the role of technology transfer agents during our seminar and also about the obstacles they encounter. For it should be noted how much our society and its economics rests on the erection and maintenance of barriers to technology transfer; institutions and institutionalisation of science; commercial confidentiality; simple inadequacy in communication; even patents. I know it will be argued that patents, commercial confidentiality, even institutionalisation of science and its disciplines are essential aids to science and technology development. Precisely! Our concern is moving, if I am right, from the need for technology development to its transfer: institutions and instruments which nurture technology creation may be impediments to its dissemination.

The second half of the question this seminar set itself remains: what contribution may research and analysis make to improving technology transfer performance? Little, I suspect, on the broad issues I have referred to concerning split of resources between generating new and transferring existing technology. Its main contribution must be in achieving an improved distribution of resources at the micro level rather than at the macro. If wisdom, case study and experimental research and analysis can identify the main problems of contextual mapping of technology on to the needs of users and so perhaps lift the eyes of the technologists from their benches and drawing boards for an occasional scan of the wider world, there may be some pay-offs in the way of greater and more rapid extension of human capability by successful technology transfer.

References

[1] Rubenstein, A.H., *R & D Management*, 6 (1976) 145.
[2] Kenward, M., *New Scientist*, 1973, 5 July, p. 26.
[3] Davidson, H.F., Cetron, M.J., Goldhar, J.D., *Technology Transfer*, Noordhoff, Leiden, 1974.
[4] Achilladelis, B. *et al.*, *Project Sappho*, Science Policy Research Unit, University of Sussex, 1971.
[5] Bradbury, F.R., "Coupling Invention to Innovation" in Davidson, H.F., Cetron, M. and Goldhar, J.D., *op. cit.*
[6] Beer, S., *Decision and Control*, Wiley, London, 1966.

[7] Rogers, E.M. & Shoemaker, F.F., *Communication of Innovations*, The Free Press, New York, 1976.

[8] Mansfield, E., *Industrial Research and Technological Innovation*, Norton, N.Y., 1968.

[9] Schon, D., *Technology & Change – The New Heraclitus*, Pergamon, London, 1967.

[10] Burns, T., "Models, Images & Myths" in Gruber & Marquis (editors), *Factors in the Transfer of Technology*, The M.I.T. Press, Cambridge, Massachusetts, 1969.

[11] Bradbury, F.R. and Loasby, B.J. *Technological Economics of Crop Protection and Pest Control*, Monograph No. 36, S.C.I., London, 1970.

[12] Simon, H., *The Sciences of the Artificial*, M.I.T. Press, Cambridge, Massachusetts, 1969.

SOME ASPECTS OF METHODOLOGY IN THE STUDY OF TECHNOLOGY TRANSFER

by *C. F. Douds* and A. H. Rubenstein*

The Present Situation

New technology does appear and move from one field or organization to another. The process is deliberately managed in part; sometimes successfully, sometimes not. Yet while there are some groups that seem to be able to make technology transfer work, there is a lot to be learned about the process. In the literature there is much in the way of description of experiences, policy recommendations, speculations, and so on, and a limited amount of field research — all of which adds to our knowledge and understanding of the process.

If we are to substitute results from the research process for rules of thumb and private experience as a basis for policy formation and transfer process design, we want assurance that these results are produced in a manner that provides high credibility, replicability, and communicability — important characteristics of "good" scientific results.

Unfortunately, we are far from this situation at present. The "research" is currently diverse, loose, full of gaps and contradictions. This is not a cause for discouragement, however, for many science-based fields such as engineering or medicine have been or still are in this condition. Much of the disorder is due to lack of standard or even fully-disclosed methodology for conducting studies, collecting data, and making inferences from the findings (despite the complex trappings of statistical tests and analytical methods).

In addition, there is the persistent problem of "amateurism" or lack of adequate training among many people who report studies of the process. This is a situation not tolerated in other fields, where adequate training is a *sine qua non* for the conduct of research.

* Northwestern University, Evanston, Illinois, USA.

A deceptive aspect of much published "research" in this area is that, for some people, all that appears to be involved in data gathering is "writing down a list of interesting questions and mailing out a questionnaire or interviewing some people." A lot of bad and useless data is collected in this way and a lot of time and patience is expended by respondents with little useful payoff.

Here we will briefly indicate some of the methodologies available and indicate some of the issues involved in assessing field research.

Fundamentally the issues are much the same as in all other areas of science and technology. One is concerned first with the state of the situation — how do things stand; what is going on; and how believable is the data presented — what is the "signal-to-noise ratio," i.e., what sorts of errors, omissions, instabilities, etc., are present in the data. Then one is concerned with understanding how the process works: What is the relationship between A and B and C — if A changes, how does C change; does it depend upon the value of B? Given a postulated theory that explains such relationship, we do not, as scientists, wholeheartedly accept it until it can be believably shown that changes in C which seem to be related to A are not being caused by some other unaccounted for or extraneous factors. Ideally, we seek to disprove our hypothesis and call it credible only when we repeatedly fail to disprove it. However, the state of our field is such that we can seldom attain this ideal — but the thought is a suitable antidote for unwarranted optimism or gullibility.

Forms of Field Research

Most of the literature on the technology transfer process takes one of three general forms — the *discursive approach*, often based on the experience of practising managers or, hopefully, astute observers; the *case study approach*, a narrative history or chronology of events usually about a single situation, event or effort; and the *field research approach*, a use of empirical data collected and structured in such a manner as to develop or test hypotheses ideally with some degree of control for alternative explanations. (Thomson [1] shows a method for inter-pelating these strategies as well as the various types of research).

Here we shall briefly consider five types of field research strategies:
— Field surveys
— Comparative case studies

- Field studies
- Longitudinal studies
- Field experiments

Surveys designed to produce data are particularly appropriate when relatively little is known about a situation. "Information," in the sense of possibly meaningful relationships, may be discovered in the data, despite lack of *a priori* theory or predictions.

Comparative case studies allow information to be extracted much more directly since an explicit basis for comparison is built into the design. The greater the extent to which the two cases are identical — except for the differences in one "independent" variable and one "dependent" variable — the more confident we can be that the difference can be attributed to the independent variable.

In real life situations, it is rarely possible to find such nearly identical cases, so the difference in outcome can potentially be attributed to many other causes. Our "information" about the connection between the independent variable and the dependent variable in the pair of cases remains somewhat questionable, and of dubious validity when we seek to apply it to other situations where even other variables and parameters are different. To potentially obtain more certain and more generalizable information other research strategies have been developed — the cross-sectional field study, the longitudinal study and the field experiment.

Field studies are frequently used to investigate one or a number of specific propositions that can be expressed in a relatively simple form. This strategy is particularly appropriate for studying relationships concerned with the states of a system. It can also be useful for exploring processes.

Longitudinal studies are needed when a process is to be thoroughly investigated. Since a longitudinal study extends through time, months or years may be required, which oftentimes leads to a considerable resource investment. A major weakness of cross-sectional field studies is that, in general, cause and effect relationships cannot be ascertained. In longitudinal studies, since the sequence of events in each focal unit is observed and measured, cause and effect can be determined more readily.

Field experiments — either natural experiments or administrative experiments — are designs that, properly done, provide the greatest potential for control of error and alternative explanations.

Natural experiments in organizations capitalize on decisions being made independently of the experimenter. *Administrative* experiments here refer to an experiment that is conceptualized and deliberately planned out beforehand so that one or more variables are changed with others being controlled in some manner. An organizational manager (administrator) is ordinarily involved in the planning, perhaps as the experimenter. In either type of experiment some "experimental treatment" occurs — a deliberate change in some controllable variable. (Such uncontrollable natural events as floods or explosions may also be considered experimental treatments in other types of studies.) In either case, control of other variables may be achieved by direct choice and action, by measurement of existing values, or by statistical randomization.

The essence of conducting a natural experiment is to be prepared to observe and capitalize on changes or variations in an on-going situation. This means that various types of data must be collected often enough so that a basis for comparison exists to permit extraction of information about the influence of factors operating in the situation [2]. In administrative experiments, the experimenter has sufficient control to deliberately introduce changes. As Campbell and Stanley [3] point out, in experimental design in the sense of Fisher, the experimenter has complete control. He can schedule treatments and measurements for optimal statistical efficiency, with complexity of design emerging only from that goal of statistical, information-generating efficiency. However, the degree of control that can be achieved in organizational experiments is vastly different from that in, say, agriculture. They develop a variety of necessarily more complex designs needed to control for eight threats to the internal validity and four threats to the external validity, and hence the generalizability, of the findings. They term these types of experiments that can be performed in the field "quasi-experimental designs."

Some Research Design Considerations

These various research strategies can be roughly arranged in the stages of acquiring knowledge about technology transfer. Surveys, unless repeated, are mostly limited to providing basic data such as how many government laboratories have how many contracts with industry, etc. Individual case studies can be a rich source of insights generating many propositions about what tends to work or not work in the process, but such insights are perhaps best expressed in the form, "I wonder if there was a connection between variable X and variable Y in this case?" There is a great deal of potential error or uncertainty. Comparative case studies can begin to reduce this uncertainty somewhat. Comparative cases can be used to begin to check a theory as well as to generate somewhat more certain insights. Cross-sectional field studies, properly designed, can carry the hypothesis building and testing process to the point where the internal validity of the study can be seriously examined. Internal validity asks the question: To what extent are the relationships found explained by the postulated hypotheses and not by other factors in the situations measured? Longitudinal studies and field experiments can carry the search for better understanding even further, such that cause and effect relations can potentially be determined and, in some cases, criteria for external validity — the ability to generalize to other situations — can be satisfied.

In any type of study we obtain a mass of data, numbers or prose, containing a great deal of variation. In testing an hypothesis, we are looking for variation in one variable (or several) that is regularly associated with variation in another. Much of this variation constitutes "noise" or "error" for the purpose of the given study. The underlying basis of the strategy and tactics of research design and the role of statistical hypothesis testing is well stated by Diamond [4]:

> "Error embraces every sort of variation in the phenomena which we are observing, except what results from the one source which is the object of our study at the moment, and which we try to bring into prominence by the design of our investigation. It includes all the accumulated effects of other influences, whether suspected, understood or not understood. (p. 6)"

> "Statistical method is only one of several ways by which we strive to isolate information — the perceived effect of the experimental (or hypothesized) variable — from error — the contamination which enters our observations because of the uncontrolled effects of other influences. The first, and no doubt the most important way, is by the *clear formulation of our problem*, which tells what kinds of data most deserve our attention. Then comes the efforts at experimental control, by which we hope to eliminate some extraneous factors and limit the scope of others (p. 7)".

"If we succeed uncommonly well in our efforts to eliminate error, the outcome of the investigation may be so clear that there will be no need for statistical analysis ... The correct appraisal of information must be preceded by an appraisal of potential error. *Experimental technique and research design strive to reduce error; statistical technique measures the error which remains.* (p. 8)"
The confidence level in statistical tests of hypotheses is a probability assessment of the likelihood of error in the results. But as noted above, and detailed more explicitly by Winch and Campbell [5], it should be the residual error remaining after all other rival hypotheses and sources of unwanted variation have been hopefully taken care of by the researcher in the design of the study.

Where We Stand

Technology transfer is a part of the research and development/innovation (RD/I) processes in our society. The total amount of published *field research* on RD/I is relatively small (probably of the order of 100 to 200 independent studies not including wisdom, speculative, and policy publications). The *IEEE Transactions on Engineering Management* has made a consistent effort to publish such research since 1960. From that year through 1973 about 42 articles containing field data more or less closely related to RD/I appeared; 37 of them field studies.

The clarity of formulation of the research problem can be aided by developing explicit researchable questions in addition to a general statement of purpose. It is here that the researcher can well sort out those parts of the problem that can be based on measurable, empirical data and those that can only be based on judgment, experience, or intuition. Of the 37 RD/I field studies in the sample, only 30% contained reasonably implicit researchable questions or a clear statement of purpose, and only 27% contained explicit researchable questions. (Of course, we have no way of knowing how many developed unreported researchable questions early in their work and how many wrote the questions after the study was completed.)

In a program of research we develop understanding by generating hypotheses in any one of many ways — from data, insight, etc. — and then subjecting them to disconfirmation. Stated hypotheses make clear exactly what information is sought and to the extent

124

they withstand attempts at disconfirmation, their generalizability is enhanced. Taking a not-too-stringent view as to what constitutes a clear proposition statement, only 24% of the articles sampled had reasonably clear statements of propositions.

The results of a test of a proposition can be no better than the measure of the variable. Reliability is a measure of the (lack of) uncertainty in a variable's measurement. In the 37 articles not one provides a reliability coefficient and only two provide some other evidence concerning the reliability of their measures.

Due to the nature of the phenomena involved and the lack of well-developed, semi-standardized instrumentation, it appears unlikely that we will ever have many measures of very high reliability. Even if we get a high reliability measure, we can only say that we are getting a strong signal — we still cannot be sure that we are measuring what we intend to measure. It is difficult to get measures of high reliability (and not always desirable to do so because of other attendant phenomena), especially when studying organizational processes. Both these difficulties may be alleviated by the use of *multiple measures*. As Webb, et al. [6] point out, no research method is without bias. The principal objection to interviews and questionnaires is that they are often used alone. Institutional records and many other imaginative methods can provide alternative or unobtrusive measures of given variables. Multiple methods having *different* methodological weaknesses from each other can enhance not only the reliability, but also the validity, of individual variables.

While reliability involves the question of how "clean" our measure is, *validity* of a construct — a variable — involves the question of how well we are measuring what we intend to measure. Campbell and Fiske [7] propose two major requirements to be met in validating a construct: 1) To demonstrate that different independent measurement methods for the same construct are convergent; and 2) To demonstrate that the measures of a construct ("trait" in their terminology, from psychology) discriminate it from other constructs ("traits") from which it is intended to differ. The relation among the constructs can be shown in a "multitrait-multimethod matrix" presenting all the intercorrelations for each of several traits measured by each of several methods. They provide several criteria to estimate construct validity. This fundamental issue of the validity of the constructs being used in the study of RD/I and technology transfer phenomena is hardly considered in the literature of the field. (Douds, [8] contains a narrow example for one construct).

Finally, in assessing our studies we can ask what is the basis for confidence in the results: In addition to the considerations above, how have the final conclusions of a study been arrived at? In the 37 field studies included in the sample, 27% used reasoning as a basis for establishing their findings. An analytical design was present in 68% of the cases. The remaining two cases (5%) presented data with an implicit design, but the relation between the data and what was said was sufficiently unclear that they could not be classified. The prior discussion emphasizes an empirically-based challenging of concepts and findings through measurement procedures. We advocate this approach strongly for any study utilizing empirical data, but not to the extent of retreating to a land of "fashionable sterility" for there is a long tradition producing useful results that utilizes intellectual reasoning based on observation, compilations of data, or historical documents.

Future Route for the Study of Technology Transfer

What way should we head as we try to understand and carry out technology transfer? It may be useful to distinguish two audiences — though the distinction fundamentally is, and should be, quite arbitrary. One audience is the administrator involved in the process; another is the researcher not directly involved. A third audience may be policy makers not directly involved in the technology transfer process and not carrying out research on it. All three seek to understand the process — but the administrator and policy maker are held accountable for results.

Perhaps this last thought indicates the nature of the route that should be followed in future studies of technology transfer. We should hold each other accountable for a steady progress in the quality of our work. We should distinguish between a study called "exploratory" because the *phenomena* has not been investigated before and one called "exploratory" because the *researcher* is not familiar with what is known about the phenomena. We should ask that the research problem statement be well identified and explicit research questions, with all their implications, be worked out. Coupled directly to this should be explicit propositions, in most instances, to assist in the design of the study's methodology. We should spend some effort on determining the reliability and validity of our variables and their measures by various means including more use of multiple measures.

126

Finally, we should ask researchers that the methods and instruments they use be sufficiently disclosed so that previous findings can be replicated, and that such replication be done to enhance the generalizability of the findings. For the administrator, who in a sense is continually carrying out organizational experiments, we can hope that he will make some of the implicit predictions in his organizational design changes explicit, introduce the changes in such a manner as to provide a basis for comparison to obtain information about some of these predictions, and keep enough records so that the human and organizational behavioral outcomes can be evaluated.

Acknowledgement

This discussion is based on Douds and Rubenstein [9] which was prepared under the auspices of the Georgia Tech Innovation Project, NSF Grant DA 39269, Melvin Cranzberg, Principal Investigator.

References

[1] Thompson, C.W.N., "Administrative Experiments: The Experience of Fifty-eight Engineers and Engineering Managers", *IEEE Transactions on Engineering Management*, May 1974.

[2] Douds, C. F., *Natural Experiments for Technology Transfer from National Laboratories*, Specification of Independent Variables and Parameters: Program of Research on the Management of Research and Development Paper 73/95, Dept. of IE/MS, Northwestern University, 9173.

[3] Campbell, D.T. and Stanley, J.C., *Experimental and Quasi-Experimental Designs for Research*, Rand McNally, Chicago, 1966.

[4] Diamond, S., *Information and Error*, Basic Books, N.Y., 1959.

[5] Winch, R.F. and Campbell, D.T., "Proof? – No; Evidence? – Yes. The Significance of Tests of Significance", *American Sociologist*, 4(2) (1969) pp. 140-143.

[6] Webb, E., Campbell, D.T., Schwartz, R.D. and Sechrist, L., *Unobtrusive Measures*, Rand McNally, Chicago, 1966.

[7] Campbell, D.T. & Fiske, D.W., "Convergent and Discriminant Validation by the Multitrait-Multimethod Matrix", *Psychological Bulletin*, 56(2) (1959) pp. 81-105.

[8] Douds, C. F., *The Effects of Work-related Values on Communication between R & D Groups*, Ph.D. Dissertation, Department of Industrial

Engineering and Management Sciences, Northwestern University, 1970.

[9]   Douds, C. F. & Rubenstein, A.H., *Review and Assessment of the Methodology Used to Study the Behavioral Aspects of the Innovation Process*, Program of Research on the Management of Research and Development Paper 73/128, Dept. of IE/MS, Northwestern University, May 1974.

THEORIES OF TECHNOLOGY TRANSFER, OR. MODELS, IMAGES, AND MYTHS REVISITED

by *R.D. Johnston* *

Introduction

In this paper it is intended to critically examine the progress made in the study of technology transfer, though not in the traditional way by reviewing the findings of various research projects; this task has been most adequately carried out by a number of people e.g. Douds, [1]; Chakrabarti, [2] and Bradbury [3]. Rather, it is the intention to focus on some of the theoretical and conceptual assumptions which have underlain much of this research. As a result, this paper is directed primarily to those engaged in the study of the phenomenon of technology transfer but, at the same time, it should be of considerable relevance, both immediately and in the longer term, for those engaged in the practical business of effecting and promoting the process.

Examination of the literature reveals that a wide range of activities are included under the label of technology transfer. Which immediately leads us to our first problem; that of definition. Technology transfer is such an umbrella term that it has become even more "de rigeur" than usual to define the particular connotation being used. Thus for Gruber and Marquis "The transfer of technology must then mean the utilization of our existing technique in an instance where it has not previously been used" [4]; for Chakrabarti "Technology transfer can be viewed as the generalized process of information transfer between science, technology and actual utilization." [2] and for Brooks "Wherever systematic rational knowledge developed by one group or institution is embodied in a way of doing things by other institutions or groups, we have technology transfer" [5]. However, for our purposes, what is most important is that we do not get bogged down in argument over the precise definition of the term. Rather we should recognise that at the most fundamental level we are dealing with the movement of

* Department of Liberal Studies in Science, University of Manchester, U.K.

129

knowledge across interfaces, while keeping in mind that there may be important distinctions between specific sub-elements within such a general framework.

To those who are familiar with the technology transfer literature, the subsidiary title of this paper will recall the contribution of Tom Burns to the 1966 M.I.T. Conference on the Human Factor in the Transfer of Technology, subsequently published in 1969 in the conference proceedings [6]. To some it may appear indecently hasty to be engaged so soon in the academic pursuit of "revisiting". However, Burns' article can be considered to have marked a watershed in studies of technology transfer. His conclusion that "the mechanism of technology transfer is one of agents, not agencies; of the movement of people among establishments, rather than of the routing of information through communication systems", marked a considerable step forward in understanding of the technology transfer process. But instead of this recognition of the importance of people in the movement of information providing a stimulus to a new generation of research [7] it has atrophied into a slogan trumpeted, without added insight, in most studies since that date. As a consequence the major problems raised by Burns have been both neglected and misunderstood.

It is the contention of this author that by re-examining the Burns' argument and developing it along a number of dimensions a basis may be provided for escape from the present doldrum state of technology transfer studies. In particular this critique is developed along just two major lines, one concerned with the state and function of knowledge in our industrial (or post-industrial) society, and the other with the nature and organisational environment of technology in that same society.

Prevailing Assumptions in Technology Transfer

One of the general assumptions underlying much study of and attempts to expedite technology transfer has been that there is some real or reified object or "package". which is to be transferred. The very verb "transfer" implies the movement of an object. To conceptualise technology as an object is to stumble into the methodological pitfall of over-reification of a concept. One consequence of this assumption has been the adoption of a "black-box" approach to technology transfer whereby the process itself is consigned to the mysterious or unknowable and research is concentrated on the inputs to and outputs from the box. Thus there have been many studies of organisational characteristics and the impact

130

of various management styles on technology transfer and innovation and on this basis prescriptions for success have been made. Similarly, at the individual level sociological and psychological factors such as social status, "cosmopoliteness" and achievement orientation have been related to success in securing the transfer of technology. While outputs have been the subject of less detailed study, the assumption behind many studies has been that success in technology transfer leads to success for the firm and for the national economy.

This reification of the concept of technology may be a consequence of the common identification of technology with hardware. However, to consider technology simply as a collection of artefacts is to make the same kind of mistake as that of the bibliometricians of science who have confused the scientific body of knowledge with the explicit content of scientific papers. Technology is not a body of systematised knowledge in the same way as science because the goals of the two forms of knowledge are different. Nevertheless, while there is little conscious effort on the part of the technologist to systematise his knowledge, it is apparent that when confronted with a problem, he does not search for potential solutions on the basis of first principles. He has a set of guiding rules composed of sets of elements of scientific law, technological "knowhow" and previous practice or which to draw. It is the essence of these guiding rules or principles which form the basis for treating technology as a system of knowledge [8].

This emphasis on technology as a knowledge system is not intended to suggest that an understanding of the function of such commercial devices as patents and licences is of no importance. However if we are seeking to gain a clearer picture of the mechanisms and roles of technology transfer at the national level, we need to probe for an underlying structure which will provide us with a knowledge basis to control and direct the production, diffusion, adaption and infiltration of technology more effectively.

Another assumption implicit in many technology transfer studies appears to be that the process is immutable and ahistorical i.e. that there exists a single most effective way of transferring technology, independent of such factors as the type of technology, environment, or cultural milieu. Some studies, such as those by Burns and Stalker [9] have examined the organisational structure appropriate to different forms of technology. Nevertheless in general, technology transfer has been examined without attention to the changing nature and role of technology in modern society. It would seem a reasonable hypothesis that the process is considerably different today to what it was twenty years ago. Similarly, just as it is now recognised that technology embodies both economic and cultural elements that may not make it appropriate for all societies, so it is possible that the process of translation of knowledge across interfaces may also vary from one environment to another.

One other common assumption is that any action or policy which increases or improves technology transfer is automatically good. As the application of technology to problems different to the one for which it is conceived leads to innovation, so the more technology transfer, the more innovation, and presumably the greater the public good. Such an assumption needs rather close examination for at the very least it might be expected that the volume and effectiveness of previous transfer affects subsequent performance.

The Structure of Knowledge in Modern Society

The first general theme I wish to examine for its relevance to the phenomena of technology transfer is the structure of knowledge in our present Western society. If there have been radical changes in the form or function of our knowledge systems, one might expect there to be corresponding changes in the process of technology transfer.

It is not startlingly novel to state that we live in a knowledge-oriented society. Such crystal-ball gazers as John Kenneth Galbraith [10] and Daniel Bell [11] have emphasised the growing importance of theoretical knowledge in the operation of the modern state. While their case may be somewhat exaggerated there can be little doubt that an ever expanding body of systematised knowledge has become an essential requisite for the kinds of economic growth we have observed in the last two decades. But what are the consequences for science and technology of being in such a situation of demand?

Here perhaps we can turn to sociology for some insight. When a particular activity is recognised as having a functional value in society it becomes institutionalised. Included in this process will normally be growth, increasing control on entry, development of accepted norms of behaviour for those within the institutions and the emergence of a career and possibly professional structure.

This is an extremely crude and mechanistic model which is capable of much more thorough development. However, it may be

132

sufficient to provide us with some useful tools for the analysis of the structure of knowledge system today. For the very demand and support for science and technology has led to its institutionalisation. Further, if we accept that the neccessary response to growth in any organisation is segmentation, then the growth of organised knowledge in response to demand has resulted in the development of a large number of relatively isolated knowledge divisions. Thus with the very success in producing knowledge, there has developed an institutional structure which divides and separates fields from one another. Furthermore each knowledge field becomes increasingly isolated from the practical problems which served as its initial focus, and concentrates on problems generated according to its own internal dynamic.

If to this argument we add the theories of Kuhn [12] and his supporters who have argued that the remarkable progress by science, and I would claim this holds equally for technology, is based on the acceptance by groups of researchers in a field of a paradigm — an accepted set of practices, models and theories which determine both problems and solutions — then we have an explanation of the structure of knowledge in modern society. While we have more knowledge, or at least information, available than at any time in our history the processes of institutionalisation and specialisation have made it less comprehendable and hence less freely available to those outside each field.

Here then is a paradox. The very system necessary for the effective growth of knowledge at the same time serves to build barriers around that knowledge and isolate it from its potential application in other areas. But technology transfer does occur, so how is it achieved? While the barriers are real, they are neither as insurmountable nor as inevitable as perhaps suggested above. Turning again to sociologists' study of science, we see that developments within a field themselves challenge the boundaries. A discovery can lead to a change of focus. At such a period of restructuring the barriers are low and movement of people and ideas into and out of a field is easier. Thus there is a continual dialectic tension between the setting of constraints around a field in order that it may progress, and the breaking down of the constraints in order to provide the basis for further progress.

The first lesson with regard to technology transfer then is that it is inherently difficult; resistance to the movement of technology is not a result of bad management or sheer perversity. The value of mobility is demonstrated — this is the origin of the "agents, not agencies" argument — but placed in context it can be seen that the

133

movement must be tied in with levels of development in appropriate knowledge fields. Future research in technology transfer should include a consideration of such factors as cognitive development and examine whether the detection of indicators of barrier breakdown is possible.

The Organisational Environment of Technology

The second major theme which it is necessary to develop is concerned with the organisational environment of technology. Just as studies of technology transfer have to a large extent ignored the institutionalised structure of knowledge in today's society, so they have failed to consider the changing nature of the environment in which technology is primarily produced and transferred i.e. industry.

This oversight cannot be attributed to a lack of information about the structure of industry today. Any number of books have been written on the growth of multi-national corporations and the power they have to manipulate the environments in which they operate to their own advantage, ensuring their supply of raw materials by participation in extractive industries, choosing their manufacturing sites on the basis of a wide range of factors including tax structures, and wages and transport costs and finally marketing the same product in many different countries.

Associated with but distinct from the emergence of the multi-national firm has been the growth of conglomerate companies, engaged in highly diversified, but mutually supporting industries. The single-product company is increasingly uncompetitive. Let us examine the business of steel-making as an example. Problems of availability of iron ore have led companies to invest in exploration and mining. The fact that this ore is increasingly located distant from European mills has led to an involvement in transport and in the construction of bulk ore carriers. The high consumption of oxygen in a modern steel plant has resulted in an involvement in industrial gas production. Developments in special purpose steels requires an availability and knowledge of non-ferrous minerals. The competition of substitutes such as aluminium and plastics have led many traditional steel companies to diversify into a general material business. Pollution legislation has required the more careful treatment of effluent leading to for example the construction of sulphuric acid plants for converting trapped sulphur dioxide. All this excludes expanded information processing, financial and marketing services involving completely new areas of competence.

Yet another development has been the growing involvement of government in industrial activities in the so-called "mixed economy" of modern capitalist societies. This ranges from the provision of relatively small-scale risk capital, as by the N.R.D.C., to the massive backing of high-technology, as in the aerospace sector, to the influence of government legislation on pollution and safety, and to the projection of government agency generated knowledge into the private sector. Also the nationalised industries are following the conglomerate trend by becoming involved in a range of activities which may be considered a spin-off from their initial concern.

I am not suggesting that there are not still a lot of small single-business companies. However, if we are interested in technology transfer and its impact at the level of the national economy, then it is in the environment described above that we must examine it. What then are the consequences of this industrial environment for technology transfer?

The first of these refers back to the assumption that with respect to technology transfer, more is automatically better. In the modern corporation there is a complex variety of factors which must be taken into consideration in the making of any decision, including that to seek or adapt new technology. Thus in the case of the steel company, the decision to diversify into plastics is a consequence of an analysis of market trends, raw material availability and cost, capital investment and likely return, technology, spare capacity, etc. There may frequently be very good reasons for deciding not to become involved in a new technology. What is needed from technology transfer studies is a careful examination of the conditions under which a company seeks new technology as there are far more important controlling factors than the availability of technology.

The process of integration and rationalisation which has occurred in industry should apparently reduce the barriers to technology transfer, as the interfaces between the various activities in which different technology is employed should be reduced. Similarly the growing involvement of government in industry should provide increased opportunities for technology transfer. There is some evidence to suggest this has actually occurred. However there is considerable scope for examination of just how technology does get transmitted in such an environment and whether sufficient attention is paid to the technological element in the process of rationalisation and diversification.

The Social Climate for Technology Transfer

No discussion pertaining to technology today would be complete without a reference to the growing unease and resentment towards technology being expressed by considerable sections of the public. To this date there has been no widespread rejection of the products of technology and it is difficult to conceive how such a rejection could occur in a society so heavily dependent on technology. Nevertheless there could be increasing resistance to the development of certain forms of technology and any comprehensive theory of technology transfer should allow for this possibility.

A considerable limitation of studies of technology transfer as previously mentioned is their acceptance of the "more is better" argument without any consideration of the ultimate purpose of the technology. Therefore one would welcome the inclusion of some form of assessment into these studies. While the growing bandwaggon of technology assessment is hardly likely to provide a panacea for technological and other social ills, there seems to be every case for including an analysis of why certain technologies should be sought, or adopted, not only with regard to the economic basis for the firm but also in terms of social value for the ultimate adopters.

Conclusion

Much of what has been argued may appear obvious but the fact remains that both studies of and programmes to foster technology transfer have been based on narrowly conceived assumptions which bear more relationship to the economist's idealised conception of perfect competition than to the actual structure of both industry and knowledge in a modern industrial society.

If research on technology transfer is to be of more use and have a greater impact on those involved in its implementation, it must be situated in a real-world environment. Two features of present day society have been developed, and a third briefly mentioned, which are of major importance in analysing the process of technology transfer. In particular, studies of this phenomenon must pay close attention to the structure of the knowledge system from which and to which transfer is occurring and also the nature of the organisational environment within which it takes place.

136

References

[1] Douds, C.F., "The State of the Art in the Study of Technology Transfer — a Brief Survey", *R & D Management* 1 (1971) 103.

[2] Chakrabarti, A.K., "Some Concepts of Technology Transfer: Adoption of Innovations in Organizational Context", *R & D Management* 3 (1973) 111.

[3] Bradbury, F.R., *Technology Transfer — Keynote Address* this volume, p. 107.

[4] Gruber, W. and Marquis, D.G., "Research on the Human factor in the Transfer of Technology" in Gruber & Marquis (eds), *Factors in the Transfer of Technology*, the M.I.T. Press, Cambridge, Massachusetts, 1969, p. 255.

[5] Brooks, H., *National Science Policy and Technology Transfer*, Proceedings of a Conference on Technology Transfer and Innovation, National Science Foundation, NsF 67-5, Washington, D.C.

[6] Burns, T., "Models, Images and Myths" in Gruber & Marquis (eds), 1969, *op. cit.*, p. 11.

[7] Johnston, R. and Gibbons, M., "Characteristics of Information Usage in Technological innovation", *IEEE Transactions on Engineering Management*, EM-22 (1975) 27.

[8] Johnston, R., "The Internal Structure of Technology'., *Sociological Review Monograph*, 18 (1972) p. 117.

[9] Burns, T. and Stalker, G.M., *The Management of Innovation*, London, Tavistock Publications, 1961.

[10] Galbraith, J.K., *The New Industrial State*, London, Penguin, 1967.

[11] Bell, D., *The Coming of Post-Industrial Society*, London, Heinemann, 1974.

[12] Kuhn, T.S. *The Structure of Scientific Revolutions*, Chicago University Press, 1962.

INNOVATION AND TECHNOLOGY TRANSFER — A NOTE ON THE FINDINGS OF PROJECT SAPPHO

by *Paul Jervis**

Project SAPPHO was a study of success and failure in industrial innovation, and the analytical results have been published widely [1, 2] as have some of the case studies on which the analysis was based.[3] During the Project 71 case studies of innovations were carried out, 36 in the chemical industry and 35 in the instrument industry, and the data gathered was used to detect differences between commercially successful and unsuccessful innovations. Much more data was gathered than has been discussed in the published reports, and if the success/failure comparison is abandoned, and the material considered as a set of detailed case studies, a number of additional analyses can be carried out. This paper examines the information about technology transfer which can be found in the SAPPHO data.

The innovation activity can involve transfer processes in a number of ways. The idea for the innovation may originate outside the innovating firm, and in some cases development may proceed as far as prototype stage before the work is taken over and brought in-house by the eventual innovator. The innovating firm may collaborate with other organisations or individuals while the development is proceeding in-house, and may call upon external assistance during production. Finally, the commercial success of the innovation will depend on its acceptance by potential users and, particularly for radical innovations, considerable user education may be needed to enable them to appreciate the advantages and make efficient use of the new product or process. In addition this description ignores what is in practice frequently a major problem, the transfer of projects within departments in the same organisation, for instance from research to production [4].

The data collected during SAPPHO includes a number of questions that yield information about the stages described above. In particular the following measures can be used:

* Oxford Centre for Management Studies, U.K.

- did the innovation arise outside the organisation that marketed it, and if so what was its source?
- was there any collaboration with outside organisations or individuals, and if so which were they?
- was there any dependence on outside technology during production, and if so was this beneficial or detrimental?
- were development engineers involved in planning and costing for production?
- were potential users involved in development at any stage?
- were any modifications involved as a result of user experience, either at prototype stage or after commercial sales?
- were any steps taken to educate users?

(i) *Source of Innovations*

In the chemical industry the majority of innovations came from ideas generated in-house. In 14 of 36 innovation attempts (39%) the ideas came from outside, and of the external sources industry received the most frequent mention. External sources of ideas appeared to be no disadvantage in chemical innovations, because of those with such sources half achieved commercial success and the remainder failed.

The instrument industry showed the opposite pattern, with 26 of 35 innovation attempts (74%) involving ideas from outside. In this case the most frequently identified sources were universities and individuals, with government laboratories and industry also quoted with approximately the same frequency. Again the external source of ideas, per se, did not appear a disadvantage although slightly more (15) of these innovations failed than achieved commercial success (11). Table 1 reports the information in this section in greater detail.

(ii) *Collaboration with External Organisations*

In the chemical industry collaboration with other organisations during the development of the innovation was reported in 23 of the innovations (64%). Collaboration with more than one external source was identified in about a third of these cases. Industry dominated the sources reported with universities and individuals receiving little mention.

The proportion of innovations involving outside collaboration in the instrument industry was almost identical (22 innovations, 63%), but the sources mentioned were dominated by universities and government with industry receiving only a few mentions. Table 2 reports the information in this section in greater detail.

(iii) *Dependence on External Technology During Production*

140

In the chemical industry nearly all the innovating organisations showed some dependence on external technology during production (33 firms, 92%). However, a clear distinction between successes and failures emerged from the result of this dependence. It appeared a benefit in the successful innovation, but a considerable hindrance in those that had failed.

The instrument innovations involved dependence on external technology slightly less frequently (21 firms, 60%), but the pattern was very much the same. Table 3 contains the information about use of external technology during production.

(iv) *Involvement of Development Engineers in Planning for Production*

In any innovation process the personnel involved in the development work are inevitably concerned in the transfer to production, whether formally or informally. In SAPPHO no absolute measure of the degree of involvement was attempted, and so information cannot be given for the individual innovations. Comparison of the extent of this involvement was made for the success/failure pairs, and this showed that more use of development engineers at this stage in the innovation process was characteristic of success. As Table 4 shows this result applied equally to chemicals and instruments.

(v) *The Users' Role in the Innovation Process*

The involvement of potential users in the development of innovations occurred more often in the instrument industry (30 cases, 86%) than in the chemical industry (15 cases, 42%), and in general although the frequency of involvement was the same in successes and failures the extent of involvement was greater in successes. (Table 5).

Again, the attempt by innovators to educate potential users was present in a majority of cases (chemicals 26 cases, 72%, and instruments 21 cases, 60%) but successful innovators devoted greater effort than the unsuccessful ones (Table 6).

One of the major findings of the success/failure analysis in SAPPHO was that successful innovators performed the development more efficiently than the unsuccessful ones and that they anticipated user requirements better. Indications of those effects were found in the frequent occurrence of technical "bugs" in production, and after-sales problems, in the failures. It has been suggested that successful innovators will anticipate and solve such problems early in development. The importance of the users' input is emphasised, however, by the fact that most of the innovations studied, whether successful or not (19 chemical cases, 53% and 28 in-

141

strument cases, 80%) had modifications introduced as a result of user experience after commercial sales (even though other user stimulated modifications may have been made during development). In general, however, failures demanded more extensive modifications at this stage than successes. (Table 7).

The Technology Transfer Process

Thus far this analysis has tried to indicate the extent to which external technology, either as an aid in development and production or, embodied in the requirements and knowledge of potential users, as a factor influencing success or failure, can be involved in and affect attempts at innovation. Each of the characteristics of the innovation process discussed above involve some kind of transfer, but there is a more specific process which is frequently implied by the phrase "technology transfer". This is the total sequence of events through which an invention which has originated in, say, a university laboratory or government research establishment is taken into a commercial organisation, modified and developed against new criteria and introduced to the market-place. There is some interesting information about this process within the SAPPHO data, but it is contained within a small subset of the case histories in the instrument industry.

In ten of the instrument innovations the technical innovator, the man who was responsible for the major technical contribution to the development and design of the innovation, was not a member of the innovating firm. In three cases a member of a university department or government laboratory who had been responsible for an invention had to try more than once (in one case it was three times) before a firm successfully marketed an innovation. Of these ten cases four were eventually successful and six failed. When failure occurred it appeared that there was insufficient or ineffective involvement of the innovator by the firm developing the product. When success was achieved the innovating firms developed and modified the innovations more than the unsuccessful firms. This suggests that when innovations are brought in from outside the innovating organisation must take the responsibility for developing them against the needs of the market-place, and with the attitudes and abilities of potential users in mind. These are features that the original, external, inventors are not always able to appreciate.

It was also noted that success depended on someone within the receiving organisation making sure the innovation received the necessary resources and support, and that his communication with the inventor was important. Some cases were also identified where transfer of staff considerably aided the technology transfer.

Conclusion

The information above is offered as additional evidence, if any is needed, of the importance of transfer processes in technical change and their close relationship to the innovation process. It may also suggest areas for future research, or hypotheses which should be tested more rigorously.

Some interesting differences between the two industries emerge, but it should be remembered when discussing these that the chemical innovations were all processes, while the instrument innovations were all products. Sections (i) and (ii) above suggest that in the chemical industry other parts of industry are more important sources of ideas and of collaboration than are the universities, while in the instrument industry universities and government laboratories are considerably more important than industry. Langrish has commented on the apparent lack of interaction between universities and industry in the chemical industry [5, 6], and the SAPPHO evidence tends to support this. However, the question which must next be resolved is whether the industry differences revealed here are inherent in the nature of the science and technology involved, or a reflection of the existing research and interests of the organisations involved.

While this information deals with innovations, and not the specific ideas which contribute to them, the importance of external inputs shown by the Queen's Award Study [7] is supported by the SAPPHO data.

The importance of the users' role in innovation and of the correct understanding of the users' attitudes and requirements by the innovator, has been widely discussed. Inter-industry differences emerge in the SAPPHO data, but it might be expected that chemical process innovators know and understand the users of their innovations from previous experience, and may need to undertake less involvement of users and user education. Indeed many process innovations are made by firms who will use the processes in-house themselves. But the instrument industry, dealing with product innovations and a more fragmented market, needs to devote considerable attention to the user if success is to be achieved. The interaction between innovator and user is clearly a transfer

143

process of great importance in the eventual success or failure of innovations.

References

[1] Achilladelis, B., Jervis, P., Robertson, A., *Project SAPPHO: A Study of Success and Failure in Innovation*, Science Policy Research Unit, University of Sussex, 1971.

[2] *Success and Failure in Industrial Innovation*, Centre for the Study of Industrial Innovation, London 1972.

[3] Jervis, P., "Innovation in Electron-Optical Instruments – Two British Case Histories", *Research Policy* 1 (1972/2) p. 174.

[4] Quinn, J.B. and Mueller, J.B., "Transferring Research Results to Operations", *Harvard Business Review*, Jan.-Feb. 1963.

[5] Langrish, J., "University Chemistry Research: Any Use to Industry", *Chemistry in Britain* 8 (1972) 330.

[6] Langrish, J., "The Changing Relationship between Science and Technology", this volume, p. 171.

[7] Langrish, J., Gibbons, M., Evans, W.G., Jevons, F.R., *Wealth from Knowledge*, Macmillan, 1972.

Table 1. *Source of inventions*

Source	Chemicals		Instruments		Total	
	Successes	Failures	Successes	Failures	Successes	Failures
Universities	3	1	5	4	8	5
Government civil	1	1	2	4	3	5
Government defence	1	1	1	1	2	2
Related industry sector	1	3	1	2	2	5
Unrelated industry sector	1	2	2	2	3	4
Individuals	—	—	3	6	3	6
Number of innovations concerned*	7	7	11	15	18	22

* Sources mentioned exceed this figure as innovations were sometimes jointly ascribed to two sources.

145

Table 2. *Outside collaboration in the development of innovations*

Source	Chemicals		Instruments		Total	
	Successes	Failures	Successes	Failures	Successes	Failures
Universities	2	2	3	4	5	6
Government civil	1	3	4	5	5	8
Government defence	2	1	2	1	4	2
Related industry sector	3	5	–	–	3	5
Unrelated industry sector	7	6	2	2	9	8
Research Associations	–	1	–	–	–	1
Professional consultants	–	1	1	–	–	1
Individuals	1	–	3	4	4	4
Number of innovations concerned*	10	13	10	12	20	25

* Sources mentioned exceed this figure as collaboration more than one source sometimes reported.

Table 3. *Effect of dependence on outside technology during production*

	Chemicals		Instruments		Total	
	Successes	failures	Successes	failures	Successes	failures
Large benefit	8	3	5	3	13	6
Small benefit	5	1	3	2	8	3
No effect/no dependence	2	1	7	7	9	8
Small hindrance	2	1	1	—	3	1
Large hindrance	1	12	1	6	2	17

Table 4. *Use of development engineers in planning for production*

	Chemicals	Instruments	Total
Successful innovation featured more use of development engineers in planning for production than unsuccessful one	7	7	14
No difference	12	12	24
Unsuccessful innovation featured more use of development engineers in planning for production than successful one	3	2	5

148

Table 5. *Involvement of potential users in development*

Degree of involvement	Chemicals		Instruments		Total	
	Successes	Failures	Successes	Failures	Successes	Failures
Potential users involved extensively	5	1	8	1	13	2
Potential users involved slightly	3	6	7	14	10	20
Potential users not involved	10	11	2	3	12	14

Table 6. *Innovators' attention to user education*

Extent of user education effort	Chemicals		Instruments		Total	
	Successes	Failures	Successes	Failures	Successes	Failures
Extensive effort to educate potential users	6	2	6	1	12	3
Moderate effort to educate potential users	10	8	7	7	17	15
No effort to educate potential users	2	8	4	10	6	18

Table 7. *Modifications resulting from user experience after commercial sales*

Extent of Modifications	Chemicals		Instruments		Total	
	Successes	failures	Successes	failures	Successes	failures
Many modifications as a result of user experience after commercial sales	1	3	4	8	5	11
A few modifications as a result of user experience after commercial sales	7	8	11	5	18	13
No modifications as a result of user experience after commercial sales	10	7	2	5	12	12

BARRIERS TO INNOVATION*

by *M.C. McCarthy***

Introduction

The purpose of this paper is to examine a simple model of innovation and its implications for those conducting research in an industrial environment. It is based on limited experience: on examination of several research projects resulting in major new products in the chemical industry, and on the examination of several years operation of the research activities of a corporate laboratory in the chemical industry.

The Model of Innovation

One simple model of innovation concentrates on the screening process by which a perceived need and the recognised qualities of a new material are brought together. The bringing together of these two patterns of properties and their subsequent modification constitute the invention, and the subsequent survival of the material whose potential usefulness has been recognised constitutes the innovation. There is a clear analogy between research activities described by this model, and the well-studied problem of search strategies. This model, and this analogy, concentrate attention on the screens adopted: the definition of relevant characteristics, the selection of particular properties as operational criteria governing acceptance or rejection, and the ability of the screener to identify in advance those criteria which will prove important [1].

Two developments to this simple model are discussed here, both of which are concerned with elaborating the concept of screening and are deliberate rejection of candidate compounds by screens

---

* The views expressed in this article are those of the author, not of Her Majesty's Government.
** Department of Industry, London, U.K.

rather than the more painful and expensive ordeal by testing in practice. The first elaboration is to consider the implications of the fact that innovation differs from most industrial problem recognition and problem-solving situations in the number of organisations and departments of organisations involved in the innovation process. It is well documented that research ideas can originate in various organisations [2]. There are important consequences of this: in the progression of an invention, there are often, and perhaps always, several organisations whose requirements must be satisfied between the original need being recognised, and the need being fully satisfied. The original need may be recognised in various places: by raw material suppliers (e.g. polythene manufacturers recognising the material's potential for shrink wrapping); by intermediate suppliers (e.g. the manufacturers of polythene film looking for new uses); by end users (e.g. the various users of Scotchtape); or by equipment manufacturers (e.g. the introduction of new techniques of making fabrics by manufacturers of knitting machinery).

But in all cases when the innovation originates other than from the end user, its success depends on persuading other organisations to participate in the innovative process. A simple example may be useful: the anaesthetic halothane was discovered by chemists in the chemical industry (the suppliers of raw materials). To succeed however the discovery had to be accepted by anaesthetists (the end users), who had to make considerable alterations to existing techniques and even to their existing patterns of thought; and changes were needed in equipment suppliers. The success of the original screens used by the chemists synthesising compounds for subsequent test as anaesthetics was directly related to the chemists' ability to identify in advance the requirements that others would have; and to their success in abstracting from these complex requirements those properties translatable into the chemist's language. Equally, the success of the original discovery owed much to the extent to which the assistance of others than raw material manufacturers was obtained.

The recognition that innovation is likely to involve several organisations has a number of features of note:
(i) the innovative process may usefully be considered as technological development within one organisation, followed by technology transfer to another organisation, which may then be responsible for its own process of development;
(ii) those who are concerned with early stages of the innovative

152

cycle may benefit from helpful and necessary feedback from technology users, and must often be active in encouraging technology transfer to other industries;

(iii)   the tasks of the discoverer who wishes his discovery to become an innovation includes those of identifying other organisations and individuals in the innovative process, of elucidating their aims, and of identifying the criteria they adopt to choose between candidate compounds;

(iv)   the identification of different operations and organisations is essential if a careful analysis is to be made of the opportunities for profitable business: it is required if the skills needed to produce a particular material, product or system are to be identified.

There is a second elaboration to the simple model of screening. This is the structuring of the barriers to innovation within the innovative chain. Here it is useful to consider problems under different headings.

(a)   *Economic barriers*

Various economic barriers to innovation may be identified. First, the organisation undertaking research will only do so if it believes this to be profitable (although not necessarily in the short run). Second, the purchaser of a new process or product must be convinced either that he is gaining the same end results as before at lower cost (e.g. a new process to produce an existing product at reduced cost) or that the extra properties which he acquires with the innovative product sufficiently compensate for any extra cost. Third, it is likely that some organisation may have to invest in capital equipment to use the research results.

(b)   *Technological barriers*

Two types of technological barriers may be identified.

First, a scientific or technological target must be achieved: a chemical yield increased to a certain percentage, or an electronic component reduced to a certain size. This particular barrier is one well-recognised by research scientists, and one to which they devote a considerable proportion of their efforts. It is perhaps not surprising, therefore, to find that analysis of the causes of failure in research laboratories has shown that failure because of unforeseen technical difficulties is not the main cause of failure: one analysis showed technical problems to be a less important cause of project failure than managerial decisions on manpower allocation; others have shown that about 30 per cent of all failures, or cost and time overruns, for research on defined targets is attributable to technical problems [3].

The second type of technological barrier is one which receives far less attention. This is the barrier related to the probability that an invention made in one organisation will be implemented by, or affect, other organisations; and must therefore be compatible with, or alter, existing techniques and processes. The experience is common: new equipment for detecting aircraft required new communication systems; new dyestuffs new dyeing techniques; new electronic equipment new standards of cleanliness among material suppliers. The introduction of a new herbicide may require new equipment and techniques to be used by the farmer; the advent of a new anaesthetic may require anaesthetists to change their ways. These changes are not optional: for the new product or process to be used, they must be made. The price of the new product may include considerable investment in new processes to use it. Despite the importance of this barrier, there is not much evidence of attention being paid to it, and of efforts being devoted to predict it; the model of innovation here discussed emphasises its importance.

(c) *Organisational barriers*

There is much discussion of organisational barriers to innovation, mainly centred round the Not Invented Here (NIH) factor. The assumption is often made that this reaction is irrational, the expected response of man in an eighteenth century environment dominated by knaves and fools. And once such an assumption has been publicised, it may well act as a self-fulfilling prophecy: the publicised assumption that someone is a knave or a fool is likely to alienate.

How far is this view justified? The model of innovation here discussed suggests a more rational explanation of the NIH factor: different organisations, and different parts of the same organisation, may have different targets and criteria, and prior commitments. Since motives may diverge, and since the language used to express even closely similar targets will differ, the innovator must be aware of many requirements on his invention, and must be able to use the appropriate method to communicate its advantages. NIH, it may be suggested, can represent not only an emotional Not Invented Here, but also an arguably logical Not Interested Here. And the latter response will be overcome only by demonstrating the potential or actual usefulness of an invention to each member of the innovative chain.

154

(d) *Personal barriers*

Organisational barriers are often compounded by the existence of personal barriers, arising from the different backgrounds and targets of different groups. Some studies have suggested conflict between the objectives of scientist and of manager, and communication problems between the two groups; others that research divided on functional lines – into, for example, a physics group and a chemistry group – has significantly greater communication problems than that organised as project teams. Again, this sort of conflict, and this barrier, is easily reconciled with the model discussed here.

(e) *Perceptual barriers*

Closely allied to both organisational and personal barriers are perceptual barriers. These perhaps more than any other type of barrier, are neglected by research scientists, and yet can profoundly influence the likelihood of an innovation's success. Two particular categories of perceptual barriers may be identified.

First, different groups in the innovative chain may possess different criteria against which to judge new ideas. An account of the difficulties encountered by an economist and an engineer when discussing a simple, but extremely effective, water pump illustrates this. The engineer was concerned with engineering complexity, the technical skill required to manufacture the pump, and its mechanical efficiency; while the economist judged the pump by comparing the costs of the pump rental against labour charges for traditional means of raising water. To the former, the device was crude and uninteresting; to the latter – and to the peasant wanting to raise water – simple and useful [4]. Another situation, not infrequently encountered, occurs when the scientist or engineer has a new product of considerable scientific complexity, which is difficult to describe in terms attractive to the customer.

Second, the new product is often judged against criteria which have been specially designed for an existing product. This may well present difficulties. Rayon, for example, was introduced as "synthetic silk" and was rejected by many since it did not approximate more closely to the properties of silk. The example shows that there are circumstances in which it is important that the new product should be seen as an entirely new product, judged on its own terms, rather than as a substitute for an existing product. If the new product is compared with the old, and judged on the terms used to judge the old, comparison may suggest that the new is more expensive or less effective, despite other cost savings or

155

advantages in the system of which the product is but one part. Thus it may be important – and difficult – to persuade customers to change their criteria in order to change their product.

So far, the discussion has suggested that the five barriers identified – economic, technological, organisational, personal and perceptual – are necessarily obstacles to the creation of an innovative pathway. It might be more accurate to claim that each represented a problem area, where barriers are likely to impede successful innovation, and where work to anticipate and overcome barriers by appropriate inclusions in the R & D programme may facilitate innovation. There is an obvious appeal between the concept of a screen within the Laboratory or research organisation, and that of a barrier existing outside. Indeed, the purpose of discussing barriers is to predict them in practical circumstances, so that work may be done early in a project's life to test the vulnerability of the project to the harshness of the environment into which it must progress.

There is a danger, however, of failing to stress the positive aspects of the model. For the concept of an innovative chain, supported by the structuring of possible barriers to innovation into five classes, allows the determined research scientist to do more than merely recognise the hazards his project must escape. One question that this analysis brings to his attention is that of motivating the protagonists in the innovative chain: "why should the engineer, or the wholesaler, or the equipment manufacturer, help realise this idea?" It is often said that "things happen because people make them happen". As important is "things happen because people see the advantages of making them happen". The model here discussed stresses the need first to identify the protagonists in an innovative chain, and then to discover their objectives and constraints. For without detailed knowledge of the protagonists' ambitions and problems any appeal to gain their assistance in furthering the innovation runs the risk of missing its target; and the danger increases that effort will be devoted to research that is not likely to complete the dangerous journey to become an innovation.

Conclusions

The simple model of innovation as a process which is similar to other industrial decision-making processes, but which is complicat-

156

ed by the number of organisations involved, has some important consequences for the industrial research scientist. The model concentrates attention not on the creation of new knowledge alone, but on the creation of knowledge of both new phenomena and of the perceived needs, in equal measure. Some other models of innovation stress the importance of invention as a separate and isolatable activity, which may be studied without reference to subsequent development [5]. The research scientist who follows this model will define his objectives as seeking new discoveries, and is likely to concentrate on the building of new knowledge. In some ways, his work will not be unlike that which he has performed at university. The work of the research scientist who adopts the model of innovation as a process involving different organisation, each with its own aims, will be very different. He will concentrate not solely on the creation of new knowledge, but also on the assessment of the significance of knowledge — either new or already existing. Scientific excellence is still required, but he will recognise that scientific excellence by itself is not sufficient. Whereas the researcher following the former model defines his targets in scientific terms, the latter is more likely to define his objectives in terms of technological achievements. The latter, operating with a wider agenda, is likely to be more aware of the constraints established by the technologies, manufacturing processes and commercial practices which connect the needs and demands of society with the scientific skills of the research scientists. He may consequently be more willing to supplement his skills with non-scientific skills.

The implications for resource allocation within a research laboratory are considerable. For the first model will lead to an emphasis on research workers at the bench, working on the discovery of new knowledge; other expense may be viewed as overheads, to be reduced as far as possible. The second model leads to a greater emphasis on activities other than those of the research worker at the bench. In particular, screening relative to the creation of new knowledge assumes a new importance, and it is recognised that the definition of appropriate screens may in itself be a major research undertaking. Finally, the two models have significance for the actual organisation of research. The former is more likely to result in research groups based on scientific divisions — a physics group, or a chemistry group. The latter suggests that in many instances a more suitable organisation may be one based on end applications — a textile auxiliaries group, for instance.

References

[1] Baines, A., Bradbury, F.R. and Suckling, C.W., *Research in the Chemical Industry*, Elsevier, London, 1969, pp. 121-129.

[2] See, for example, Peck, M.J., "Inventions in the post-war American aluminium industry" in *The Rate and Direction of Inventive Activity*, Princeton, 1962.

[3] Mansfield, J., *Industrial Research and Technological Innovation*, New York, 1968, p. 59; Scherer, F.M., "Economic and Social Factors" in *The Rate and Direction of Inventive Activity*, Princeton, 1962, pp. 498-500.

[4] Sansom, R.L., "The motor pump: a case study of innovation and development", *Oxford Economic Papers* (New Series), 21, 118-119.

[5] Jewkes, J., Sawers, D., and Stillerman, R., *The Sources of Invention*, London, 1969.

TRANSFER OF TECHNOLOGY IN THE TEXTILE INDUSTRY

by *H. Catling* *

General

There are many examples of the transfer of technology from other industries to the textile industry. Generally these transfers have done little to change the basic textile technology but have contributed greatly to the means by which the textile technology is realised. The use of PTFE coated cylinders for the drying of sized warps and finished fabrics is a simple example. Advanced automatic temperature control equipment developed for a variety of other purposes has found application in the extrusion of synthetic fibres, in texturing continuous filament yarns and in the dyeing and setting of fabrics. Electronic digital control is being applied to give precise draw ratios in sizing and filament yarn processing where gear trains and mechanical variable gearing are conventionally used.

One of the more spectacular true transfers of recent years has been in the field of pattern reproduction in textiles. In medieval times intricate patterns were woven by a master weaver assisted by a number of draw boys who manually raised and lowered the appropriate warp thread to produce the pattern. In 1801 Jacquard introduced a system of automatic pattern weaving based on the use of punched cards which is still in use today. Although a great boon to the weaver the Jacquard system had a weakness in the considerable effort involved in the conversion of the artists design into a chain of punched cards. For many years now there has been a great deal of interest in devices to render this task less laborious. Until recently the outcome has been no more than the provision of gadgetry for the easier implementation of the Jacquard system but we now have new systems breaking completely with earlier concepts of how a textile design may be automatically reproduced.

* Shirley Institute, Manchester, U.K.

A number of technologies are contributing to these developments. Early picture transmitting systems such as the Mufac "pictures by telephone" device, television and computer technology together with electro-magnetic gadgetry and fluid logic are all involved and it seems highly likely that the traditional Jacquard will be displaced in the forseeable future. A glance at the efforts of one particular company working in this field will serve as an example of how technological transfer into the textile industry is proceeding.

A surge of interest in Jacquard patterned double-jersey knitted fabrics stimulated development amongst knitting machine makers. Although to a purist the mechanism employed in the knitting of patterns is not a true Jacquard as used in weaving it does involve exactly the same problems in the conversion of the artists design into a form suitable for the control of a textile pattern weaving mechanism. A number of companies throughout the world attacked the problem in a variety of ways. Wildt Mellor Bromley, a Leicester based British company with a long history of knitting machine manufacture, working in conjunction with a company specialising in computer control and a third company specialising in photo-sensitive and electro-magnetic devices developed and is now producing and marketing an extremely sophisticated system.

Known as the "Computaknit" electronic pattern preparation system it works directly from the original artists' drawing, painting or photograph. The original need not be to any particular scale as the digitiser, after scanning the picture assembles all the information needed to knit the pattern within a rectangle of a previously specified number of stitches and rows. Before proceeding to actual knitting, the design stored in the computer can be displayed in colour on a "television" screen and the designer can make correction or additions using a joystick which controls a flashing cursor dot on the screen. When he is satisfied with the picture on the screen the designer, by means of a control console, instructs a knitting machine which is directly coupled to the computer to proceed, and within a few minutes a piece of fabric is available for appraisal.

Further amendments may be necessary but these can be done quickly and easily by recalling the pattern to the screen and sufficient fabric can then be knitted to provide samples to show to customers. It is envisaged that ultimately even long production runs will be done on computer controlled knitting machines but in the meantime punched paper or other pattern storage devices for conventional, mechanically controlled, knitting machines are pre-

160

pared automatically from the design information stored in the computer.

The Computaknit is an example of a very successful exercise in the transfer and integration of concepts and devices from other industries to solve a readily identifiable problem in the textile industry. It would be both interesting and pleasant to explore in greater detail just how the transfer took place but this would be rather like sailing on calm waters in fine weather and I have no doubt that this work will, in due course, be well documented and the various contributors will receive their deserved accolades. There are, however, more important lessons to be learnt on rough seas in foul weather and the mechanics of disaster should be compulsory reading for all sailors. I feel, therefore, that it would be more instructive to us all to look closely into a very considerable exercise in technology transfer which, because it ended in virtually total failure, will attract neither technological historians nor accolades.

A Notable Failure

The Situation

In the late 40's and early 50's two aspects of engineering technology were developing very rapidly and finding successful application in a number of diverse situations. One was the application of automatic control theory and practice, the other was the employment of automatic transfer devices to progress a work piece through a succession of processing machines. Both appeared to have considerable potential for application in the preparation of both natural and man-made short staple fibres for spinning.

When development work started the first stage of preparation of short fibres for spinning generally employed a single-process opening line, a highly automated assembly of units involving a minimum of handling of the material and incorporating simple and reliable, yet adequate, automatic control devices. The output from this stage was a uniform fleece of fibres about a metre wide and a centimetre thick delivered automatically in 40 lb rolls known as "laps". The production rate of a typical single process opening line was about 1,000 lb per hour. The state of development of the next stage, the conversion of the laps into bobbins of roving, was very much less satisfactory. It involved:

(i) Carding the lap, one yard of which weighed about one pound, to produce a "sliver", of which about 100 yards weighed one

161

pound. The production rate of one carding engine (card) was about eight pounds per hour and the sliver was delivered coiled into cylindrical canisters each holding about 10 lb of sliver.

(ii) Drawing the sliver through a succession of accelerating rollers with the object of parallelising the fibres preparatory to conversion into roving. Typically six sliver from six cans were fed into each drawing unit. The draw ratio would be about six so that the delivered sliver had roughly the same weight per unit length as the individual input slivers and differed only in the degree of orientation of its component fibres. The production rate of each drawing unit was about 100 lb of sliver per hour, delivered in cylindrical cans exactly like those used at the card. To achieve the requisite degree of fibre orientation it was usual to pass all sliver through three successive stages of drawing.

(iii) Production of roving from sliver. This was done on "spindle and flyer" frames fed from 10 lb cans of sliver and producing roving on bobbins weighing from 1 to 3 lb depending on the fineness of the yarn to be produced by the spinning frames. A typical roving frame would have from 100 to 150 spindles.

A percipient visitor to a mill of that period would have been immediately struck by the early-industrial-revolution atmosphere of this stage of yarn manufacture and must surely have felt that something should be done about it. In the smallest mill equipped with only one opening line (1,000 lb/hour) he would have seen 125 cards — each a large machine occupying about 100 square feet of floor space — with a part exhausted 40 lb lap of cotton on its feed table and a part filled 10 lb sliver can under the delivery coiler. Downstream from the cards would be a cascade of three sequences of drawing each consisting of 12 or 14 drawing units, each fed from six sliver cans and delivering into a seventh. Downstream again from the draw frame would be the spindle and flyer frames with a total of 250 to 500 spindles each fed from one of the sliver cans delivered by the final draw frames. Thus at successive processes there were:

	IN	OUT
carding — 125 carding engines	125 x 40 lb laps	125 x 10 lb sliver cans
1st drawing — 12 drawing units	72 x 10 lb sliver cans	12 x 10 lb sliver cans
2nd drawing — 12 drawing units	72 x 10 lb sliver cans	12 x 10 lb sliver cans
3rd drawing — 12 drawing units	72 x 10 lb sliver cans	12 x 10 lb sliver cans
roving — 350 spindle and flyer units	350 x 10 lb sliver cans	350 x 2 lb roving bob- bins

A dominating feature of the scene was the amount of manual creeling and doffing going on and the number of cans of silver about the place. In addition to buffer stocks of full and empty cans there were seven hundred and twenty five cans actually in use each, at any one time, holding on average 5 lb of sliver and each representing a creeling or doffing point requiring more or less frequent manual attendance. At the cards it was necessary to creel in 25 laps per hour; and doff 100 cans per hour. The drawframe section presented the scene of most frenzied activity with a need for creeling in 300 cans per hour and doffing a similar number, each creel can remaining in position for about 42 minutes and each of the 36 delivery stations requiring the doffing of a can approximately every 7 minutes. The spindle and flyer frame section was relatively tranquil with 350 cans, each remaining in place for about $3\frac{1}{2}$ hours.

It is difficult to give a clear yet concise picture of the tasks involved in marshalling, doffing and creeling sliver cans. The cans themselves were generally 9 or 10 inches in diameter and about 30 inches high — not by any means ideal for handling but necessarily of that shape for proper functioning of the coiling mechanism and the stacking requirements for a satisfactory creel. Doffing required only the removal of the full can followed by deft replacement by an empty can and severance of the sliver. Creeling required timely removal of the emptying can, replacement by a full can and neat and skillful splicing of the new sliver to the tail of the old one.

There was obviously a case here for at least consideration of the possibility of introducing automatic transfer means between process sequences and it quickly became apparent that some radical

163

redesign of machinery would be necessary. The situation was complicated by the fact that recent research into the relationship between sliver uniformity and yarn properties had shown that improved sliver uniformity could give greatly enhanced yarn properties and it was known that a number of factors were combining to create a strong demand for better yarns. It was also appreciated that a number of imperfectly understood features of the drawing process itself were the cause of much of the sliver variability which adversely affected the yarn. This had stimulated scientific interest in the causes of sliver irregularity but a stronger "practical" school was advocating acceptance of these features and the application of automatic draft control devices to remove irregularities introduced at earlier drawing stages. The influence of this school was greatly strengthened by the success of automatic control in other industries and particularly by the extremely successful introduction (by Prince Smith & Stells of Keighley) of the Raper autoleveller for worsted (long staple) drawing. Thus the scene was set for a revolution in short staple drawing practice by transfer from other industries of two distinct and separate technologies.

The progress of Technology Transfer

Movement started in the early 50's. It quickly gathered momentum and very soon textile machinery makers and research establishments throughout the world were working towards the goal of a completely automated carding and drawing sequence. The Japanese were particularly active and many prototype installations were put into service in Japan. In Britain Textile Machinery Makers Limited (now Platt International) developed two systems and the Shirley Institute developed one.

Development of the Shirley "Automated Card Room" was a major item in the research programme of the Institute for about six years. Although primarily financed from the Institute's central research fund it received substantial financial support from the National Research Development Corporation and was guided by a Steering Committee consisting of representatives from both the production and R & D interests of the spinning industry leavened by a sprinkling of academics and machinery makers.

From the outline of the processes given above, the general nature of the problems encountered can easily be appreciated. Automatic feeding of the cards presented no insuperable difficulties but there were two views as to how it could best be done. Some favoured the radical solution of conveying the fibre from the opening line either pneumatically or on a lattice directly to chutes behind the card without ever forming it into a lap. Others developed automatic handling equipment to convey and deliver the traditional laps to the cards. At the outset the difficulty in automatic card feeding by either system lay in the divergence required to pass the flow of a single channel delivering c. 1,000 lb of fibre an hour through a large number of parallel channels each passing approximately 8 lb/hour. Later the situation changed materially as a result of independent advances in carding technology.

Transfer at the next stage in the process sequence, cards to draw frames, posed the opposite problem. It was necessary to pass the flow from six cards through each of the drawing channels. Again some workers developed automatic handling equipment to doff, transport and creel the traditional package of sliver, others developed novel packages more convenient for automatic handling whilst a further school (of which the Shirley system was an example) coupled a number of cards together to produce a rate of material flow to match the feed requirements of a draw frame and combined this with novel forms of package. Generally a great deal of ingenuity was shown in the design of gadgetry for transporting the packages used and for doffing and creeling.

Most systems provided automatic linking of two drawframe sequences but did not go on to automate the transfer to the spindle and flyer frames.

In parallel with this work on automatic handling, various systems of automatic draft control were developed to complement the new handling systems by eliminating the need for manual monitoring of sliver weight and improving the quality of the sliver produced in terms of freedom from both long and short term variability. Every conceivable type of transducer was used, from simple direct mechanical displacement devices measuring the thickness of the sliver, to pneumatic devices measuring the air permeability of the sliver. Control mechanisms covered an equally wide range and the result was a bewildering variety of regulators and auto-levellers all capable of making useful contributions to sliver quality.

By the late 50's mills throughout the world were beginning to install prototype automated card room sequences. Most were in Japan, several, usually by local makers, were dotted about in Europe and two or three of Japanese design were installed in America. In Britain Platts made two radically different mill installations and the Shirley Institute provided a third. All, without exception, failed in that they did not become established as viable systems and it is doubtful if any are in use today. As this was a world wide attempt at technology transfer which was initially extremely attractive and on which many millions of pounds was spent we must ask what went wrong, to the end that an understanding of the mechanics of failure will be useful in the future.

The Causes of Failure

With the benefit of hindsight one can see that the root cause of the trouble was the failure of the technology transfer advocates to appreciate the significance of the better understanding of the basic textile technology which was being gained by fundamental studies in this field. In the event this better understanding has so revolutionised the basic textile processes that neither automatic handling technology nor short term draft control can contribute usefully to the operation of a modern process sequence. The situation did not change overnight but, during the ten year period from 1955 to 1965, both card production rates and sliver drawing speeds were increased ten fold whilst at the same time producing a significantly better product. The surprising thing, in retrospect, is that, as production rates were increased step by step development engineers working to produce automated systems saw, in the increasing speeds, only a challenge to their ability – not a disappearance of the need for automatic transfer devices.

The two developments in textile technology, improved carding and improved drawing, were mutually independent and had little in common except their near co-incident arrival on the scene and their implications for the process sequence. The more important implications were:

(i) Increase in card production rates reduced the number of cards required to take the output from an opening line. It had long been technically possible to feed cards directly from an opening line. The practical objection to direct feeding was the high cost of the ducts or lattices and the metering equipment needed when 125 cards were involved. Reducing the number to 12 or 16 transformed the situation making direct feed arrangements so cheap and simple that it was no longer worthwhile entertaining the idea of scutcher laps with or without automated handling.

(ii) Increase in drawing speeds of the same order as the increase in carding rate meant that the most economic size of sliver package was also increased. The size of intermediate package used in process sequences of the sort with which we are here concerned is always a matter of compromise. Handling labour costs can general-

166

ly be reduced by the use of larger packages but only at the expense of increased space requirements, increased cost of work in progress and constraints on machine design. With the old card and drawframe speeds a 10 lb package was near the optimum but with the 10 fold increase in speed there has been roughly a 10 fold increase in optimum package size and cans holding from 80 to 120 lb of sliver are now being used.

(iii) The increase in drawing speeds was the serendipitous outcome of work done with the primary object of improving sliver quality. Briefly, many irregularities introduced during drafting were traceable to machine imperfections such as imprecise location of rollers, torsional vibration in shafts and gearing inaccuracies. It was found that when these weaknesses were removed by greatly improved standards of machine design and construction not only was sliver quality dramatically improved but in addition it was found that the process could be carried out at much higher speeds. The significance of the speed increase is dealt with in (ii) above. The improvement in drafting performance was significant in that it (a) reduced sliver variability to such an extent that there was no longer any point in even contemplating the use of an autoleveller to remove irregularities introduced at earlier drafting stages and (b) it enabled the number of drawing sequences needed to be reduced from three to two.

Thus the modern machine line-up to be compared with the typical line-up of the 1950's shown above, is:

	IN	OUT
carding – 14 carding engines	Direct feed	14 x 100 lb sliver cans
1st drawing – 4 drawing units	32 x 100 lb sliver cans	4 x 100 lb sliver cans
2nd drawing – 4 drawing units	32 x 100 lb sliver cans	4 x 40 lb sliver cans
roving – 250 spindle and flyer units	250 x 40 lb cans	250 x 3 lb roving bobbins

(The use of smaller cans for sliver for the delivery from the second stage of drawing is dictated by economic considerations in the design of the spindle and flyer frame creel).

It is immediately obvious, particularly in considering the carding and drawing sequences only, that the amount of package handling required has been drastically reduced. At the cards no creeling is now needed and the doffing requirement has been reduced from 100 cans per hour to 10. The drawframe creeling requirement has been reduced from 300 cans per hour to 20, and drawframe doffing reduced from 300 to 35. It is easy to see why, in the new situation, there is little need for automatic handling and why all attempts to provide completely automated card rooms have failed.

Reflections

The surprising thing is that, when the improved cards and improved drawframes became available in the very early 60's, the corporate planners controlling the purse strings did not clamp down on the automation development work. In many instances the resources available were actually increased in an attempt to overcome the practical problems which had arisen as a result of increased machine speeds. At the Shirley Institute the continuation of work beyond the point in time when rational appraisal of the situation should have counselled a withdrawal can be attributed to three factors:
(i) Because the work received support from NRDC it was directed by a committee. The terms of reference of this committee were, not unreasonably, limited to pursuance of a defined goal — the development of an automated cardroom sequence. The committee had no mandate to question the soundness of its objective.
(ii) R & D staff directly concerned with the work tended to be euphoric about their actual achievement and were consequently unable to make a truly objective assessment of the implications of the changing situation. To some extent this situation must always obtain if a research team is to have a chance of success. A team lacking confidence in the worthwhileness of the project on which it is engaged is extremely unlikely to succeed.
(iii) Long term arrangements had been made in regard to the mill trials of the system and it could be argued that the mill concerned would have been seriously embarrassed had the equipment not been installed at the scheduled time. It was in fact operated for more than two years providing a significant proportion of the total capacity for spinning preparation in that mill.

Similar considerations were, no doubt, operating in other establishments and these together with such sentiments as "It is a pity to withdraw after spending half a million pounds and no machinery to show for it, let us spend another half million and at least there will be a concrete outcome which will be of some use to someone," led to work being continued long after it should, logically, have been terminated.

It is estimated that, world wide, upwards of £25 million was spent and in the event very little has been salvaged from all the effort which went into this considerable exercise in technology transfer. Some of the process control work has found application in the control of direct feeding to cards but none of the automation gadgetry has any relevance to the technology of todays industry.

There is a temptation to put forward the above case history as constituting a case for the frequent re-appraisal of all major R & D projects by qualified people without a direct involvement. Unfortunately it is by no means certain that such a practice would have been effective even in this instance and it must be admitted that too-frequent re-appraisal of projects can seriously inhibit the performance of a research and development team and lead to distortion of the work schedule.

THE CHANGING RELATIONSHIP BETWEEN SCIENCE AND TECHNOLOGY

by *J. Langrish* *

Introduction

Results from studies of the inputs from Science to Technology suggest that the relationship between the two has changed in the past and is about to change again.

In recent years, the belief that technological change is somehow based on scientific advance has been increasingly challenged. Price, for example, has claimed:

> "The naive picture of technology as applied science simply will not fit the facts. Inventions do not hang like fruits on a scientific tree. In those parts of the history of technology where one feels some confidence, it is quite apparent that most technological avances derive immediately from those that precede them". [1]

Technological change has been increasingly seen as the adaption of existing technological concepts in response to the pull of demand. Schmookler, for example, has attempted to show that the variation in inventive activity between different American industries is explicable in terms of the variation in demand, concluding that economic growth determines the rate of inventive activity rather than the reverse [2] None the less, Governments have continued to invest in scientific research at a level much greater than other activities which can also claim cultural and prestige benefits. Science receives much more money than the Arts because it is believed to be useful. When science is not used, it is claimed that there is a communication barrier; the alternative possibility that it is intrinsically of no use is not examined.

One of the major problems in looking at the usefulness of science is a matter of definitions. What is Science? What is Technology? To avoid this problem, it is possible to ask such questions as what is the effect of university research and research in govern-

* Institute of Science and Technology, University of Manchester, U.K.

ment laboratories on industrial change (or on improvements in health, agriculture etc.).

A study of 84 British technological innovations [3] showed that "demand pull" occurred more frequently than "discovery push" and that out of 158 key technical ideas made use of in innovations, 56 originated within the innovating firms and of the remaining 102, 7 came from a British university and 17 from a British government laboratory (including Research Associations).

The apparent conclusion that ideas from British universities had little effect on British innovation was challenged in a variety of ways. One of these was the claim that although industrial innovation may be based on industrial research, the day to day progress of industrial research depended on university research in ways that would not be revealed in looking at "key ideas". It was pointed out, for example, that industrial chemists spend time reading the results of university chemical research.

In order to examine the relative contribution of university research in the literature input to industrial research, seven review articles written by British industrial chemists were examined [4]. The reviews contained 567 references to other publications (including patents) and the institutional origins of 396 of them were identified. Only 23 out of the 396 references were to the work of British universities and of these, 7 stated that some industrial finance had been involved in the research. British government institutions appeared to be more interesting to the industrial reviewers in that 45 of the references were involved. Table 1 compares the relative importance of the institutional origins of the 102 "key ideas" with the origins of the 396 references and also the origins of 452 abstracts to be discussed later.

Table 1. *Institutional Origins of Knowledge Inputs to British Industry*

Origins	% of 102 ideas	% of 396 references	% of 452 abstracts (1952)
U.K. Industry	22	10	19
U.K. University	7	6	1
U.K. Government	19*	11	1
Foreign Industry	40	40	68
Foreign University	3	21	5
Foreign Government	9*	12	6

* Government and Military combined

172

German Industry Rested on German Science

Table 1 seems to show that the results of British university research have little impact on British industry. Why then does the British Government continue to finance university research? One possible reason is that university research only occasionally produces results of economic benefit but when it does the benefits are so large that they outweigh the total costs of all university research for several decades. A possible example of this kind in the present century is the research that led to atomic power. A more fruitful source of such examples is the last half of the last century.

There is little doubt that German university research in organic chemistry, for example, provided the foundations for the German synthetic dyestuffs industry and subsequent advances in pharmaceuticals, synthetic rubber and plastics. Similarly the electrical industries can be seen as being based on nineteenth century academic research.

At the time of the First World War Britain realised that Germany had advanced industrially by using the results of scientific research and, in 1917, the Department of Scientific and Industrial Research was established. Since then, the British Government has ploughed an increasing quantity of money into scientific research in the belief that what was good for Germany in the last century should be good for Britain in the present century.

Times Have Changed

Reliance on the German example does not seem to have been justified. One possible explanation is that the relationship between science (university research) and technology (industrial practice) has changed since the last century. In order to test this hypothesis, abstracts produced by the Journal of the Society of Chemical Industry were examined. For some eighty years, this Journal produced abstracts of the world's literature that might be of relevance to industrial chemists. Even in the last century, large teams of abstractors were used, reducing the possible bias of an individual. The abstracts were classified according to industrial subject matter, and those classes which might be considered to rest on organic chemistry were chosen for examination.

The original publications selected by the abstractors as being worth the attention of industrial chemists were consulted and wherever possible, institutional origins identified. Initially, the years 1884, 1917, 1935 and 1952 were examined but the differ-

Table 2. *Change with Time of Institutional Sources of Abstracts in Journal of Society of Chemical Industry for Industrial Area Connected with Organic Chemistry*

Year of Journal	1884	1899	1917	1935	1952
Institutional Source of Abstract	%	%	%	%	%
U.S. Industry	—	4.8	14.5	38.1	53.8
U.K. Industry	8.8	17.3	6.2	9.3	19.0
European Industry	23.5	44.7	52.4	24.1	13.6
Other Industry	—	1.0	0.7	0.5	0.9
TOTAL INDUSTRY	32.3	67.8	73.8	72.0	87.4
U.S. Government	—	1.0	1.4	1.9	3.6
U.K. Government	—	1.0	—	0.5	1.1
European Government	5.9	1.9	2.1	3.4	1.3
Other Government	—	1.0	2.1	0.5	1.1
TOTAL GOVERNMENT	5.9	4.8	5.5	6.3	7.2
U.S. University	3.0	1.0	1.4	1.9	2.6
U.K. University	—	7.7	6.2	0.8	0.7
European University	58.8	18.7	13.1	15.3	0.2
Other University	—	—	—	3.7	2.0
TOTAL UNIVERSITY	61.8	27.4	20.7	21.7	5.5

ence in institutional origins between 1884 and 1917 was so great that the year 1899 was added to the investigation.

Table 2 shows the institutional sources of abstracts in randomly selected editions of the Journal for the given years. (A small proportion of abstracts in all years defied attempts to identify origins. The figures given are for identified sources).

Teaching establishments (e.g. the Vienna Engineering School, Austria, and Kanazawa Technical High School, Japan) are included under the category of University as are research laboratories and institutions attached to universities (e.g. the Zelinsky Laboratory Moscow). The "Government" category includes Research Associations (e.g. Rubber Producers' RA), Government-financed industrial laboratories (e.g. the Imperial Fuel Research Institute, Japan) and military establishments (e.g. the U.S. Naval Powder Factory and the USAF Materials Laboratory).

Several of the abstracts were to patents some of which caused difficulties in the assignment of origins. Early patents usually give the name and profession of the inventor. In most cases the profession enabled a classification to be made e.g. "professor" – university "merchant" – industry. However descriptions such as "gentleman" or "subject of the Czar" had to remain unclassified unless the inventor could be identified from other sources.

Papers by joint authors from different types of institutions were scored $\frac{1}{2}$ each.

It can be seen from Table 2 that there has been a marked change in the relative importance of the institutional origins from European university (mainly German) to European industry and then to American industry as being the major contributors selected by the abstractors.

Although some of the change may be due to changes in abstractors, journal policy etc., the large decline in the relative importance of university publications from 61% in 1884 to 6% in 1952 and the steady growth in the importance of American industry from 0 in 1884 to 54% in 1953 can be assumed to be the result of a change in the relationship between university research in organic chemistry and those industries which use organic chemicals.

The data for 1952 is included in Table 1 for comparison with the studies previously mentioned. This data is based on an examination of 544 abstracts of which 59 could not be found, 6 had insufficient information and 27 were unclassifiable patents, leaving 452 identified origins. The three different studies give different percentage inputs but it should be noted that in all three studies:
a) "Foreign Industry" was the major source of inputs;
b) "U.K. Industry" was the 2nd most frequent source in two studies and the 4th most important in the other;
c) "U.K. University" was either the least important source or next to the least.

Why the Change?

The dramatic change which has taken place since the days when German university research was providing results of direct relevance to the German dyestuffs industry may be explained by two alternative hypotheses:

1. *Industry has taken over its own research.* The massive growth in industrial research since German industry employed teams of chemists to search for new dyes may explain the decline in appar-

175

ent relevance of university research. However, university research has also grown enormously since the last century. (An interesting account of the growth of British industrial research has been given by Sanderson [5]).

2. *A new branch of science is only useful in its early days.* The early days of astronomy as a science were linked with economically important attempts at improving navigation but astronomy has hardly been useful since then. (Even earlier, astronomy was used to maintain the power of priestly castes). The early days of atomic power involved theoretical physicists; since then the theoretical physicists and the designers of nuclear power stations have moved further apart.

The early days of organic chemistry involved the production of new chemical substances and new ways of making them. Since then the university chemist has been more concerned with understanding the results of early research; the industrial chemist has been concerned with using the early knowledge and is not too interested in later theoretical developments.

This hypothesis can be illustrated diagrammatically as in Figure 1.

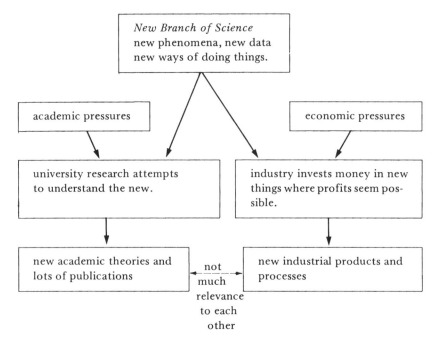

Figure 1. *Differences between University and Industrial Research.*

A New Branch of Science

One of the seven review articles referred to earlier was about "polyolefins" and only 14 out of 102 identified references were to university research in spite of the fact that the present industrial importance of such materials as polypropylene started with the non-industrial research of Ziegler and Natta who may be considered to have founded if not a new branch of science, at least a new stem entitled "stereospecific polymerisation."

It was decided therefore, to test the above hypothesis by looking at earlier reviews of "polyolefins" by industrial chemists with the results given in Table 3.

Table 3 shows that the relative importance of university contributions dropped from 50% in 1957 to 14% in 1967, although the absolute number of university contributions remained constant.

Another point of interest is that British industry began publishing items of interest to the reviewer before British universities.

Table 3. *Change with Time of Institutional Source of Publications Referred to by British Industrial Chemists in Reviews of "Polyolefin" Chemistry*

Date of Review	1957	1961	1967
Institutional Source	% (n=28)	% (n=71)	% (n=102)
UK Industry	3.5	12.0	12.0
US Industry	41.5	46.0	} 69.5
European Industry	5.0	7.0	
TOTAL INDUSTRY	50.0	65.5	81.0
UK University	—	—	2.0
US University	7.0	—	} 12.0
European University	43.0	28.0	
TOTAL UNIVERSITY	50.0	28.0	14.0
UK Industry-University Collaboration	—	—	3.0
US Industry-University Collaboration	—	6.5	} 2.0
European Industry-University Collaboration	—	—	
TOTAL INDUSTRY-UNIVERSITY COLLABORATION	—	6.5	5.0

This was not because British universities ignored sterospecific polymerisation. It was because universities concentrated on the scientific problem of describing and explaining the mechanisms involved and the structure of the polymers produced whilst industry concentrated on obtaining manufacturing processes and improving properties such as light resistance. From a common origin, the discovery of sterospecific polymerisation, academics and industrialists have moved in different directions.

It would seem, therefore, that the relationship between university research and industry may be a function of the degree of development of the area concerned. Once a new area has been established, the aim of science is to understand; the aim of technology is to make it work and industry has been very successful at making things work without too much reliance on understanding.

Industry makes use of the trained manpower supplied by universities. It also uses new techniques developed in universities. However the new products and processes of industry seem to depend on a combination of existing technological concepts, economic pressures and empirical research with scientific understanding not being very relevant.

The Future

This does not mean that university research is a waste of money; the situation may be changing. Concern about such matters as resource depletion, ecology, pollution, fire risk, health hazards, quality of working life etc. coupled with the increasing scale of industrial operations may mean that industry will have to pay more attention to understanding what it is doing.

In the study of 84 innovations mentioned earlier, the only example of theoretical work in a British university assisting British industry was in the area of steel frames for building construction. A concern for human safety together with a shortage of steel led to the use of Baker's theory of plastic flow to design buildings which are safe but use less steel.

It could be that in the future, many sections of industry are going to require an increasing reliance upon theoretical research aimed at understanding as the empirical approach, which has been so successful, joins the quest for economic growth as a thing of the past.

It would seem, therefore, that there are both macro and micro effects leading to changes in the relationship between science and technology.

178

At the micro level, the relevance of a particular part of science has depended on its degree of development. At the macro level, the relationship seems to move in cycles, with the first half of the nineteenth century involving little reliance upon scientific theory (although the scientific technique of methodical observation was made use of) the second half of the nineteenth century being characterised by a series of inputs from research concerned with exploring scientific problems, the first half of the present century being a triumph of industrial methodical empiricism and the future requiring an increasing dependence on understanding.

Acknowledgements

The Department of Education and Science and the Programmes Analysis Unit funded parts of the research described above. Also, tribute is due to the considerable ingenuity of Trevor Parkinson in tracking down the institutional origins of some of the more obscure references.

References

[1] Price, D.J. de Solla in Gruber & Marquis (eds.), *Factors in the Transfer of Technology*, M.I.T., Cambridge, Massachusetts, 1969, p. 97.
[2] Schmookler, J., *Invention and Economic Growth*, Harvard University Press, Cambridge, Massachusetts, 1966.
[3] Langrish, J., Gibbons, M., Evans, W.G. and Jevons, F.R., *Wealth from Knowledge*, MacMillan, London, 1972.
[4] Langrish, J., "University Chemistry Research: Any Use to Industry?" *Chemistry in Britain* 8 (1972) 330.
[5] Sanderson, M., "Research and The Firm in British Industry 1919-39" *Science Studies* 2 (1972) 107.

INDUSTRIAL INNOVATIONS FROM MANCHESTER UNIVERSITY

by *K.P. Norris**

The concept of innovation in which the oak of technological advance typically grows from an acorn of scientifically-motivated research in a university is now somewhat discredited. Nonetheless, examples of this kind of process occur with sufficient frequency to justify paying some attention to the problem of ensuring that when a valuable innovative idea occurs in a university, it is taken up and utilised. Some evidence on the nature of this problem has been provided by studies made by members of the R & D Research Unit at Manchester Business School of the incidence and fortunes of innovative ideas in the University of Manchester. "Innovative idea", and, especially, "originator of an innovative idea", are expressions which are too clumsy for frequent use, and therefore "invention" and "inventor" will be used here in a special sense, to express the same meanings.

The method by which information about inventions was obtained was semi-structured interviewing of samples of the academic staff. In the first phase of the studies, carried out in 1971, the main emphasis was on attitudes towards contact and collaboration with industry, and in particular towards the inventor taking on an entrepreneurial role, and attempting the commercial exploitation of the invention himself. At that time, there was still a good deal of discussion of the Route 128 phenomenon, in which new businesses in advanced areas of technology were being set up by staff and former staff of the Massachusetts Institute of Technology. In the second phase of the studies, carried out in 1972-3, and sponsored by the National Research Development Corporation, the emphasis was more on the means by which inventors had attempted to secure utilisation of their ideas, the degree of success attained, and the relation of both of these to the inventor's personal background and to the kind of work from which the idea emerged.

* Institute of Science and Technology, University of Manchester, U.K.

181

Incidence of Inventions

Both phases provided information about the incidence of inventions. Deciding whether an idea was an invention for the purpose of the study was sometimes difficult, and depended to some extent on subjective judgments. The criterion was whether an idea was of potential commercial significance, and this implied that on the one hand it should have apparent advantages over a wide field of application, and on the other that it should lead to a distinct and identifiable product or technique. This ruled out, for example, ideas for experimental equipment unlikely to be useful outside a specialised research area, and ideas of wide but non-specific application, such as contributions to design methods and data. Ideas of the latter type are an important part of the universities' output, but they do not lend themselves to commercial transactions between the inventor and other parties, nor do they usually require such relationships for their development and utilisation.

The samples of people to be interviewed were drawn from those parts of the University where inventions seemed most likely — initially, the Faculty of Science and the Faculty of Technology (i.e. UMIST), and later, in the second phase, from the Faculty of Medicine, and the Departments of Architecture and Education. The numbers in the samples were 86 for the first phase, and 95 for the second. From the first sample, it was roughly estimated that in the University as a whole there were 86 inventions per year. The second sample, with a different estimating method, gave 60 inventions per year for a total academic staff of 1100 in the Faculties and Departments i.e. one per 18 staff. This result is very close to the figure of one per 20 staff obtained by Launder and Webster in their rather similar study of Imperial College, London [1]. An alternative way of seeing the same figures is that the average person produces two inventions in the course of his academic career. On the whole, therefore, an invention is a fairly rare and unusual event in an academic life, though the distribution of inventions is unequal, and some people have quite a strong propensity to invent.

Industrial Experience and Contacts

An analysis of the second-phase data was made to determine how the incidence of inventions varied according to the nature of Departments (scientific or technological) and according to whether the people had previous industrial experience or had good industrial contacts. The results are summarised in Table 1.

Overall, omitting Medicine and Education, 41% of people had industrial experience. The proportion was higher in the Faculty of Technology (UMIST) (51%) than in the Faculty of Science (31%) and much higher in technological departments (e.g. chemical engineering, metallurgy) than in scientific departments (e.g. chemistry, botany) — 61%, compared with 11%. It should perhaps be pointed out that, since to a large extent UMIST is a university within a university, Technology includes scientific departments (e.g. phys-

Table 1. *Characteristics of Staff Sample*

Industrial connections of staff

	Faculty of Technology	Faculty of Science	Technological Depts.	Scientific Depts.	All
With industrial experience	% 51	% 31	% 61	% 11	% 41
Without industrial experience	51	41	61	26	47

	Industrial experience	*No industrial experience*
Good industrial contacts	68%	32%

Incidence of Inventions

	% staff having made inventions at any time.
All sample	43
Faculty of Technology	51
Faculty of Medicine (inc. Dentistry)	45
Faculty of Science	35
Technological departments	57
Scientific departments	26
Industrial experience	
Yes	42
No	47
Good industrial contacts	
Yes	63
No	26

183

ics) and Science includes technological departments (e.g. electrical engineering).

The distribution of good industrial contacts showed a very similar pattern. Overall, 47% had good contacts, and again the proportion was higher in Technology (51%) than in Science (41%) and higher in technological departments (61%) than in scientific departments (26%). As might be expected, good industrial contacts were quite strongly correlated with previous industrial experience — 68% of those with experience had good contacts, against 32% of those without experience. There were enough examples to the contrary, however, to show that previous experience is no guarantee of continuing good contact, and that good contacts can be established by those without the benefit of experience, if they have the will to do so.

Overall, 43% of the people interviewed had produced an invention at some time during their academic careers. The proportion was rather higher in Technology (51%) and in Medicine (45%) than in Science (35%) but much higher in technological departments (57%) than in scientific departments (26%). Not unexpectedly, the proportion was much higher among people with good industrial contacts (63%) than among those without such contacts (26%). What was unexpected, however, was the reversed difference

Table 2.

	Classification of Inventions
Medical and dental devices	11
Electrical and electronic devices (except computers)	10
New processes	9
Mechanical devices	4
Chemical products (except pharmaceuticals)	4
Scientific instruments (except for chemical analysis)	4
Computer programs	4
Instruments for chemical analysis	3
New materials	3
Teaching aids	3
Pharmaceutical products	3
Computer components	3
Building systems	2
Games	2
	65

184

(though it was not substantial) between those without industrial experience (47%) and those with such experience (42%).

An attempt was made to classify the inventions, based rather more on observed similarities between the inventions than upon any ideal general classification, and the results are given in Table 2. The main features are the relatively large groups of electrical and electronic devices, which is not surprising, and of medical and dental devices, which is rather more surprising. A number of other medical and dental devices were in fact encountered during the study, but were not admitted as inventions, because they were for research, rather than diagnosis or treatment, and did not have sufficiently wide application. Dentists, in particular, were prolific inventors.

Methods Tried for Promoting Inventions

The methods by which people tried to secure the utilisation of their inventions are analysed in Table 3. The grand total of the categories comes to more than the number of inventions, since an invention can appear in more than one category. In many cases, the method was determined by prior commitments; thus, 6 inventions were offered to the National Research Development Corporation under the terms of Research Council grants or Government contracts and 13 went to firms under the terms of contracts for research or consultancy. Where there was a choice, rather more inventions were offered to the NRDC (21) than were offered to firms directly (16). Five inventions were patented by the inventors at their own expense, but only one of these was taken beyond the provisional stage. The two inventions marketed by the inventors were computer programs. One case was met of a more concrete

Table 3. *Methods Tried for Promoting Inventions*

	No. of Inventions
Offered to NRDC — as per terms of grant etc.,	6
Offered to NRDC — Voluntarily	21
Taken by firms, as per terms of contract	13
Offered to firms voluntarily	16
Patented by inventor	5
Marketed by inventor	2
Current — no action yet	8
Published — no further action	1
No action	2

185

invention – an educational game – being manufactured and marketed by the inventor, but this was too specialised and limited in application to be admitted as an invention for the purposes of the study. For two inventions, the inventors had made no attempt to secure utilisation.

Successful Inventions

Assessment of the success of an invention, in any ultimate sense, is subject to considerable difficulty and uncertainty; success may not be clearly established until an innovation has been in commerce for a number of years. In this study, assessment of success was necessarily limited to two initial stages. The results of analysing the inventions in terms of these are given in Table 4.

Table 4. *Initial Success of Inventions*

Origins of successful inventions

| | Number of Inventions | | |
	Offered	1st stage success	2nd stage success
Offered to N.R.D.C.	27	20	5
Offered to firms			
– as per terms of contract	13	13	10
– voluntarily	16	3	1
Other	–	–	3
All	56	36	19

Characteristics of inventors with 2nd stage successes

	Number of inventors
All	13
Technological departments	10
Scientific departments	2
Medical departments	1
Industrial experience	
Yes	4
No	8
Good industrial contacts	
Yes	11
No	1

186

A first stage of success was considered to be attained when a second party became sufficiently convinced of the merit of an invention to spend some of his own money on patenting, developing, or attempting to sell or license it. Of the 27 inventions offered to the NRDC, 20 were accepted in this way, but of the 16 offered directly to firms, only 3 were accepted. All 13 inventions taken by firms under the terms of contracts must also be considered first-stage successes. Only 5 of these were patented; in some of the other cases, it was known that the firm believed that the invention was not patentable, or that there was greater advantage in avoiding disclosure. In total, 36 inventions out of 65 achieved first-stage success.

A second stage of success was considered to have been attained if an invention had been known to have been used or produced commercially, and there was no evidence that it was ultimately a failure. By this standard, only 19 of the inventions were successes. Five of these were inventions accepted by the NRDC: three contributions to computer technology, one improvement in an existing successful invention (a dental cement) and one metallurgical technique which was eventually used in the United States, where patent cover had not been secured. One invention was offered directly to a firm, and two were marketed by the inventors, being computer programs. One invention which had been abandoned by the inventor was eventually marketed independently, without benefit to him. All the remaining 10 inventions which were second-stage successes arose out of research contracts and consultancies, and were adopted by the firms which had paid for the work. Thus, the proportion of second-stage successes among inventions arising in this way (10 out of 13) was very much higher than among the rest of the inventions (9 out of 52).

Associated with the 19 second-stage successes were 13 inventors, not counting the two already noted whose inventions were not successful in their own hands. Of the 13, 10 were in technological departments, and 3 in scientific departments. One was in medicine and therefore was not classified with respect to industrial experience and contacts. Of the remaining 12, 4 had industrial experience, which is a rather lower proportion than in the whole sample. On the other hand, 11 had good industrial contacts, which is a much higher proportion than in the whole sample. Thus, it appears that successful invention was strongly correlated with good industrial contacts, but not with industrial experience.

Discussion

Although a few naturally inventive individuals were encountered, who had produced several ideas in unconnected areas, the great majority of the inventions in these studies were out of the inventor's teaching and research, either directly, as one of the objects of research, or indirectly, as tools which he devised to help in his work. In a university, inventions are usually a by-product, occurring comparatively rarely in relation to the number of people employed. Apart from trained people, the main output consists of ideas and information of a general kind, which can be taken up and used by the outside world in a variety of applications. Thus, much of the output of university civil and mechanical engineers consists of methods and data for the design of broad classes of structures and machines. Even where university staff are consulted on a specific industrial problem, their function is more often to contribute ideas and information towards a solution than to devise a complete new product or process. In the studies described here, 10 cases of substantial contributions to industrial technology were found, which were too general in application to be regarded as inventions.

Where an invention does occur, the results of these studies strongly suggest that its chances of being utilised are greatest if its author has close contacts with industry, and especially if it has arisen out of a contract with a firm for research or consultancy. The likely reasons for this are not difficult to suggest. In such cases, the inventor has no need to convince the firm that he knows something about their business, and that they have a need which his invention may meet; the existence of the contract or consultancy already implies a relationship of esteem and confidence (which has usually taken some time to build up), and also the recognition by the firm of a need or opportunity, to the specific meeting of which the inventor can direct his efforts. Further, the technical staff of the firm are involved from the start, and are more likely to become champions of any resulting invention than opponents, since they can acquire a personal interest and commitment, and perhaps a claim to some of the credit.

In contrast, the inventor who has to "sell" an invention made in isolation, perhaps a little premature, perhaps not quite adapted to the market need, necessarily faces a very uphill struggle, even if the invention is basically sound. To overcome inertia, aversion to change, and reluctance to accept ideas from outsiders, a great deal of persistence and persuasion, time and effort, are required.

For the inventor with faith in the merit of his invention, a possible response to the short-sightedness of others is to set up his own business to manufacture or otherwise utilise the invention. In the first phase of these studies, people were asked whether they would consider going into business in this way, and a relatively high proportion (16%) said that they would. This was a hypothetical question, however, and the histories of actual inventions which were collected suggested that among British academics, unlike American ones, setting up a business to secure utilisation of an invention, or for any other reason, was very rare. No such cases were encountered, other than the trivial ones of the educational game and the computer programs already mentioned, and only one person could recall such a thing happening, some years ago, at UMIST. They may perhaps be a little less rare at Imperial College – Launder and Webster found two cases.

Most of those interviewed agreed that such a business required full-time attention, and therefore necessitated a break with academic life. The main drawbacks quoted by those who would consider setting up a business, which were also the main reasons given by those who would not consider it, were doubts about their own managerial and commercial abilities, and a preference for the satisfactions of the university, relative to those of the business world. In short, men with entrepreneurial talents and inclinations do not usually become academics. A further point is that, if an able academic wishes to enlarge his interests and his income, consultancy, not manufacture, is the obvious kind of business, and can be combined with his academic work.

Considerations arising from the nature of university life also affect the inventor who relies on others to take up and utilise his invention. If he tries to promote it himself, and to interest firms, he will be involved in considerable expenditure of time and effort. If he manages to interest an intermediary (normally the NRDC) he may then think, as many do, that his part is done, but in fact it seems likely that in many cases the enthusiasm and special knowledge of the inventor still needs to be used in approaches to firms, if the invention is to have its best chance of success. In return for his effort, the inventor has an uncertain and, unless the invention has unusually high commercial value, small financial return, especially after NRDC, university, and perhaps even department have taken their share. Inventions have little academic value. The same effort devoted to research and the writing of papers, and thus to the enhancement of promotion prospects, could be considerably more rewarding, even in financial terms.

For these reasons, little reliance can be placed on the efforts of the university inventor to secure utilisation of his inventions, unless he already knows of receptive potential users. Asked what institutional means were desirable to provide a bridge between inventor and potential user, most people proposed something very much like the service provided at present by the NRDC. Such a service is clearly necessary for those whose work, by its nature, does not bring them into contact with industry. It is difficult to provide, since it involves sifting a great many inventions of which only a few are viable, but may be justified by the occasional major success which can happen when an unconventional link is established between an area of research and an area of application.

The main conclusion to which the results of these studies seem to point, however, is that the best way of ensuring better utilisation of university inventions is to encourage closer contacts with industry. This will work partly by making it more likely that independent inventions will receive friendly consideration, but mainly by influencing the content of research and the nature of inventions, by drawing the attention of academics to the needs and opportunities seen by industry. To this end, movement of people from industry is helpful, but does not appear to be essential.

In principle, the attitude of most people (95% of those interviewed in the first phase) was favourable towards closer collaboration with industry, largely because of a natural desire to see their ideas and inventions put to some useful purpose. Most people, however, also expressed reservations about the way in which such collaborations should be conducted. The most frequent of these was that the academic must guard against excessive dependence on industry, since this would endanger his freedom to chose areas of research and his freedom to publish. Next, industry was thought to be short-sighted and interested only in short-term work, whereas the university should have long-term research objectives. There was also suspicion that academics risked being exploited as sources of cheap consultancy and research. This is a less fundamental argument, since essentially it reflects doubts about their own commercial abilities. Finally, since a large part of university research is in fact carried out by research students, it was generally agreed that the primary requirement for a research topic was that it should have adequate educational value.

There is substance in some of the arguments, and it is neither possible nor desirable for university research, even in technological subjects, to be governed entirely by the needs voiced by industry.

Nonetheless, there are large areas where, from the point of view of educational value and professional interest, questions of immediate practical importance can be as good subjects for research as any others. If closer contacts with industry can make academics more aware of these, it seems likely that the number of useful inventions will be increased, and the value of the universities to society will be enhanced.

Acknowledgement

The author wishes to thank the National Research Development Corporation for permission to draw upon the results of work undertaken on their behalf.

Reference

[1]   Launder, B.E. and Webster, G.A., *University Research and the Considerations Affecting its Commercial Exploitation*, Technological Development Capital Ltd., London, 1969.

TECHNOLOGY TRANSFER BY HATRA – ONE RA's APPROACH

by *T.S. Nutting**

Introduction

HATRA's approach to the techniques of technology transfer have developed progressively over the past 20 years. They have been moulded by a consistent philosophy on the part of our organisation of the need for such activity and by the size and general structure of our industry.

We define our industry as covering weft knitting, dyeing and making-up of knitted fabrics. Approximately 120,000 people are employed in 850 establishments with a turnover of £600M. The industry is concentrated (about 65%) in the Midlands with smaller but significant concentrations in London, Manchester, Hawick, and Glasgow. The entire range is from Shetlands to Penzance.

Of great significance is the size distribution of firms in membership with Hatra:

	%
Up to 49	52
50- 99	18
100- 199	14
200- 499	10
500- 999	3.5
1000-1999	1.5
2000 plus	1.0

Our industry is in fact typical of many with a high proportion of small firms.

Technology Transfer in our terms means the solving of four problems:

(i) to transfer technology resulting from our own research to members of the RA;

* Research Centre for Knitting, Dyeing and Making-up of Knitted Textiles, HATRA, Nottingham, U.K.

193

(ii) to encourage the use of that technology;
(iii) to obtain feed back from the industrial members on current or potential future research;
(iv) to provide a source of, and encourage the use of, information and technology not originating in the RA.
Of these four problems the first two are really inseparable, the third important, and all these are more important (to us) than the last one.

The Basic Concept

Our basic philosophy has always been that research work done by us and not applied in our industry is a waste of effort — it is no good for the RA and no good for the industry.

What do we see as the major steps given the success of research in producing technology, recognising that technology in our terms may be hardware, or a concept, an idea?

We see things in the following way:

This represents the ideal, the simple way where industry positively seeks and is provided with technology. If this were always the case then perhaps technology transfer would not rate its present importance.

The first stage we regard as a conversion operation — almost an inversion.

That is, rather than present the information from the researchers point of view, — the problem, the analysis, the logic, the general solution — we turn it on its head and seek to have answers to the questions industry will ask.
Why should I use it?
How much will it cost?
How much will it save me?

194

The second stage is to recognise that industry is not a person — industry is made up of a number of people at different levels. Although the formal hierarchical structure is usually clear and well defined, acceptance of technology by no means follows the formal routing. In our conversion of technology from research to user acceptance we need to structure our appeal to different levels; technology transfer in depth.

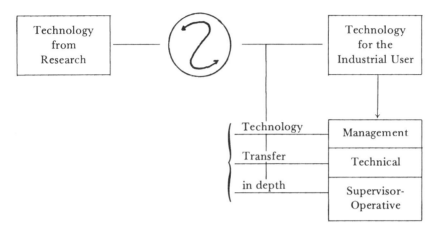

Industrial Factors

Before dealing in a little more detail with the methods that we use, consider the situation from the industry's viewpoint. We see three factors of relevance to technology transfer. First, the overwhelming problem that managers have in our industry is that of current production. Of finding work if there is a shortage; or of producing it if the orders are there. The short term "today" problems overwhelm most of the others. The smaller the firm the more likely is this to be the case.

Written information on any subject is the cheapest way of distributing it. By definition most written information is generalised, and we think this is particularly true of research type information. This requires the recipient to de-generalise it and look for applications within their own situation. This we see as the second factor of importance, since in general the necessary time and skill is scarce.

A third item that also plays a big part in blocking technology transfer is the problem of internal communications within an organisation. It is this particular problem that places usefulness of written material in such doubt. We are in full control until the

195

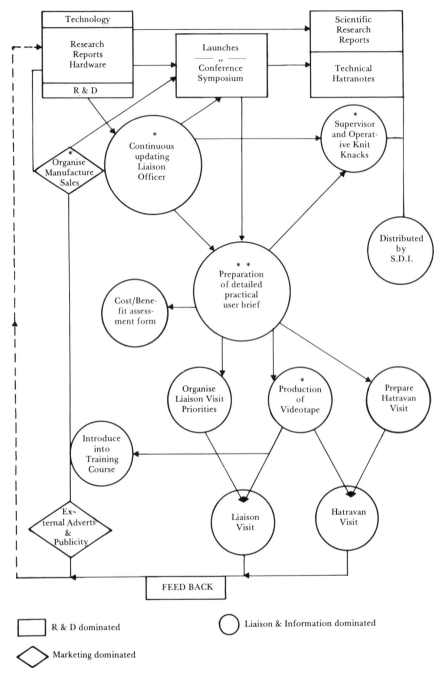

Figure 1. *Routes from Technology to Transfer*

written material is posted. We have no say in its distribution within a company.

It is our experience that the combined effect of these three factors poses the major block to the technology transfer of potentially useful technology.

Internal Preparation for Technology Transfer

The detailed route from technology resulting from research to Technology Transfer will vary according to circumstances. We have, however, a general pattern that is followed, and this is shown in Figure 1. All links in the chain are important, but those marked* we regard as very important and the one marked** as of vital importance. This latter step is the prime move in our inversion concept from research technology to receiver technology. Although the outline indicates spheres of influence the system only works if we have adequate co-operation and communication between the three major groups; research, marketing, liaison.

Figure 2, by way of a simple instrument called the V-bed Knock Over Depth Gauge, illustrates a real example of the progression towards technology transfer.

Staff for Technology Transfer

By far the greater part of our technology transfer is undertaken by Technical Liaison Officers. Our major reasons for having special staff rather than allowing research staff to be their own technology transfer agents, are partly problems of cost and logistics of coverage, and partly because of our basic philosophy. We believe in the need to deal with technology transfer in depth, by helping an individual in a company to utilise our information within his company for his needs. For example, a new quality control instrument that measures a specific parameter is no real use if it is just dumped in the factory. The use of the instrument has to be integrated within the total existing factory quality control system. This we think can be best achieved by people who spend the majority of time in industry. Such people are chosen because their ability and personality promotes good personal communications.

We attempt to visit each unit a minimum of once per year. Because of the essential vagaries of research project fruition, we cannot rely on having a new piece of information each year for each sector of industry. Because of this and the wide geographical

197

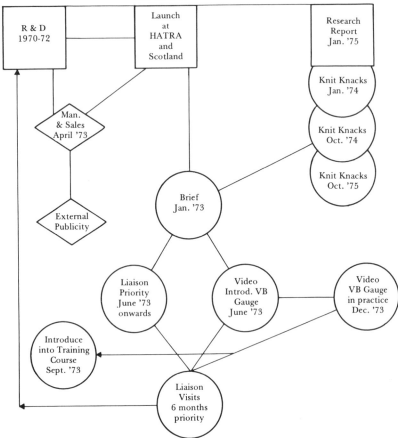

Figure 2. *HATRA VB Knock over Depth Gauge*

spread of our members we work with liaison officers covering a geographical area.

Like most organisations, involved in technology transfer, we have found the most effective method is by talking face to face with people. The chance of technology transfer being acted upon is increased when there is mutual confidence between the people concerned: mutual confidence is best built up by regular personal contact. Successful personal contact of this kind not only generates good feed back on current technology application, but also provides discussions likely to lead to additional fruitful research. These are other reasons for choosing Technical Liaison Officers as media for technology transfer.

It would be unrealistic to suggest that the research worker plays no part in technology transfer. The research worker will have been involved with firms in the latter part of any project, and will probably have taken part in initial visits to firms. In some instances a specific piece of technology has been transferred by the research team — but this is an exception.

Techniques for Technology Transfer

(i)   Hatra Publications

In its main series of publications, Hatra aims to provide technical information in a variety of forms adapted to the needs of staff within member firms — described earlier as dissemination in depth.

Hatra Research Reports describe original Hatra work in the traditional form of a scientific paper, are each concerned with a single topic, and are intended for scientists and technologists within the industry elsewhere.

Hatranotes are the main vehicle for communication with management and technical staff in member firms. Each deals with a single topic and emphasises the practical applications of research and the implications of new production techniques.

Knit Knacks is a magazine for mechanics and supervisors showing in detail, and with many illustrations and examples, how new techniques developed from our research can be implemented on the shop floor. It is, in fact, the most widely read of all our publications at all levels.

Newsletter is a monthly news sheet sent to the senior member of staff in each unit.

Research Reports and Hatranotes (and any other special publications) are selectively distributed based on a firm's technical interest profile. This profile is computer based and the system can

199

be searched for individuals or firms having a particular interest. The computer prints out the name (and title) and firm's address. Our aim is to reduce the quantity of redundant paper that firms receive.

(ii) Visits by Technical Liaison Officers
(iii) Video-tape. We have a small TV studio and produce short (10-15 minute) TV programmes on new Hatra information and hardware. Each of the Technical Liaison Officers has a VCR and monitor and hence the capability of showing the programmes to small groups of people in a factory.
(iv) A travelling class-room (Hatravan)
(v) Conferences

Some Comments on Technology Transfer Techniques

One danger in discussing technology transfer techniques is the temptation to get too involved in the technique and lose sight of the main objective. The technology and its objective should decide the technique and not the other way round. The cost of techniques and of the whole technology transfer programme needs to be kept in balance and will vary from technology to technology and project to project.

For reasons stated in the introduction, Hatra tends to spend, or acknowledges the spending of, more money in proportion to R & D than most RA's (about a quarter on liaison compared with R & D).

The preparation, and continued updating, of the User Brief and the use of video-tape play major roles in our technology transfer methods. The reason for the former, as an inversion concept, has already been dealt with. The latter we find important because it offers us a method of getting a group of people together in a firm – usually a good hierarchical cross section – and transferring the technology to them all at once. Dissemination in depth at a blow! The most important man to convince is the Managing Director; the next most important person is the man who is going to use the hardware or idea!

Other Technology Transfer

The majority of what has been written concerns the methods by which we transfer home-produced technology; in other words the answers to three of the questions posed at the beginning. Masses of other technology is available to our industry from many sources, fibre and yarn producers, the dyestuff makers, the machine builders. We deal with this by publishing Hosiery Abstracts once per month: having a first class information centre where questions can be answered by telephone, letter, or via photocopies and loans: and from the accumulated experience and wisdom of *all* our staff. The fact that this latter part has only been dealt with briefly does not mean that we underestimate the massive importance of other technology. This other technology provides answers to question four.

The paper now presented is based on one given two years earlier. The written word, although it gives a reasonably accurate account of the mechanical aspects of technology transfer cannot purvey the personal flavour of the activity: the joys and frustrations; the arguments and discussions to hammer out a route from technology to transfer. It is people who use technology — or who do not use technology.

Technology transfer is about people; about their vagaries; their entrenched positions; about their successes and hopes. After the technology itself, transfer techniques help, but the people at each end of the transfer are vital.

SPECULATIONS ON A RECIPIENT, NEED ORIENTED, APPROACH TO TECHNOLOGY TRANSFER

by *C.S. Morphet**

The Concept of "Need" in Innovation Studies

Idealised linear models of the innovation process fall into two categories: — the "idea push" model sees a sequence of events initiated by a scientific or technological discovery; the "need-pull" model sees a sequence of events initiated by a perception of need upon which invention and innovation are consequent. Langrish et al [1] analysed 84 innovations which had won the Queen's Award to Industry and concluded that the reality of the processes that they studied was too complex to be represented by any form of linear model. But by restricting their view of the process to activities within the innovating firm they showed that in around two cases out of three a perceived need was instrumental in initiating the activity that led the firm to a successful innovation.

In a comparable study of minor innovations in the U.S.A., Myers and Marquis [2] were able to show that in three out of four cases the primary factor in undertaking work on the innovation was a recognised market potential or a recognised need in the production process.

The other cases described by Myers and Marquis, and Langrish et al, are viewed as "idea push" in the sense that the innovative activity was initiated by the recognition of a technical potential which might be exploited. But as Myers and Marquis point out: "The idea or concept for an innovation is necessarily a fusion of both demand and technical potential". In particular it must be recognised that the awareness of a technical potential cannot be a *sufficient* condition for innovation to take place. The ensuing technology transfer (maybe even the perception of the technical potential itself) depends on the firm being on some state such that it can realise the technical potential which is evidenced.

* Manchester Business School, University of Manchester, U.K.

To describe an innovative act as being consequent on "need-pull" or on "idea push" is to describe how the process took place but not to explain why. The dichotomy is between alternative triggers in a process whose common factor, the co-existence of compatible states of technical and commercial potential, is the more significant. The state of commercial potential is hitherto referred to as the firm's receptive state.

That view of technology transfer at the organisational level characterised by reviewers such as Chakrabarti [3] as the R & D perspective supposes that the process of technology transfer consists of a series of orderly steps from research through development to innovation and diffusion. Where transfer fails the model implies that some agent or agency has acted imperfectly. The structure of the model directs attention away from the needs of the recipient who is assumed to be a passive actor who would accept the idea if it were delivered in the right way at the right time through the right channel.

A more realistic structure is supposed by, for example, Havelock [4]. Here the process is viewed as one of problem solving involving both source and user in mutually reinforcing collaboration. Such a framework is assumed in Morphet [5]. Successful innovation is assumed to result when linkage is achieved between states of technical opportunity and practical receptivity. This approach directs attention to the recipient and in particular to his receptive states. It suggests that a potentially fruitful question is to ask not how a particular piece of technology achieved utilisation but how a particular receptive state came into existence, and was satisfied; the emphasis is the reverse of that implied by the R & D perspective.

Some Implications of a Rigorous Interpretation of "Need"

A recent paper [5] will be described which uses this approach to develop a framework within which can be analysed the timeliness factor which, it is suggested, partially governs the acceptance or rejection by industrial firms of innovative technical ideas.

The concept of the receptive state was presented in the guise of the New Idea Point (NIP). An argument was based on the paradigm case of profit maintenance by periodic product innovation in the single product firm. The NIP was identified as the point in time at which the firm had to have assembled a portfolio of new product ideas in order that subsequent development could result in a new product launch at a time when profits from the existing product began to decline.

Given the relative abundance of technical ideas (Booz, Allen & Hamilton [6], Bales [7] and NRDC [8] are cited in support) the firm is faced with a stream of innovation opportunities from which it must eventually choose one in order to satisfy the imperative of the NIP. Consistent with the firm's ambivalence towards innovation described for example by Schon [9] is the assumption that ideas impacting on the firm early in the period between NIPs will be relatively less likely to be adopted. In a postulated hyper-rational organisation this effect will be minimal; at the opposite extreme will be a pronounced tendency to overlook opportunities evidenced early, and a consequent predisposition towards ideas the awareness of which coincides with an imminent NIP. The determinant of a firms position between these two extremes is defined as the firm's z-value. Low z-values are associated with the hyper-rational end of the scale, and high z-values with the opposite extreme.

If this timeliness factor is separated out from all other influences, technical, economic and social, which determine whether an idea will be adopted, a probability profile can be defined. This shows the "ceteris paribus" probability of adoption (P) of an idea of which the firm becomes aware at a time t. It is argued that a plausible shape of this profile is as in Figure 1.

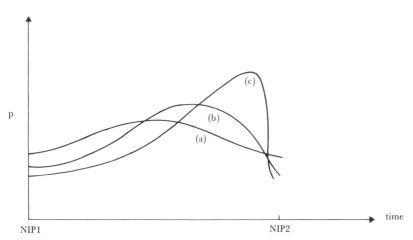

Figure 1. *A plausible pattern of variation in P over the NIP period (see text)*

Figure 1 shows a family of curves and it is argued that the profile exhibited by a particular firm will depend upon its z-value and also on its ability to store and retrieve, or remember, information about technical opportunities. The shift of the curve from (a) to (b) to (c) is broadly the result of an increasing z-value or a decreasing memory.

The general applicability of the model in this simple form demands the assumption that a large complex organisation can be treated from the point of view of its receptivity to new ideas as no more than the sum of a number of dependent parts each of which has a desire for survival and a concomitant demand for periodic innovation. It is also necessary to assume, in order that the probability profile might take the smooth form sketched in Figure 1, that the firm reacts to future NIPs and must therefore have prior knowledge of them, if only tacitly. These assumptions are discussed in an earlier paper [5].

The outcome of the approach described is the recognition that transfer is most likely to be initiated at the peaks of the probability profiles defined above. Firms with higher z-values and shorter memories will exhibit higher peaks and if these peaks can be predicted, sources of technical ideas can optimise their technology transfer. The identification of such peaks is of course more than a simple problem of industrial intelligence since it necessarily relies on data which are dependent on the theory of the model. In particular it depends on the concept of the NIP. This is discussed in the final section of this paper.

Implications of the above View for a Theory of Diffusion

Conventional studies of the diffusion of innovation are underpinned by an epidemic theory of change whereby increased adoption results in an increased probability of adoption within a decreasing pool of non-adopters and a classical logistic adoption curve results.

Such an approach has been partially successful in explaining adoption rates in terms of the profitability and the investment requirement of the innovation, but largely unable to explain which firms will be early adopters and why a firm which adopts one innovation earlier than another firm is little more than 50% likely to be the earlier adopter a second time [10].

Such studies are akin to the R & D perspective on technology transfer in that they focus attention onto the technical innovation and leave the changing needs of the firm largely unexplored. The firm is assumed to be a passive receptor who will innovate when uncertainty is reduced, after a certain amount of adoption, to some tolerable level.

The influence of the contagion factor must not be discounted; but the view of technology transfer described in this paper has implications for the study of the diffusion of innovations. If firms are only prepared to innovate at largely predetermined points in time the early adopters will be quite simply found among those firms whose NIPs are imminent when the innovation is first launched.

If we take the case of a particular innovation, and assume that it is not unique in its ability to satisfy the imperatives of a NIP, we would expect its rate of adoption to vary with its profitability etc. in accordance with the results described above — the higher its perceived value the more likely it is to be used in preference to its competitors. But the rate of adoption will also be consequent on the spacing between NIPs in the industry concerned, and the particular shape of the adoption curve will depend on the extent to which the NIPs in the industry are in phase. It can also be argued that the shapes of the probability profiles (see above) which are evidenced in the industry will also determine the pattern of adoption.

Such an approach to diffusion studies appears, in this embryonic form, to offer some potential in addition to that revealed by the epidemiological tradition.

A Wider Framework for the Analysis of Need

It is clear that the NIP is descriptive of an idealised situation. It is perhaps unlikely that innovation takes place at times which are totally inelastic with respect to technical opportunities. To be able to put the problem in these terms, however, is perhaps indicative of some heuristic value in this recipient-oriented approach.

Field work is at present being undertaken by the author. This in its initial stages is using a questionnaire to gather data on the nature of the receptive states which (as the questionnaire explicitly asks the respondent to acknowledge) must exist in the organisation if innovation is to take place. In particular it is concerned to establish for specific instances of innovation the particular circumstances which brought the receptive state into existence, and to discover how long the state had existed before it was satisfied by an act of innovation. It is hoped that the results of this survey will be reported in due course.

The intention of this section is to present a speculative account of an extended framework within which the emergence of receptive states might be analysed.

We can divide the firm's world into:
(i) Its practice;
(ii) All factors external to its practice.

We note that these externalities include:
(i) The firm's value;
(ii) Imposed rules and practices e.g. legislation;
(iii) Perceived technical opportunities;
(iv) Financial constraints.

We can introduce the notion of optimal practice which is a function of the firms world – i.e. it depends on current practice and on changing externalities – and it defines the state of practice towards which the firm will tend. Optimal practice will be continuously shifting but we would not expect actual practice to move in dynamic equilibrium with it – partly this will reflect the firm's dynamic conservatism and partly the economically rational avoidance of too frequent expenditure on change in the face of uncertainty. We therefore expect the firm to make occasional quantum changes in the direction of optimality.

At any one time there is likely to be a degree of mismatch between actual practice and optimal practice – in this sense latent needs always exist but are not a sufficient condition for action. However we would expect that at some critical level of mismatch innovation will be indicated. This point can be associated with the NIP; the period of time that precedes it will see the build up of perceived need and the consequent variation in the interest in new ideas which has been described above.

This model enables us to encompass a time-elasticity in the NIP with respect to technical opportunity, for optimality is defined by an (albeit uncertainly) *possible* alternative world. The advent of a new technical opportunity may define a new optimality which is beyond the critical level of mismatch – thus we would witness an instance of innovation resulting from "idea push" although in a sense differing from that supposed by the simple linear models described in a previous section.

It should be noted that this overall view of technical change is not developed to the state of a practical research tool, nor is it implied in the field work described above.

Acknowledgement

The ideas on which this paper are based arose out of a research project supported by the Programmes Analysis Unit.

References

[1] Langrish, J., Gibbons, M., Evans, W.G. and Jevons, F.R., *Wealth from Knowledge*, Macmillan, London, 1972.

[2] Myers, S. and Marquis, D.G., *Successful Industrial Innovations*, NSF 68-17, 1969.

[3] Chakrabarti, A.K., "Some Concepts of Technology Transfer: Adoption of Innovations in Organisational Context", *R & D Management* 3 (1973) 111-120.

[4] Havelock, R.G., *Planning for Innovation*, Ann Arbor: The University of Michigan, Institute for Social Research, 1969.

[5] Morphet, C.S., "A Probabilistic Model of Time Dependent Factors Governing the Acceptance of Innovative Ideas by Industry", *R & D Management* 4 (1974) 3.

[6] Booz, Allen & Hamilton, *Management of New Products*, Booz, Allen & Hamilton, Management Consultants, U.S.A., 1968.

[7] Bales, P., "Background and Philosophy of Navan Incorporated" in Blood, J.W., *Utilising R & D By-Products*, American Management Association, New York, 1967.

[8] N.R.D.C. (1972) – Annual Report 1971/72, H.M.S.O.

[9] Schon, D., *Technology and Change: The New Heraclitus*, Pergamon, London, 1967.

[10] Mansfield, E., *Industrial Research and Technological Innovation*, Norton & Co., New York, 1968.

TECHNOLOGY TRANSFER – THE INTERNATIONAL DIMENSION

by *J.S. Millar**

Introduction

The transfer of technology between nations over the last thirty years has developed into a trade of considerable economic importance to both developed and developing countries. The payments and receipts arising from this trade have become significant features in the invisible trade balances of many countries and the consequent effects on their foreign currency resources has influenced fiscal policy. It has also become increasingly evident that economic and material progress of nations is dependent on their store of available technology and that this store needs to be continuously replenished and maintained. Although strenuous efforts have been made to increase indigenous sources of technology, nations which seek an international trading status in goods and services realise that the marketability of these goods and services cannot rely solely on such indigenous sources and that much of this new technology must be purchased abroad. There is a degree of conflict between these two considerations; every government would like to see an increase in the import of foreign technology, but many governments are unwilling to leave this to normal economic forces.

One of the primary objects of this paper is to take an overall view of the nature of this trade over the specific period 1960-1971 inclusive to see what general conclusions can be drawn in terms of its economic effects.

Technology is generally but not exclusively transferred under a licence arrangement between at least two parties. The arrangement may be in the express form of a legally binding agreement, the general style and content of which is common and conventional to those involved, or, it may be implied. The technology which is licensed may consist of statutorily protected rights in the territory

* Imperial Metal Industries, Ltd., Birmingham, U.K.

of the licensee, namely, patents, design registrations or copyright, or it may be in the form of rights created and protected by contract dealing with technical information and "know-how". Any one or more of these elements may be present in any particular licence. In express licences the nature of the rights is set out often in considerable detail and the consideration payable by the licensee for these rights is generally in the form of a single or recurrent lump sum possibly contingent on the happening of certain events, and a running royalty related to the profit which arises from the exercise of the rights.

It is also common to transfer technology with an implied licence. It may be incorporated in machines or equipment or even in the price of goods. Transfers of technology between companies which have associated shareholdings (referred to in this paper as Affiliates) occasionally takes place without any identifiable payment on the basis that the value of the technology transferred will be reflected in profits. Furthermore, it is not uncommon for payments for technology licences to be ascribed for tax purposes to the provision of technical assistance or managerial or other services.

Clearly, the effect of using implied licences or of attribution of payments to other causes, makes it difficult to rely on the available statistical information too heavily. It is however assumed here that the available evidence is sufficient to indicate relationships and consequently to show a pattern of international trade in technology which is worthy of examination.

International Comparisons

The figures shown in Table 1 are taken from published information relating primarily to express licences. This needs to be looked at first of all from a country by country viewpoint.

1. *The United States*

It is clear from the size of US receipts in 1971 of $ 2590m against payments of $225m that it is the principal provider of foreign technology for the Western World. It is however particularly noteworthy that only a quarter of US receipts from foreign licensing arises from non-affiliated companies. It is also interesting that in the period 1964-1970 inclusive the licence receipts of US companies from non-affiliated licensees rose by 92% whereas receipts of licence income from affiliates rose by 148% [1].

On the other hand it will be seen from Table 2 that European

Table 1. Revenue and Expenditure in the Licence-Trade of Specially Selected Countries (1960-1971) (in mm US Dollars)[1]

	Country	1960	1961	1962	1963	1964	1965	1966	1967	1968	1969	1970	1971
Revenues (= Exports of Licences)	United States of America	650	711	837	927	1,057	1,259	1,378	1,488	1,664	2,205	2,459	2,590
	Federal Republic of Germany	–	–	–	50	62	75	73	89	98	97	118	141
	France	48	56	55	139	144	168	180	194	164	207	213	248
	Great Britain	–	–	–	–	123	138	162	154	204	211	263	282
	Italy	–	–	–	32	39	43	48	61	65	65	78	78
	Japan[2]	2	3	7	5	7	14	19	27	34	46	59	60
Expenditure (= Licence Imports)	United States of America	67	80	100	111	127	133	139	137	181	192	193	225
	Federal Republic of Germany	–	–	–	135	153	165	175	192	218	252	304	358
	France	91	105	120	189	191	213	243	228	275	323	319	445
	Great Britain	–	–	–	–	115	130	135	143	185	212	249	263
	Italy	–	–	–	138	157	155	182	191	219	271	312	–
	Japan[2]	95	112	114	135	155	165	192	239	314	368	433	488
Balance	United States of America	+583	+681	+737	+816	+ 930	+1,126	+1,239	+1,351	+1,473	+2,013	+2,266	+2,365
	Federal Republic of Germany	–	–	–	–85	–91	–90	–102	–103	–120	–155	–186	–217
	France	–43	–49	–65	–50	–47	–45	–63	–35	–111	–116	–136	–197
	Great Britain	–	–	–	–	+ 8	+ 8	+ 27	+ 11	+ 19	–1	+ 14	+ 19
	Italy	–	–	–	–106	–118	–112	–134	–130	–154	–206	–234	–
	Japan[2]	–93	–109	–107	–130	–148	–141	–173	–212	–380	–322	–374	–428

– unavailable

1. To the extent that this was necessary, the payments have been converted on the basis of the 1972 official dollar parities.

2. The Japanese financial year starts on April 1 of one year and ends on the March 31 of the following year.

Table 2. Capital Flows European Direct Investments in the Unted States

(in millions of dollars)

	United Kingdom	EEG	Benelux	France	West Germany	Italy	The Netherlands	Other	Total
Net trans-actions									
1966 . . .	114	18	− 7	− 5	− 21	− 1	52	83	216
1967 . . .	70	1	−10	−15	− 51	10	67	− 15	56
1968 . . .	56	−101	−20	1	− 27	− 1	− 54	86	41
1969 . . .	99	−229	−12	− 5	−194	5	− 23	− 31	−161
1970 . . .	−348	− 1	4	37	− 35	3	− 10	23	−324
1971 . . .	44	77	21	− 7	− 29	− 8	99	143	264
Capital flows to U.S. affiliates									
1966 . . .	23	66	9	8	28	1	20	1	90
1967 . . .	65	113	18	26	65	− 8	12	72	250
1968 . . .	114	212	25	10	34	2	141	− 29	297
1969 . . .	86	363	19	17	204	− 2	125	101	550
1970 . . .	529	136	6	−27	48	2	107	65	730
1971 . . .	203	60	−17	18	48	13	− 1	− 35	228
Income received by owners									
1966 . . .	125	85	2	3	7	*	73	73	284
1967 . . .	124	117	9	12	14	2	80	46	287
1968 . . .	149	111	5	11	7	1	87	48	308
1969 . . .	159	132	6	12	10	3	101	57	348
1970 . . .	164	132	9	9	13	5	96	67	363
1971 . . .	236	134	3	10	19	5	97	96	466
Royalties and fees received by owners									
1966 . . .	12	− 1	*	*	*	**	− 1	11	22
1967 . . .	11	− 3	− 1	− 1	*	**	− 1	11	19
1968 . . .	21	*	*	*	*	**	*	9	30
1969 . . .	26	2	1	*	*	**	1	13	41
1970 . . .	19	3	1	1	*	**	1	21	43
1971 . . .	11	3	1	1	*	**	1	12	26
Six-year summary All trans-actions . .	37	−235	−24	6	−357	8	131	289	92
Capital flows to U.S.A. . . .	1,020	950	60	52	427	8	404	175	2,145
Income to owners . .	957	711	34	57	70	16	534	387	2,056
Royalties and fees .	100	4	2	1	*	**	1	77	181

* Less than $ 5000,000.
** Figures not available.

companies which had US affiliates relied much more heavily on dividend income as compared to licence income than did US companies with European affiliates.

The first and obvious observation that may be made on these points is the support which is given to the impression that US companies preferred to enter foreign markets by establishing or acquiring their own subsidiaries or forming joint ventures. This may very well be attributable to their experience in treating the United States as a single market; in a single market local requirements are more likely to be met, unless there is a resources problem, by setting up a local facility than by transferring the technology concerned to another party under licence. This experience has no doubt been sharpened by distance factors. Lack of regular intimate contact with other countries, and the linguistic and cultural inhibitions in making contact probably create doubts as to the energy of foreign management in exploiting American technology and business techniques and create the impression that control can only be effectively maintained by having an organisation that is properly attuned and oriented to the US parent.

The increase in licensing income of the United States would appear to reflect an increase in world trade in technology over the period under consideration rather than inflationary factors. Corresponding increases in the volume of this trade are evident in the case of the other industrialised countries.

It would seem to be a reasonable deduction that the transfer of American technology to non-affiliated companies is only a secondary means of exploitation and is only preferred when the resources available for financing and staffing affiliated companies to use it are not available.

On the other side of the coin it is clear that there is a magnitude of difference in the level of payments made by the United States for foreign technology as compared to its receipts. This may be ascribed to a number of factors. It may reflect a general superiority or higher intensity of US technology compared to that available outside USA. It may also reflect a relatively higher concentration of investment in service industries in USA by European companies as opposed to US companies' investments in Europe. In addition it may be a function of the difficulties of licensing into USA by smaller less specialised and less well serviced organisations which may be deterred by the more sophisticated and intricate business and legal climate of the United States. In particular the difficulty and cost of enforcing US patents and the hazards of US anti-trust law would appear to support this view.

In all probability each of these factors has contributed something to what has become known as the "Technology Gap" to which Sir Harold Wilson referred as being one in which: "we in Europe produce only the conventional apparatus of a modern economy, while becoming increasingly dependent upon American business for the sophisticated apparatus which will call the industrial tune in the 70's and 80's."

2. *The United Kingdom*

Next to the United States, the United Kingdom spent during this period the highest proportion of GNP on research and development (c. 3%) compared to the other countries under consideration. It also had the highest income from sale of technology abroad. In 1970 27% of UK's receipts of $263m from sale of technology came from the United States, 22% from the (then) six EEC countries and only 3% from EFTA. It seems reasonable to suppose that the major reason for the small amount received from EFTA was that this was effectively a single market in which commodities could be traded relatively unhindered by tariff or transport costs. It seems likely that the same pattern will emerge in EEC trade, and that this will be encouraged not merely by the removal of tariffs but by the trend of EEC competition law. The effect of recent decisions of the EEC Commission in implementing the competition provisions of the Treaty of Rome [2] is positively to discourage trade in technology between non-affiliated companies in EEC. Primarily this is due to the current interpretation (although still not finally determined) that a licence to sell in one member state is a licence to sell in them all and therefore every licensee is also a potential competitor. It seems reasonable to deduce that EEC will tend to follow the pattern of US anti trust law and that this will lead to a trend for UK technology to be transferred in EEC primarily to affiliated companies.

Again it is interesting to note (Table 2) that British companies with US affiliates drew only 9.5% of income in as receipts for technology compared to the overall US figure of 18.0% [3].

The most interesting feature of the UK position is that despite the investment made by the UK in research and development its share of world markets has been steadily reducing. It needs to be borne in mind that the bulk of British manufacture is in the low to medium value per ton bracket, and that this is the area most susceptible to competition. In its endeavour to improve the value per ton of exports the British Government has sponsored heavy investment in advanced technology such as computers, electronics

216

and aerospace [4]. In fact these constitute only a small proportion of GNP and show no signs of developing faster than the rest of the economy; aerospace has actually declined since 1963. One of the fastest rising sectors has been the chemical industry and this is an industry which has paid the closest attention to the exchange of technology. However, the chemical industry receives more than it pays from technology trading [5].

It seems worthy of consideration whether on the one hand the UK's level of receipts from sales of technology is not too high and does not reflect a tendency to transfer technology under licence where it should be transferring it in support of investment. Furthermore, it raises the question whether some part of resources being deployed to developing indigenous technology in low growth industries would not be better used in purchasing more technology overseas. Has the existing policy not in fact been a major factor in the low growth rate of the UK economy? It is interesting to contrast the UK's position with that of Japan.

3. *Japan*

In 1973 the Japanese negative balance of payments arising from technology trading was $495m. This represented payments of $570m and receipts of $75m and placed Japan in the position of being the world's largest importer of foreign technology. It remains to be seen whether this trend will change as a result of increases in world commodity prices.

It has to be noted that during this period the growth rate of GNP in Japan was approximately 11% p a. This naturally raises the question: was there any relationship between intake of foreign technology and growth of the economy, and if so can the Japanese experience be generalised?

Without necessarily offering any final answer to this proposition, there are a number of particular features of Japanese approach which are empirically valuable in this context. First of all there appears to be very little of the "not invented here" attitude; the source of technology is clearly of less significance than in the West. This may well be the natural result of decades of willing absorption of foreign technology as the only policy to wrench the country quickly from a closed medieval society to a modern industrial state. This in turn has led to a very positive attitude towards the use of outside technology which is characterised by the process of "inward diffusion", that is, an objective analysis and criticism of technology at all levels in the recipient company. This is facilitated by the facts that improvements are not made for their own sake and that genuine improvements are always sought. The process is aided by the availability of a plethora of medium level technologists with considerable freedom to comment, argue and dissent.

Furthermore, the dedication and tribal loyalty of employees in Japanese companies is in itself significant in helping to overcome the inertial forces to be met in launching new projects. The active planning and sponsorship by Government of the search for and application of outside technology provides in this situation an important element of leadership, if not direction. This collaboration of state and industry is aided by the skills of the half dozen or so world wide trading companies such as Sumitomo, Mitsui and Mitsubishi whose scale of operation and resources are vast by European standards. These companies are highly conversant with the technology needs of their clients and are well staffed to cover any technology on which they may be required to advise. Their services are also available to other Japanese organisations which do not have adequate resources of their own.

This would appear to add up to a powerful combination of resources to seek, obtain and ensure effective use of outside technology backed by positive encouragement and economic planning to ensure such effective use.

It seems doubtful that the "inward diffusion" of outside technology is the only reason for Japan's remarkable growth. However the effect of continuously broadening and modernising the technology base must be regarded as an important feature of success in an economy which is in no way economically autarchic and must depend on trade.

Japan has not relied as heavily as the United Kingdom on indigenous research. The patent activity of Japan is substantial by world standards (in 1974 8% of patents filed in UK were filed by Japanese [6]) but is basically related to development activity. This whole situation contrasts vividly with the position in the United Kingdom to an extent that the United Kingdom should at least be asking itself whether its position on the transfer of technology inwards is really adequate.

4. The rest of Europe

It will be seen from Table 1 that France, Italy and the Federal German Republic each appeared to be importing more foreign technology during the period than the United Kingdom and also as opposed to the United Kingdom were each apparently net importers of technology. Again, each of these territories had a faster rate of growth of GNP than the United Kingdom.

Although, it would be tempting to draw the conclusion, particularly with the Japanese situation in mind, that there was a positive relationship it seems necessary to consider whether the amounts of payments and receipts are significant taking into account the quickening effect during this period of the development of EEC and also the nature of the technology transferred. With reference to this latter point it has already been recorded that the United Kingdom was making strenuous efforts to develop high technology industries which had a disappointing growth performance. Consequently, to the extent that outside technology was acquired for these industries, the effect of such technology on the economy would have been less evident. However, there was very little emphasis in France, Germany and Italy on such technology during this period and these countries acquired the bulk of such advanced technology as they needed under licence from abroad.

In addition, it will be seen from Table 2 that something like half the payments for technology arising in EEC in 1971 were remitted to US companies from their affiliates. This suggests that there may also be a tax effect of uncertain dimensions.

Factors Influencing Technology Transfer

Up to now consideration has been given to some tentative conclusions on what the available statistics suggest in regard to the pattern of technology transfer which relates to the industrialised countries. It now seems appropriate to introduce some general factors which have a bearing on the interpretation of these statistics.

First cognizance must be taken of the taxation effect. The primary importance of this arises from the observation already made that technology tends to follow investment unless it is inhibited from doing so by, for example, lack of resources or governmental intervention. There are advantages in taking profit from an affiliate by way of royalty for technology rather than as dividend, as the former is usually treated in the host country as a cost which is deductible for tax purposes. As a result it is difficult to ascertain from the statistics available how much really represents an economic payment for technology transferred and how much is in fact a payment for risk capital, i.e. masked dividend. There have been enough cases of rapacious royalties being paid by affiliates to

219

alert governmental authorities to this practice and it is now common in developing and newly emergent countries for statutory limitations to be placed on the rates of royalty payable to parties who are also shareholders. Unfortunately, these limitations usually represent an overreaction by the host government, the effect of which is to introduce distortions which make it impossible to obtain an economic arms-length return for the use of technology. Examples of this are the Andean Pact guidelines and the licensing criteria of countries like Argentine, Brazil, Spain, Iran and India. A good example of the distorting effects of taxation on statistics is the case of Switzerland (see Table 2) which would appear to be a source of major activity in technology trading but on analysis this turns out to be little more than an entrepot trade more concerned with tax avoidance than industrialisation.

Secondly, it must be borne in mind that there are certain inhibitions on the transfer of technology which vary from territory to territory but have a pronounced effect on the handling and placing of transferring technology. The most effective body of doctrine is that found in USA embodied in the Sherman and Clayton Antitrust Acts and the consequent rules and practices of the US Departments of Justice and of Commerce. The object is to remove unjustifiable restraints on competition which directly or indirectly affect US trade; the criteria applied for this purpose are as much economic as legal and consequently leave a large indeterminate area where law is a matter of judgment rather than certainty. The same object is to be found in the rapidly growing body of EEC competition law derived from Articles 36, 85 and 86 of the Treaty of Rome, and in the domestic law of most member nations of EEC and of other industrialised countries such as Japan.

One effect of anti-trust/competition law is likely to be an increasing emphasis on the transfer of technology only to affiliates of the company which owns the technology. The restrictions imposed by these systems of law on limiting the recipients' rights of sale and field of use could have the effect of making every licensee a competitor of the licensor. Unless the owner of the technology can control its use through controlling the user, the transfer of the technology under licence could undermine his long term market position. Exercise through an affiliate may not always be a solution however; it could be prone to attack in USA on the basis of inter-merger conspiracy and in most jurisdictions if it leads to monopolisation or a sufficient degree of market dominance.

A further inhibiting effect is the intervention or possible intervention of host government authorities. This may result as mentioned above in licence terms which are uneconomic. It is unfortunate that a history of rapacious licensing, abuse of tax systems, investment grants, pioneering terms and other host government incentives has led many of those countries which most urgently need Western technology to set up controls which make the transfer of such technology hazardous and unattractive.

Thirdly, there is a notable concentration in the transfer process. The effect of the uncertainties referred to above is an inevitable tendency for technology to be transferred more readily outside the territory of the owner by owners who are large enough to be knowledgeable about the technique and its intricacies. This tends to place the business of technology transfer in the hands of multinational companies and large corporations where expertise in handling the complex transactions involved is usually centred in a specialist department. These organisations represent a "comity of licensing".

In countries where technology is transferred through a State trading organisation there is a further clear example of the concentration of the transfer process. This process is apparent in the West as an increasing trend. Many large US companies have highly developed programmes for promoting technology transfer, a few are willing to extend their services to promote the transfer of other parties' technology. Further evidence of the trend towards concentration can be seen (Table 2) in the extent to which technology transfer by US companies took place with affiliates rather than non-affiliated organisations.

Fourthly, it may be reasonably concluded that there is a preference for transfer to an affiliated company. This is to some extent due to the taxation effect and to some extent to the inhibitions on licensing other parties. In addition there are more positive reasons to be considered such as the wish to retain long term control of the technology where there is for example limited, narrow or short term patent protection or indeed none at all. Furthermore, there is usually a higher profit potential than from simple licensing of other parties bearing in mind that given adequate resources the object of industry is to earn profits from risk capital. In this connection the conclusions of the second Reddaway report on the relationship between long term investment overseas and the balance of payments indicated that there was a clear effect after eleven years on the balance of payments of policies limiting overseas investment [7]. It seems reasonable to conclude that dispensing technology under licence (the normal length of which will be about ten years) rather than in support of an investment suggests that the latter is a better economic policy for the donor country — assuming availability of resources.

Finally, as the corollary of the last point above there is an apparent correlation between receipt of foreign technology and growth of GNP. As mentioned above the example of Japan suggests that this may be a real effect. It is likely, if applicable to other territories, that it would require the same degree of planning as in Japan and a similar set of attitudes on the part of the recipient.

General Discussion and Conclusions

It has to be admitted that the observations made above are the result on the one hand of empirical observation and on the other of interpretation of very crude statistics. It is doubtful whether the statistics noted in Tables 1 and 2 have arisen from identical criteria; it is not clear what they include under the label of a payment for technology nor whether they capture all technology which is transferred. A close scrutiny of contracts relating to transfers and of payments made in respect to them would improve the accuracy of the figures but probably would still not make them wholly reliable. Some governmental authorities such as those in Japan and Spain already undertake such an examination to assist economic planning and the direction of governmental contracts for research and development into the most productive channels.

There would appear to be a clear need for both government and industry to be better informed of the pattern of technology transfer both as regards the economic effect of topping up the national store of technology from abroad and as regards the best methods from the national point of view of exploiting domestic technology abroad. It seems reasonable to suppose that domestic technology is not in fact simply an invisible export to be encouraged primarily because of its short-term effect on the balance of payments.

There is also a need to establish what technology transfer means in terms of economic models. It could be useful to assess the effects of varying levels of technology transfer on different phases of the economy.

It is concluded that a greater understanding of the international dimension of technology transfer is required to be sure that the scarce technology which is available for transfer is not squandered.

References

[1] Teplin, M.F., "US International Transactions in Royalties and Fees: their Relationship to the Transfer of Technology", *Survey of Current Business*, December 1973.

[2] See: "Treaty of Rome Articles 36, 85 and 86 and Centrafarm Bv v. Sterling Drug Inc.", Court of the European Communities, Case 15/74.

[3] US Department of Commerce, Office of Business Economics, *Quarterly Report*, March 1971.

[4] *Industrial Research and Development in Government Laboratories*, HMSO, 1970.

[5] Taylor & Silberston, *The Economic Impact of the Patent System*, Cambridge University Press, London, 1973.

[6] *Report of Comptroller General of the Patent Office*, HMSO, 1975.

[7] *Reddaway Report on Effects of UK Direct Investment Overseas*, Occasional Paper No. 15, Cambridge University Press, London, 1968.

RESEARCH ON TECHNOLOGY TRANSFER AND INNOVATION

by *R.M. Bell** and *S.C. Hill**

1. The Relation between Knowledge and Technique — Some Basic Definitions

Technology has been the subject of ordered study in the social sciences for long enough to suggest that a preamble on definitions must be redundant here. However, the extraordinarily rapid rate of growth of technology in recent years has almost been matched by the rate of diversification of interpretations given to the term itself — explicitly given by definition or more often by implication in use. Before saying anything about transferring it, we shall try to clarify what we think "it" is.

We take as a starting point the type of definition used by economists — or at least by those economists who have been more careful in their use of the term. For example, Freeman and Pavitt, [1], pp. 3-17, or Mansfield, [2], pp. 10-11. In this view of things technology is (a) words or knowledge (logos), (b) about the arts (techne) — usually thought of quite narrowly as the practical, productive arts. Thus a machine is in itself not technology, nor is a consumer product, nor is a method of production *per se*. Knowledge about a machine, about a product or about a method of production *is* technology. So also is the underlying knowledge which was drawn on to produce the machine, product or method. The latter, in their concrete forms in use within production, are techniques. Thus we start with a distinction between knowledge and the artefacts and operating procedures which have drawn on and embody that knowledge. (Those who find this distinction difficult to accept might examine the meaning of some other -ologies. Biology is not animals and plants etc. Sociology is not social

* University of Sussex, Brighton, U.K.

225

structures and systems, nor, to the best of our knowledge, is theology identical with God.)

This certainly runs counter to some popular forms of usage which tend to equate technology with the artefacts into which it is embodied. This definition also runs counter to another aspect of popular usage in that it implies nothing about the timing of the origin of the knowledge. Knowledge need not be "modern" knowledge and need not be relevant to "modern" techniques to qualify as "technology". On the contrary the stock of technology consists of knowledge accumulated since the relevant records have been maintained. In fact, it is an interesting peculiarity that technology is expanding "backwards" as well as "forwards". Historians and archaeologists expand the current stock of technology as they acquire, record, and systematise knowledge about techniques used by producers before recorded history e.g. about methods of producing tools, keeping livestock or growing crops in neolithic periods. At the same time, and again counter to some forms of popular usage, the term "technology" does not necessarily imply anything about the "sophistication" or "complexity" of the knowledge itself or of the techniques to which it relates. Therefore, if we wish to refer to "modern", "sophisticated" technology, to "modern", "simple" technology, or to "old", "complex" technology we shall try to use the appropriate qualifications and definitions.

Related to this distinction between technology and techniques is a distinction we make between technological change and technical change. The former relates to a change in knowledge – be it by the addition of knowledge about phenomena previously not established, or be it by the combination, manipulation, transformation or elaboration of existing information to provide knowledge that was not previously available. Technical change on the other hand, is a change in the *used* methods of production. Conventionally, two types of technical change are distinguished – innovation and the "replications" of that innovatory technical change that takes place in a succeeding process of diffusion. Innovation is defined as the application and use in a technique of an element of technology previously unused, i.e. the term refers to the *first* use of a technique. Subsequent to its use in innovation a technique may be replicated in succeeding technical changes. This spread of a technical change following its innovation is often referred to as a *diffusion* process. However, as Rosenberg [3] has

226

stressed, it is hard to identify examples of this non-innovatory form of technical change, i.e. *pure* replication.

This last point is particularly important for what follows, and a little elaboration may help. A particular example from agriculture — the technical change consisting of the use of hybrid corn varieties — is useful to illustrate the interaction of innovation with what is described as a diffusion process following the first application of hybridised corn seed. The spread or diffusion of this innovation to new areas of use required an ongoing process of research and modification (of new knowledge creation) to develop varieties suited to varying soil and climatic conditions even within the relatively narrow area of the American Mid-West [4, 5]. Almost every step in the widening area of application of hybridised corn involved a "first application" of some elements of knowledge. Industrial technology provides numerous illustrations of this point.

The so-called diffusion of numerical control techniques for manufacturing operations is one useful example. These have "diffused" through a variety of different types of application — within the machine tool field and outside it. It is almost impossible to separate this process into innovative and replicative technical changes. A constant process of adaptation and change — both of the control systems and of the equipment to which they were applied — has accompanied spreading application. Even at the level of adoption of replicated hardware systems for use in production there is very frequently a need for modification of the system of production itself. In many instances such changes in technique which are necessary to absorb the replicated hardware will result in unique "first applications" of some elements of the technique — sometimes in the absorbed hardware, often in the related hardware and very frequently in the organisational and procedural elements of the technique. For one example of this type of absorptive adaptation in apparently replicative technical changes see [6].

For some purposes, then, it may be useful to distinguish between technical changes that are innovations and those that are "replications" in a "diffusion process" — as that is usually defined. However, to do so may hide both the extent to which technology is drawn on to produce "neo-replications" that are unique, and the extent to which new knowledge may be generated in the process. Indeed for some purposes it may be more helpful to abandon the distinction and to conceive of technical changes as incorporating a variable proportion of elements that are "first applications" of knowledge (i.e. that are innovatory) — from 100 per cent (most unusual) to zero (perhaps equally unusual). A very large proportion of all technical changes result in a system of production (a technique) that has some unique elements previously not used. In other words very few technical changes involve no "innovatory component", although this may be very high in some cases and very low in others. If this is so, almost all technical changes draw "directly" on technology as knowledge as well as "indirectly" in the form of knowledge *already* embodied, "fixed", or encapsulated within elements of the techniques that are brought into use. The incidence of technical change that is effected by "pure replication" of all elements of the technique and without any direct drawing on technology for unique application is, we suggest, probably very low. If such cases exist, the technical changes themselves do not involve a direct transfer of technology, but a transfer of technique. The technology involved has been transformed (or embodied) into the technique, and only in this "frozen" form is the knowledge transferred to application. We shall not be much concerned with this form of technology transfer, but only with the transfer to application of technology *per se*, i.e. of knowledge, rather than of information "encapsulated" in artefacts or in well-established, codified procedures.

Before moving on to discuss transfer, we ought to clarify how we see two other terms ('R & D' and 'science') fitting into this scheme of things. "R & D" is systematic activity directed to the advance or change of technology.[7] This is relatively wide-ranging since "systematic activity" may be far broader in scope than those activities which happen to go on under the formal label of "R & D". On the other hand, to some this definition may seem narrow. By being defined in relation to changing technology, "R & D" does not in itself produce technical changes, but rather new knowledge in some form. Only incidentally may "R & D" produce techniques rather than knowledge — as when the tooling and production schedules and methods needed to produce prototype aircraft for technological investigations can be switched unchanged for use to produce for the market; or when a pilot-plant which was initially set up to establish knowledge about, for example, optimal plant designs and operating procedures is subsequently used for commercial production. Usually a further set of activ-

228

ities beyond R & D is needed to *use* knowledge and produce innovative techniques — be they concerned with processes, with products, or with methods of organisation or procedure, or all three combined. This activity which uses knowledge or inventions to generate innovations may be one form or another of engineering.

A technical change (whether an innovation or not) may be described as being effected with or without R & D. In part this depends on whether R & D generated any of the knowledge used. In part it also depends on the institutional or temporal separation of the R & D activity from the innovating activity. If some of the knowledge used in innovation was generated by R & D, it may have been generated in an institution or at a time that was widely separated from the innovative activity. The gap may have been so wide that it makes no sense to say that the innovation process "involved" R & D. On the other hand, the institutional or temporal proximity of the knowledge-producing R & D to the technique-changing activity may be so close that the technical change process can be described as "R & D-intensive".

What about "science"? How does that fit into this outline of our basic concepts and definitions? We find it instructive to use two concepts of science: science as knowledge, and science as method. Science as knowledge differs from technology in that the knowledge (about natural phenomena) has no *perceived* relevance to techniques. Although it serves our purposes here, this distinction is too harsh and unidimensional. Science can be distinguished from technology in a variety of ways. These would include distinctions relating to the sociological context of the activities, the motivations of participants behaviour and the form and degree of "publicity" given to the knowledge outputs[8]. These are all, however, consistent with our crude distinction here that the body of knowledge that we call science has a low level of perceived utility for application in connection with techniques of production. Science as knowledge is the product of scientific research, or perhaps of "basic" technological research — i.e. of search for new knowledge which does not have foreseen possibilities for use in connection with technology, but which it is expected/hoped may come to have such possibilities. Science as knowledge may be transformed into technology when its relevance for techniques comes to be perceived and when it is therefore drawn from the stock of science and incorporated into the stock of technology. This time-lag between the origin of an element of scientific knowledge and its incorporation into technology may be very long. In situations where it tends to be short, we would describe the technology as being "science-intensive" or "science-based". Similarly, an industry which tended to incorporate into its techniques knowledge which relatively recently was science would be described as science-based.

The term science is used often to refer not so much to knowledge about phenomena as to a set of particular methods for acquiring and validating knowledge — scientific method and/or scientific procedures. In this sense, science may be used in "R & D" in the process of acquiring and validating technical knowledge (technology). The relatively intensive use of scientific methods in the search for knowledge might be used as a dimension that helps to classify an area of technology or a sector of industry as "science-based". Since R & D is almost by definition based on scientific method, we shall use "R & D-intensive" to refer to this method of acquiring technology. Thus "scientific" referring to method is redundant. For our purposes, "scientific research" is research to produce science as knowledge. As an activity it differs from technological research less (if at all) in the methods used, but more in the social context and "meaning" of the activity. We shall keep "science-intensive" to relate to the frequency of use, in areas of technology or in sectors of production, of knowledge that relatively recently was science. It may nevertheless be useful to distinguish between technology that is acquired by the use of scientific method (i.e. by definition through R & D) and technology that is generated by other methods — for example, luck, accident, casual observations, "experience", unsystematic "trial and error", etc. When this distinction is necessary we shall try to make clear that we are referring to the use of science as method rather than science as knowledge.

The preceding paragraphs outline how we prefer to define technology and a number of related terms. Defining "transfer" should not delay us too long. Clearly the origin of an element of technology has a fixed location in time — even if this location cannot be empirically identified for all elements of knowledge. More important for our purposes is the fact that elements of technology have a bounded location in space at any time. Particular items of knowledge may be "stored" in one or more people at given places, and not "known" at that time by other people in other places. Similarly, elements of technology may be stored in some "documentary" forms that are located at some places (perhaps only one) and not at others. Usually we can draw various types of institutional boundary around particular "stores" of particular elements of technology, e.g. an R & D department, a laboratory, a firm, a library, a computer-based information system, a university professor, his department, production engineers in general or some subset of them, technical college graduates in general or the class of '75, and so on. For some purposes we may wish to draw regional boundaries around the particular storage "locations" of some components of the total stock of knowledge e.g. American laser technology, East Anglian axe-head technology, or the industrial technology of the "developed" countries.

In general, what we understand by the "transfer" of technology is the movement of knowledge from a defined "store" in one "location" to storage in another. This usually does not imply that it ceases to be stored at the initial location, and hence we might use a concept like the "expansion" of the stores of knowledge. However, this would not be appropriate to cases where individuals or groups move with their knowledge from one location to another leaving no trace of the knowledge behind them; or when some "documentary" store is not duplicated but physically removed from one place to another. This may be simply an inter-personal movement, e.g. from professor to student, or from Smith to his laboratory colleague Jones. It may involve knowledge crossing institutional boundaries, e.g. from laboratory to "shop floor", from firm A to firm B, or from "university to industry". It may also involve crossing regional boundaries e.g. from America to Europe, from East Anglia to Wessex, or from developed to developing countries.

However, we are not concerned here with all technology transfer in general, but only with those transfer processes that are related to, and lie behind, technical innovation. A considerable part of the totality of change, or expansion, in the location of "stores" of elements of technology may have nothing to do with innovation. For example, much of the technology that is transferred through the various forms of educational process finishes up being used to *operate* given, existing techniques of production. Some of it may be used to effect replicative, non-innovatory technical changes (if they exist). Other parts of this totality of educationally-transferred technical knowledge probably finishes up not being used for anything at all, but other parts do finish up being drawn on directly in innovative activity. Similarly, of the mountains of documentary stores of technical knowledge, a large proportion finishes up being used for nothing at all — often despite being duplicated and dispersed to innumerable locations. In the same way, an individual may carry out research, acquire technology, document some of this (for use or not, perhaps in innovation), but continue to "store" the rest in himself. Much of what he accumulates in his "mental store" may never see the light of day (never mind be used for anything). Other parts may be used, perhaps for innovative activity — with or without interpersonal transfer in the process.

This obviously raises the question of time. The knowledge that finishes up being used to effect an innovation may not be transferred from its location of origin to the point of application in a smooth, continuous flow over time. Much technology may lie "dormant" in the stock of knowledge for some considerable time before being "activated" and drawn into an innovation process. Other elements of technical knowledge may be drawn on repeatedly to effect innovations that are spaced out over considerable lengths of time. Almost all innovations will simultaneously draw on elements of technology that are scattered across a range of different "vintages" in the stock of knowledge. The proportions from each "vintage" that are used will vary between innovations. Those innovations that draw relatively heavily on vintages of knowledge that were recently science would be "science-intensive" innovations, and an analyst might be interested in the transfer process that "moved" the scientific knowledge into the "locations" where it was used as technology. Other innovations may draw on knowledge that long since ceased to be science — if it ever was. Indeed, in drawing on technology, "innovators" may draw an overwhelming proportion that is of considerable age, reorganising only some small part of this to produce the new information which, on application, constitutes the innovatory element of the package that is classed as "an innovation".

It is conceivable, but most unlikely, that *all* the elements of knowledge that are used to effect an innovation can be generated *de novo* in the location of use of the knowledge for innovation. In almost all cases — even those of the lone, individual innovator — *some* elements will have moved from storage somewhere to storage in the location of application in innovation. This movement of knowledge across interpersonal, inter-institutional or inter-regional boundaries, which lies behind innovatory technical change, and which is an integral part of the process of effecting such technical change, is the phenomenon with which we are concerned – that subset of all technology transfer processes that is related to effecting innovation.

It might be helpful to summarize this discussion with a highly simplified descriptive "model" of our subject of interest (see Figure 1).

At the centre of things is the stock of technology – the whole diversity of existing technical knowledge, including both that which has and that which has not, been used. The "system of production" is the location of use of innovations that result in "better" or cheaper goods and services. Between this system and the stock of technology lies the key activity of "technique creation" or innovation (by definition a technique is an *applied* method of production). The diagrammatic separation of "technique creation" from the system of production implies nothing about the institutional location of the two activities. Both may (and often do) occur in the same institutions. Indeed the same *person* may do both at different times. However, sometimes a large proportion of the necessary innovative activities are clearly separated institutionally from the ongoing business of production – as in product design departments or capital goods firms. Since the innovation finishes up being integrated into the ongoing production systems, it is inconceivable that the *totality* of innovative activity relating to a particular change can take place in institutional separation from the ongoing business of production. As we shall suggest later, the contribution to innovative activity that is made by people who are located within the production system and who are not specialised change agents, is probably far larger than is recognised in most studies of innovation. The diagrammatic separation simply indicates that they are different activities. Technique creation whoever does it and whether it consists largely of "engineering" or of the unsystematic application of "hunch", is a qualitatively different activity from the day-to-day, ongoing operation of the existing production system.

The stocks of science (as knowledge and as method) are linked to the "science creation" activity. There is a one way flow of scientific knowledge (transformed to technology) to

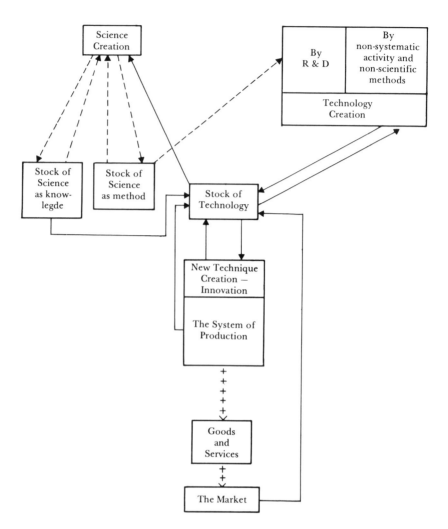

Flows of technology involving transfers across inter-personal, inter-institutional or inter-regional boundaries.

+++++ > Flows of goods and services with "encapsulated" technical information and perhaps accompanied by technology.

– – – ▶ Flows of scientific information (science as knowledge and science as method).

Figure 1. *Technology Transfer and Innovation*

234

the stock of technology, but science creating and the stock of scientific methods may draw on technology, while "R & D" may draw on the stock of scientific methods and procedures.

For our purposes here we are concerned with the market for goods and services only as a generator of relevant technical knowledge. In effect, the market can be regarded here as a giant "test-bed" or simulation model through which are run various technical configurations of goods and services. The output information (some expressed in technical terms, some not) consists of data regarding the extent to which the configurations of the techniques achieve (actually or prospectively) their objectives. As such, this information is critical knowledge about techniques of production − often as critical as the knowledge about technique that can be gained from design manuals, pilot-plants, or laboratory experiments.

The last element of the "model" is the activity of "technology creation" which changes or augments technical knowledge. In part this is effected by "R & D" − a *systematic* activity probably involving science as method, but not necessarily an activity carrying the institutional label of "R" or "D". To remind ourselves that technology can be changed or augmented by unsystematic activities based little, if at all, on scientific procedures, we have identified a separate category of technology creation.

Within this "model", the relevant flows of technology (transfers of technical knowledge from one storage location to another) are obvious. They may take place *within* any of the activity elements e.g. between people or institutions concerned with "R & D" or with new technique creation. To simplify things and to remain consistent with our earlier discussion (and hopefully to accord with reality) such intra-activity transfers take place via the stock of knowledge, i.e. once generated an element of technical knowledge instantaneously becomes part of the stock of knowledge, and then may or may not be transferred somewhere. The other transfer processes take place *between* the various elements − again via the stock of technology. We should emphasise that the transfer links illustrated are only those that are relevant to our immediate problem: innovation. Thus, for example there do exist transfers of technology, and of course even of science, from the stocks to production that by-pass the new technique creating (innovating) activity. They may be critically important for ongoing operation or for replication-type technical change, but only that knowledge which is used in innovation is of concern to us now.

Fairly obviously the diagram omits a host of institutions (e.g. educational or other information dissemination institutions) which help to mobilise the flows of knowledge around the system. One final point to note is that although goods and services are not themselves technology, they incorporate embedded or encapsulated in themselves elements of knowledge. Actually, the supply of a product may be accompanied by the supply of technology in some form, e.g. the supply of the mechanical component of the technique for opening food cans (a can-opener) may be accompanied by information about when the technique will work optimally and when not at all, and about how to operate the technique – all knowledge about the technique and hence technology. This encapsulated (crystallised?) knowledge may be extracted and activated – as when an industrial machine or a domestic hi-fi system is taken to pieces to see (in part) "how it works" in order perhaps to effect better operation or repair (or perhaps simply to satisfy curiosity). This indirect method of transferring technology – by encapsulation in goods and services – is not of concern to us here, except in those cases where it forms a means of transferring knowledge that enables subsequent innovation to take place.

Aimed with this stock-centred model of the processes of technology transfer for innovation, we now proceed to review a number of the more prominent research studies that have been conducted in this field in industrialised societies.

2. Innovation and Technology Transfer Models – What they Assume

i. The Linear Sequential Model of Technology Innovation and Transfer

The familiar view of technology transfer in advanced countries which characterised much of the literature into the late 1960's is that of a linear flow process from research through to final industrial application and diffusion – a model which Langrish et al. [9] call the "discovery push" model. Two examples from disparate sources illustrate an oft-recurring theme: Blackett [10] characterised innovation as a sequence of related steps from pure science through applied science, invention, development, prototype construction, production, marketing, sales and profit. Participants at an MIT Conference on technology transfer [11] added feedback loops to their "probabilistic model II" in which the core is a sequential, connected flow from idea through research – development – production – innovation – diffusion.

It is this linear model which underscored the original retrospective studies of innovation-technology transfer processes related to Defence Department applications in the United States – "Project Hindsight" [12]. This study was mounted as an attempt to justify government expenditure on fundamental research. It was set in the prevalent American (and European) government attitudes about technology transfer. Tom Burns [13], with reference to attempts of the USA space programme to foster industrial application of government research, characterises this view:

> "technology transfer is a matter of either the unplanned percolation, or the planned transmission, of ideas, technical routines, or information from research (scientific and technological) to manufacturing industry and so into commercial exploitation and eventual use."

Belief in the connectedness and coherence of the linear model was temporarily disturbed by the results of Project Hindsight. This study, based on a 20 years time scale and on a somewhat questionable methodology, [14] suggested that only 0.3 per cent of research "events", which were relevant to a set of defence technology applications, came from basic research funded by the Defence Department. Predictably, this demonstration of a possible chink in the armour of the conventional view was seen as threatening by both the government and scientific establishments. The threat was quite explicit. Following the earliest publication of the Hindsight results in 1966, the journal "Science" published an article [15] and later an editorial, both of which questioned the utility of academic research [16]. However, relief was on hand to restore peace of mind to the faithful. It was no coincidence that at this time the US National Foundation commissioned "Project Traces", [17] the terms of reference of which allowed a much greater chance of fundamental science being shown as relevant. This study essentially replicated Project Hindsight, but on a longer time scale (50 years) and using a methodology relying on a more circumspect selection of cases and armchair reminiscence.

From Project Traces it was demonstrated, not unexpectedly, that 70 per cent of inputs to innovation came ultimately from fundamental research see [18]. *Science* was now able to publish an article [19] which stated:

"basic research was of overwhelming importance in five recent technological innovations of wide value."

The National Science Foundation then sponsored a follow-up study of Project Traces by a project team from Battelle laboratories. Cases for study were selected jointly by the National Science Foundation and the Battelle project team as of "high social or economic impact"; three Traces cases were re-analysed and an additional eight added. This study concluded that basic research contributed to 57 per cent of events in the "pre conception period", 16 per cent of events in the "innovative period", and 10 per cent of events in the "post-innovative period". Publishing in 1973, the authors still held a "discovery push", linear process — view of innovation, and thus of technology transfer. Innovation is conceived by them as not

"... merely a marginal improvement to an existing product or process. Rather it is a complex series of activities, beginning at 'first conception', when the original idea is conceived; proceeding through a succession of interwoven steps of research, development, engineering, design, market analysis, management decision-making etc.; and ending at 'first realisation', when an industrially successful product, (which may actually be a thing, a technique, or a process) is accepted in the marketplace." [17]

In spite of the continuing return to a rather linear view of the innovation-technology transfer process reflected particularly in these US sponsored studies, there has been mounting evidence of both the variability and complexity of innovation and technology transfer. Schon [6] for example, in analysing numerical control innovations in the US machine tool industry noted the complexity in a second wave of innovation. This second wave was directed towards programming sequences for very simple machine operation whereas the first had been more concerned with similar systems for machining intricate and complex parts. However, this change was not simply taking technology from one place and applying it elsewhere; it *depended*, amongst other things, on a revolutionising of market strategies. Variability in the starting point of the process was recognised by authors such as Holloman, [21] in the development of "need pull" models, where perceived need precedes

238

the invention-innovation sequence. Even Globe, Levy and Schwartz [20] concluded in their "Traces" follow-up study that 69 per cent of decisive events in innovation were characterised by "recognition of need" though this was outweighed by 87 per cent attributable to recognition of "technical opportunity".

SPRU's Project "SAPPHO" on paired "successful" and "unsuccessful" innovations in the British chemical processes and scientific instruments industries demonstrated the influence of "need pull", in that successful firms pay more attention to the market than do their unsuccessful counterparts [22, 23]. Gibbons and Johnston [24] and [25] conclude, counter to the linear research-based concept of innovation, that "need pull" was important and no innovations they studied were induced by a particular scientific discovery. What led to innovation was not "need pull" alone, "rather it was most frequently the conjunction of technological *need* or *opportunity* and a positive *assessment of* actual or potential *market* that acted as joint stimuli". Langrish et al. [9] recognise the complexity of a comprehensive innovation/technology transfer model and synthesise the "discovery push", "need pull" models into a four-way classification: the (a) "science discovers, technology applies" (b) "technological discovery" (c) "customer need", and (d) "management by objectives" (where need is perceived by management rather than customers) models. Whereas they observe that some of the Queen's Award Innovations can be classified as predominately stimulated by "discovery push" or "need pull", very few can be fitted into any one of the four models — thus demonstrating the alternatives and complexity or technology transfer.

Feedback within the technology transfer process has also been recognised as *transforming* the sequence. Smith [26], for example noted that the development of ductile tungsten filaments for incandescent lamps led to more fruitful studies of "grain boundary" behaviour than had previous scientific research. Baker, Siegman and Rubenstein [27] also recognised the feedback from technology to new scientific effort. Price [28] rewrites Toynbee's [29] earlier observation that "science and technology behave like a pair of dancers to the same music, though it is imperceptible who is leading and who following" to read, "the well-known lag between scientific and technological advance would seem to indicate that the dancers hold each other at arms length instead of dancing cheek to cheek".

Gibbons and Johnston's [25] study added empirical support to Price's contentions: they observed the gap between the scientific and technological systems such that there was either no interaction, or once a useful bridge was established, an avalanche. Consequently, although over a third of inputs to innovation originated from scientific activity (one third of these stemming from original scientific research), the relevance of scientific research to innovation was characterised by a bimodal pattern — zero or multiple interaction. The most fruitful links were those established by people who had their feet planted in both the academic and industrial technology camps. Mensch [30] observes a lag between basic science inventions and subsequent basic innovations, but demonstrates that once a basic innovation is made, a "bandwaggon" effect of related basic innovations follows — again suggesting the containment of both the scientific and technological systems.

This gap between scientific and technological systems can be attributed partly to a gap between organisations and organisational commitments (with little motivation to cross this threshold), and partly to an institutional inward-referent character of the scientific and technological professional organisations (and communication and reward systems; see Hill [31, 32]). For many scientists, as an example, attention to application orientations outside the internally reinforced consensus can not only be at cost to career but may threaten the essential elitism of the system. See, for example, Hill, Frensham and Howden [33, 34]; also Greenberg [35]. With an inward referent character of scientific and technological systems, and location in separate organisations, for example, research in a government institution, and application of technology in an industrial firm, the moat which must be crossed is very broad indeed. Bridges have been built, however, particularly in firms which *depend* on exploitation of the science and technological frontiers. Survival for them, depends on controlling or at very least, having access to, relevant scientific and technological advances. Consequently, research is likely to be built into the firm — the scientific and technological systems are integrated under a single organisational roof; perhaps more importantly, based on in-house capability, the firm becomes a very receptive customer for relevant scientific ideas promulgated elsewhere. Freeman [36] demonstrates by taking a historical perspective that over time, as characteristics of industrial production systems have changed, the connectedness of science and

240

technology in the innovation processes directed at these systems has changed: insulation of the science from technology system may have been, in an earlier period, much as Price suggests. However, as those industries which are dependent on exploiting the frontiers of existing technology have become increasingly important, and as the process of industrial change and growth increasingly has come to rest on moving the technology frontier outwards, so the science/research intensity of innovation has increased, as has the connectedness of science and technology in the innovation process.

It is important to recognise then that even a casual glance at the interaction between scientific and technological systems suggests:

(1) that a view of innovation depending upon a linear and sequential science-application process is not necessarily generalisable beyond a particular context and, depending on the levels of discontinuity as one moves away, may be quite wrong in other contexts;

(2) that the level of connectedness of science and technology (or, as a related point, the level of research input in generating technological change and thus in generating innovative technical change) varies, perhaps in systematic ways, with the nature of the production system towards which innovatory change efforts are directed. Thus when the context of innovation is considered over a wide enough range of differences there may be no such thing as process of innovation and its related technology transfer. There may exist a number of "species" of that process which differ qualitatively in their fundamental character.

ii. *Basic Assumptions and Consequent Bias in the Selection of Phenomena for Analysis*

From the above revisions and critiques of the linear innovation-technology transfer model, it is clear that a model which views technology transfer as a sequential process running on from research through application to diffusion is inadequate as a general model. This, of course, has probably always been obvious to many practitioners and is becoming increasingly obvious to analysts. What is not so obvious is the way that conceptual frameworks and methodologies of alternate approaches to analysis are also contained by similar assumptions as characterised by this simple model. Except perhaps for Freeman's analysis [36], none of the studies questions the way in which shifts in industrial context may lead to shifts in theoretical schemes not just re-apportionment of inputs into the process; for example the studies do not question *a* role for scientific research. As we go on to show later, as the industrial context shifts, such assumptions are particularly constraining of theory. The existence of such unexamined assumptions is, we believe, a product (a) of treating a very particular industrial context of experience of technology transfer and innovation as parametric, not variable, and (b) of research focus and methodology being set in this parametric context: whereas definitions and methods used are appropriate to detailing the "science research" centred paradigm of innovation-technology transfer they are inappropriate to questioning its assumptions. We can establish this argument best by approaching these two points in reverse order.

The starting point of all the innovation studies cited above is the identification of *"innovations"*, followed by retrospective analysis of events or inputs to the process. Gibbons and Johnston's study [25] is unusual in covering contemporary innovations, but it is still based on a retrospective rather than longitudinal methodology. Innovations identified vary from those of "high social or economic impact" in the Battelle study through those nominated for Queen's Awards in Langrish et al.'s study, and through "significant" innovations in the (essentially research based) chemical processing and scientific instruments industries studied by Project SAPPHO ... to a population sampled from reported "new product features" in British Technical Journals in the Gibbons and Johnston study. What remain, as yet, largely outside the scope of these studies are the "minor" incremental improvements in process, organisation or product which form the on-going background to the more "significant" advances. Gibbons and Johnston recognise this bias and seek to overcome it. They do to some extent, but their population is still sampled from those product improvements significant enough to be publically reported. Without real-time studies, or very detailed studies of everything that happened to a complete manufacturing process, there is no way of knowing either how important these incremental changes are to increased production efficiency nor what variables and processes may be involved in "successful" innovation of this type. We have no assessment of this essential backdrop to the periodic "significant" innovation activity.

242

Further, ongoing work on Project SAPPHO may help to map the character of this backdrop. Studies of the coal mining industry although necessarily retrospective, identify the innovation *process* by examining its origin in the total production technology and in the changes occurring in it over time. Studies of the textile industry are attempting to analyse the relationship of general patterns of incremental and substantial technical change to the success and failure of firms. Another ongoing study (of organisational innovation and its communication in Australia) has been using longitudinal methodology. Preliminary results suggest that what happens (particularly for the more minor incremental changes) may be a rather different process from that which is assumed to characterise "significant" innovation activity. Although there is a continuing background noise of innovation activity, there are significant social and organisational barriers to more general implementation. For example, attempts are frequently made to fit innovative communications into routinised paths, but there is a far greater dependence on mimetic process rather than on free flowing communication. The results seem to suggest rather less functionally rational behaviour in innovation than appears to be assumed in most retrospective studies. This is not an unexpected contrast in view of (i) the Western cultural imperative on rationality, and (ii) the methodology of all the innovation-technology transfer studies which have relied on data from personal reconstructions of the past.

It seems reasonable to suggest that this type of "minor" innovative activity differs significantly in many respects from innovation in "more significant" steps. Improvements of a less radical nature are more likely to evolve from the production floor, are more likely to be centred within in-house problem solving ability and to draw on technology accumulated more by various types of "learning" rather than in a research capability, particularly in one outside the firm. Some indication of the greater importance of in-house capability and the lesser role of external scientific research to the less radical innovations is suggested both by Project SAPPHO and Gibbons and Johnston's study: in Project SAPPHO, Rothwell [22] notes that contrasted to the more radical chemical processing innovations, those in the scientific instruments industry were less radical and more associated with an in-house technical innovator. Gibbons and Johnston [25] whose focus rested on innovations closer to (but not identical with) the "backdrop improvements" we are discussing, found that none of these originated from scientific discovery, although scientific inputs were relevant to subsequent problem solving.

Thus we are suggesting a related argument to that posed earlier concerning the variability of the degree of integration of science and technology, and hence of the significance to innovation of inputs from scientific knowledge. There we were suggesting that the more industry depended on pushing forward the frontier of knowledge in order to develop innovative techniques the higher would be the demand for integrating science into the innovative process. The proximity of industrial operations to the frontier of knowledge might vary over time or between sectors and would reflect, among other things, the degree to which inter-firm competition had come to depend on a constant process of technical change. We were therefore concerned with the resulting variation in the integration of science and technology within a general type of innovation process.

Here we are suggesting that across a range of different types of industrial milieu the importance of particular "species" of innovation will vary. These differing "species" will involve processes of innovation and technology transfer that differ qualitatively from each other. For example, at some point as one moves towards "minor" and "incremental" types of innovation, the connectedness of science and technology, or the importance of research inputs may not simply be lower, but may become of no importance. Indeed, they may become factors that are negatively related to success. Thus in an industrial context in which production operations are far from the frontier of knowledge, the low actual and necessary connectedness of science and research with innovative technical change might be reinforced again by a rational, priority concern with "species" of innovation (e.g. "minor" or "incremental" types) that involved very low frequencies of temporally remote linkage with science or research. It might even be that these species of innovation would be *less* effective (or less cost-effective) the greater were the efforts to "force" higher frequencies of more direct linkage.

This biased focus of research on *particular* types of innovation phenomena may, then, contribute to maintaining the science and research intensive view of "innovation" (as well as other forms of non- and mis-understanding of the full range of innovation phenomena).

244

A second type of methodological bias with similar consequences arises in other aspects of the definition of innovations used in the predominant retrospective studies. These studies tend to focus specifically on the machines, the processes, the products and not on their surrounding organisation context. For example, Langrish et al. [9], pp. 42-43 approach their definition through the hardware-oriented view of Schon's that technology is "any tool or technique, any product or process, any physical equipment or method of doing or making, by which human capability is extended". They broaden this to include software elements: "the concepts and knowledge which are embodied within the hardware", concluding as a result that "technology transfer may be reduced simply to the movement of ideas and information from one context to another". But even though this study, as an example of others, is broadened to include information, this information and thus the content of innovation tends to be anchored in the hardware component of techniques. This kind of information usually implies a linkage between innovation and scientific research inputs; in the Battelle study this link is stated explicitly, "basic to the process of information are the tools-discoveries, and techniques of science and technology" [17]. In addition, all the innovation and technology transfer studies we have cited discern ultimately that an "innovation" has occurred when an advance has been made in technology hardware.

Defining innovation in such singular terms seems, on the surface, eminently sensible and quite legitimate. But it assumes a particular significance of changes in the "core", "hardware" activity within a total production organisation. See Kreilkamp [14] for specific comments on this aspect of the methodology of Project Hindsight. It focusses attention away from for example, machine peripheral, inter-machine, organisational or inter-firm changes which may employ no machine innovations as such but which still may represent important, innovative technical changes, and which are certainly part of the complete "process" by which innovations are embedded into the production system.

In addition to shifting the focus of concern away from those types of innovation which have low or non-existent "hardware-symptoms", definition of the phenomena of interest in hardware terms tends to introduce another type of bias. Starting from such a definition, the investigation moves to the identification of the novelty element of the innovation. This search is likely to focus around differences in the configuration of the hardware and thence to the sources of knowledge contributing to those differences. Inevitably this leads towards hardware-engineering and thence towards the sources of knowledge about engineering phenomena. This is a route which inherently has a high probability of leading "back" towards research and science. Thus, even in situations where core-hardware changes *are* the more significant types of innovation, the dominating concern with these symptoms of the change reduces (perhaps to zero) the investigation of sources and transfer mechanism of knowledge and information concerning the "software" components of the technical change. Are these components — even of innovations that are most sensibly defined in hardware terms — important? What are the sources and transfer mechanisms of the relevant knowledge and information? Are they any different from those of knowledge and information relating to the hardware components? Our own review of the innovation literature suggests that we do not have convincing answers to these types of questions.

Finally, of course, the focus of much of the research about technology transfer onto the phenomenon of innovation is in itself a bias. As we noted in the first section of the paper, innovative technical change (involving the "first application" of at least some element of knowledge within the whole set in the change) is only part of the totality of technical change. We suggested there that the distinction between innovative and replicative technical change was probably hard to establish empirically, and we put forward the opinion that the incidence of "pure", replicative, technical change was probably very low. Immediately above, we have suggested, in effect, that the particular selections of innovative phenomena for analysis in most research have not even entered the "grey" area of indistinction between innovation and replication. To the extent that purely replicative technical change exists and is important, then the results of technology transfer research that is concerned with innovation may be totally irrelevant to that important set of technical change phenomena.

A great part of "technical progress" in the developed countries results from technical change involving little imurative novelty. A number of institutions that are concerned with technical change (e.g. some of the UK Research Associations or some management consultants) are heavily involved in transferring "old" technology to replicate "old" techniques. In many

246

cases the consequences are, in fact, probably more than technical change of the "pure", replicative type. There probably remain, of course, the other cases in which they are not. As we
shall suggest later, if the context of concern shifts, for example to the developing countries, different patterns of technical
change may be called for, even to the extent that the innovative novelty in technical change becomes socially less important, and perhaps only marginally relevant.

In such a situation the irrelevance of innovation-based technology transfer studies may not be fully compensated by the
greater relevance of "diffusion" studies. Beyond this, the par-
donable faults of omission become transformed into faults of
commission if the methods or conclusions of studies of technology transfer and innovation in particular are used to guide
research or action about technology transfer and technical
change in general. As we shall suggest, something of this sort
seems to have happened.

iii. *Bias in Selection of Variables brought into Analysis of the
Innovation Process*

We have suggested then that a general bias in the selection
of phenomena to be analysed ("significant" innovations primarily concerned with novelty in "hardware" elements of techniques of production) is likely to lead to general bias which
may leave out of account, for example, types of innovation
phenomena which are particularly important to LDC's. Before
turning to these countries, we shall illustrate another type of
bias which may be important — bias in the selection of variables brought into the analysis of the innovation process. What
are considered (perhaps justifiably given the methodology and
definitions used), as parameters to some innovation processes
may in others be variables to be manipulated in the interest of
socially effective innovation.

For example, most innovation studies have focused primarily
on the variables involved in the innovation process itself. In
general they have not incorporated analysis of the institutional
and socio-economic context within which that process operates. Kreilkamp's discussion of the methodology of Project
Hindsight draws attention to this issue in a not atypical case.
When such studies have considered variables "outside" the innovation process, they have found such variables to be relatively unimportant. [17] Thus the research approach seems to
have some justification — for the context in which it has been

used. However, the institutional and socio-economic environment of the innovation process may vary from that of the innovation processes which have been the main subjects of study. We shall consider only a few ways in which this environment may differ.

We shall confine our attention initially to the relatively large and significant innovations. In this type of case, most of the innovative activity takes place in some sort of institutional structure that is more or less separated from the ongoing production institutions — in a Research Institute, or in a Research Department and/or Development Section of the producing firm. Most of the innovation studies have not been concerned with the characteristics of the ongoing production institutions within which the innovation activities are located, or to which they are related. They have at times been concerned with relationships *between* the two systems, (as for example, in Project SAPPHO's concern with the *overall* management of the innovation process), but not with the characterstics of the production system itself.

However, for example, we might consider the managerial and technical capabilities within the production system. These capabilities play a key part in the innovation process. At one end of the process they constitute (or at least determine) the capacity of the system to absorb innovation. In the extreme, this absorptive capacity will determine whether the innovation is introduced at all. At the very least, it will be largely responsible for all minor modifications, trouble-shooting, and "bedding-in" of the innovation. Perhaps most importantly, these capabilities will be responsible for carrying out the host of adjustments in those parts of the production systems that are related to the innovation itself. The introduction of any innovation into the production system usually generates a ramified complex of complementary *change* requirements — for example, in labour skills, maintenance procedures, materials supplies, capital goods production, marketing relationships and so forth, all in addition to adjustments in related stages of the production process. Examples of such ripples of necessity for change which reached as far as the design and marketing/customer areas were noted in a study of the introduction of new techniques into tool making production in the U.K.

> "Detailed changes in both component design and tool design may be necessary to accommodate the needs of both computer aided design and numerically controlled manu-

facture ... (such as) ... the minimisation of sharp corners in component design ... ."

Or again,

"prior to the general acceptance of electrical discharge machining (edm) customers were used to the surfaces produced by milling then filing and polishing. The surfaces produced by edm tended to be of a different character than those produced traditionally and initially customers were not prepared to accept them ..." [37]

For successful transfer there must exist adequate capabilities to respond effectively to these types of ripples of secondary change requirement. These adjustments are necessary if the system as a whole is to absorb the impact of the specific innovation, and hence maximise the net gains from the change.

The managerial and technical capabilities of the production system may also be critical variables at another point — at the "other end" of the innovation process. These capabilities play key roles in identifying problems for which innovation may provide solutions, in defining innovation possibilities and in initiating the innovation process. To the extent that recent innovation studies have reversed, or at least circularised, the linear model, they have indicated the importance of these capabilities for identifying and defining innovation possibilities and for initiating the innovation process. For example, the "customer needs" and "management by objectives" models of Langrish et al. [9] draw attention to the rather obvious requirement for customers who can identify and specify their needs, and for managers in supplier firms who can define their customers' needs and who can formulate objectives for innovation. To the extent that these studies have begun to look at the ongoing backdrop of "minor" and "incremental" innovation and technical change, they have drawn attention to the fact that the more radical innovations often emerge from this ongoing process of minor technical change. This process, of course, is heavily dependent on the managerial and technical capabilities within the production system. Thus these capabilities, their activities and the ways in which they are organised can play a crucial role in initiating the innovation process — even the process concerned with large-scale and radical innovations. Without these capabilities there may not even be an innovation and technology transfer process. Certainly such a process would probably be more biased towards irrelevance and lack of success. Thus in certain situations, characteristics of the production system may not be parametric to the innovation process, but may include variables that are critical to determining its success — even its existence.

Of course, it is useful to consider how these capabilities are *related and linked to* the innovation process. However, if the context is one in which these capabilities do not exist to an adequate extent, then questions about relationships become less important. Other questions may become more important. Two alternative situations can illustrate the point. First, there may exist neither the institutional structure for innovation itself, nor the innovation-initiating capabilities within the production system. The crucial policy questions are unlikely to be about how to manage an innovation process or about how to improve it, but about how to get such a process to exist at all. The starting point is unlikely to be in the area of managing and marginally adjusting relationships between one system and the other, but in *creating*, building or enhancing elements of capability within, or close to, the production system. Without thought about how to build institutions incorporating the innovation executing capabilities in a context where initiating capabilities are severely limited one simply runs into a second type of problem.

This second situation is perhaps more common. Despite limited capabilities in the production system, there may exist the institutional structure of an innovation system. Concern with questions of relationship and communication is again likely to be misplaced if there is little or nothing to relate to, or communicate with. Again we may have to worry less about managing and marginally adjusting a given system.

We have reached this point in the argument about capabilities within the production system while retaining the assumption that the main phenomena of interest are the large, radical and significant innovations. Quite obviously as we shift our focus towards the minor and incremental innovation phenomena then questions about the managerial and technical capabilities of the production system become even more important. They, and the activities in which they are used, become important not merely for their role in initiating the innovation process and in absorbing the output of that process. Their role becomes increasingly concerned with actually executing the process itself.

In focussing on questions about the capabilities and activities within the production system we have illustrated some ways in which parameters in one situation may have to be considered variables in another. However, in doing so we have tried to make two points. First, we have tried to make the obvious point that some of these variables may be critical, particularly if the basic questions in the research are shifted to focus on other types of innovation or to ask why innovation does and does not exist. Secondly, we have suggested that with the particular methodological approach of most innovation studies, a marginalist approach to the problems has been reinforced. "Better" innovation performance is seen as resulting from better management, control and adjustment of given systems. However successful innovation, or any innovation at all, may require an approach involving fundamental restructuring and creation of systems.

A variation on this last point can be taken from within one of the main sets of conclusions of the body of recent innovation studies. Results of DC technology transfer research emphasise how important broad ranges of technical and managerial capabilities are for firms to innovative successfully. For example, from the Battelle study, the seven most important factors in innovation (down to 50 per cent of "decisive events") were − recognition of technical opportunity > recognition of need > internal R and D management > management venture decision > availability of funding > technical entrepreneur > in-house colleagues. External economic, political and social factors were rated low [17]. A heavy emphasis on these types of capability is also reflected in Project SAPPHO results. The five factors which discriminated for successful innovation were: strength of management and characteristics of managers, marketing performance, understanding user needs, R and D efficiency of development, communications, [22]. In all the studies discussed in this paper, transfer of information from outside the innovating institutions depended on competent in-house technical capability.

Thus, it seems clear that a necessary condition for success is some minimum level of a wide range of technical and managerial capabilities for executing the central innovating activities themselves. To have identified some of the necessary types of capability, and to have indicated something of the level required, have been valuable contributions. But the main concern so far seems to have been about the *relative* importance of these, and about ensuring the appropriate balance between them. If we drop the assumption that the necessary range and

251

levels of these capabilities exist, and that the main problem is about how to mix them together, then the central issue is again about creating, not manipulating capabilities.

To summarise this second section of the paper, we have suggested that the underlying models and the methods used in research about technology transfer and innovation may have seriously constrained the utility of the research.

More specifically, we suggested that:

1. The approach to research has not yet managed to throw off the constraint imposed by the assumed connectedness and coherence of a "linear" model — particularly with respect to the necessary connection of science and research to the rest of innovative activity.

2. Even when attempts have been made to cope with such problems as the multiplicity and interaction both of different stimuli and of different inputs relating to "success", research has been constrained by the nature of the particular innovation phenomena that have been selected for analysis in most of the research — for example in the selection of "significant" rather than "minor" innovations, or of innovations that consist (totally or predominantly) of "hardware" rather than "software" changes.

3. There has been a repeated tendency not to explore the relevance of variables relating to the institutional and socio-economic environment of the "central" activities in the innovation process — for example, the managerial and technical capabilities within the production system which may be critically important for absorbing innovation, for effecting the bulk of activities in certain types of innovation process and in a variety of ways for initiating the innovation process itself.

4. These limitations become particularly important if the context of innovation is shifted from that which has been explored by the majority of these studies, or if the basic questions asked in the research shift from being centred on marginalist considerations of improving and optimising a particular category of innovation process to more structural explorations of, for example, whether there are significantly different types of innovation process, or why the phenomenon of innovation (in any form) exists at all where it does and why it does not where it is absent.

Beyond these observations, we suggest that there is probably an interaction between these various features of the field of research that reinforce each other. The articulation of the basic model is reinforced by the selection of phenomena and variables. The basic questions asked lead towards continued reference (if only grudgingly and in part) to the basic model and towards the various forms of biasing methodology. Attachment to the methodology probably reinforces the tendency to explore phenomena within a particular context, and so on. A contributory factor to the continuing integrity of this intellectual structure has probably been the particular interests of the scientific community and its relatively powerful "lobby". Quite frequently perceptive researchers have moved outside one or more of the constraints, but most of the results have been used to contribute to further articulation within the boundaries of the existing structure of knowledge. Those results which lead outside this structure, and which suggest the need for new models, methodologies and basic research questions do not seem as yet to have been pursued with vigour. In other words, at the risk of sounding pretentious, we suggest that research on technology transfer and innovation is predominantly caught up in a self-reinforcing paradigm — a consensus formed around the basic dimensions of the area of intellectual enquiry.

We were led to the more detailed conclusions in this section, and hence to the more general observations directly above, by the fortunate experience of trying to explore technology transfer and innovation processes in the context of the developing countries and Thailand in particular. Forced into this different research environment we found, to put it simply, that the questions, models and methodologies which we could draw from the previous research were of limited helpfulness. Most importantly we found that they tended to focus attention away from the types of explanation and types of phenomena which appeared to be of greatest practical importance and social relevance.

We cannot hope to reproduce this experience for the full evaluation of others (or for their vicarious experience). However, in the next section we shall try to outline some of the relevant information, not only to indicate ways in which research in this field would probably have to be different in this type of context, but also to raise the question of whether it might be more useful if different in the context of the developed, industrialised societies.

3. Some Significant Differences in the DC and LDC Contexts for Innovation and Technology Transfer

We shall confine ourselves to a discussion of some of the characteristics of the industrial and manufacturing sectors of developing societies. We should also stress that much of our comment on the LDC industrial system is primarily (but not exclusively) derived from research in only one developing country — Thailand — which has been going through a particular historical period of industrialisation in a particular way, and building an industrial structure with a particular composition of subsectors. However, in general terms this phase, manner and composition of industrialisation, is, has been, and will be, common to a number of other countries. Obviously, however, the wider one attempts to generalise across the "LDC context" the more careful one must be. Therefore, throughout this section we shall use the term "developing country" (or LDC) as shorthand for "developing countries with a techno-economic structure similar to that in Thailand".

One striking feature of the industrialised societies is that the industrial production system operates very close to the universal frontier of advancing technology. On average the "age" of the elements of knowledge embodied in advances in production technology is short — relative to that in the LDC context. The leading growth sectors of the DC industrial system are heavily dependent on scientific and technical knowledge that is relatively new — electronics, petrochemicals, military hardware, transportation and so forth. Right across the board industrial change and advance depends upon creation of new knowledge, on exploiting elements of relatively new knowledge, on developing new combinations of existing knowledge, and on embodying those elements of new knowledge in new techniques. In this context "new" is defined not in relation to some local, national or regional entity, but in relation to the total, universal stock of technology. Quite obviously there are differences between sectors. Some are close to the frontiers of technical knowledge and exploring beyond them. Others are primarily concerned with utilising "older" technology in novel forms — perhaps only in the more trivial forms of product differentiation.

The advancing technological basis of production is very different in the developing countries. Products, processes and materials that are new to the *particular* economy are introduced into the production structure by the process of industrial growth and change. However, technology incorporated into these local novelties is often of considerable age. A few examples from recent industrial development in Thailand will illustrate this rather obvious point.

In the mid 1960's a major investment in the metal products industry consisted of the establishment of tinplate manufacture by the hot-dip process — utilising techniques that were developed in the nineteenth century and obsolete in the industrialised countries by the 1950's. When there arose problems of cost and product quality in tinplate production, effective "technical progress" was achieved not by research personnel but by a retired tinplate production manager from a developed country who was able to drag up from his experience the necessary knowledge to make the "innovations" required. Technical progress in this sector in the earlier 1970's in Thailand involved the replacement of the hot-dip process by the electrolytic process — based on technology of the early part of this century and utilising techniques developed in the 1930's, brought into use in the industrialised countries in the early 1940's and already "mature" by the late 1950's.

In the development of the food processing industry in Thailand, the establishment of metal container production was, in local terms, a major technical advance. Core elements of the techniques required were already mature in the industrialised societies in the 1930's. In fact, it seems likely that the more "appropriate" method of production was a slightly modified version of that used in the industrialised societies in the late nineteenth and early twentieth centuries [38].

The point hardly needs further elaboration. In a society like Thailand many parts of the leading edge of economic advance rest on technology that is far behind the leading edge of current advance, and on techniques which have long since "stabilised" and ceased to change in significant ways. In many cases it is so far behind that it is close to, or behind, the *trailing edge* of technology — the historical phase boundary at which technology passes out of use in the industrialised societies.

Quite obviously, as in the DC situation, the picture is not homogeneous — neither within a particular innovation nor between different innovations. For any particular innovation one will have to draw simultaneously on a spectrum of different "vintages" of technology. Beyond this the average "age" of the technological elements needed for technical and economic

255

advance will probably vary between innovations — almost certainly between innovations in different sectors. In some cases the average age of the relevant items of technology will be very high. In other cases it will be necessary to engage in research to develop universally new knowledge in order to make the desired step forward in economic performance.

Somewhat paradoxically it may be in the area of "traditional" production systems that research and/or development may be most frequently necessary. In some of these areas the scientifically derived knowledge of the production techniques may never have been developed. Without it, economic advance may not be possible. However, even in these *relatively* new knowledge-intensive cases it is likely that the ultimate "package" of the technique brought into use will have drawn on some items of new knowledge with large proportions of old, and will incorporate a large proportion of elements of "old" techniques.

The point we are suggesting is simply that, across the board, the average age of elements of technology embodied in advances in production, which can be absorbed into the technical system of production and its socio-economic context, will probably be substantially higher than in the industrialised societies.

Clearly we must seriously question the relevance to the LDC's of analyses of innovation and technology transfer which concentrate on the processes of research, technological change and the development of techniques of universal novelty, and which are primarily concerned with mechanisms for transferring and interrelating knowledge of relatively recent vintage.

Let us turn to some of the specific features of the prevailing innovation analyses — the methodological bias towards focus on "significant" innovations involving elements of universal novelty, particularly in the core of "hard" technology.

There is good reason to believe that "radical" and "significant" innovations — even if they are innovative with reference only to the locality and even if they utilise predominantly "old" technology — are not as important to the process of economic growth and transformation as they are in the industrialised societies. This, of course, is a difficult statement to support since no one has as yet demonstrated how significant "minor" and "incremental" innovations are in the DC contexts.

There has been frequent reference to the need in LDC's for

types of technical change that are "adaptive" or modifying — directed at making more "appropriate" the old techniques introduced from the industrialised societies. This thesis hardly needs repeating here, but two comments will be made. First, this type of "innovation" conforms quite closely to the "minor" types of innovation neglected by almost all innovation studies (so far). Secondly, in the majority of cases, this adaptive type of innovation is likely to draw mainly on available knowledge and technique. Only rarely will it require some exploration beyond the frontiers of what is, or has been, known. This is one reason why those versions of the argument which talk of "adaptive *research*" rather than "adaptive innovation" can be highly misleading.

What is normally referred to in the argument for "adaptive" innovation is pre-investment innovation — the modification of processes before they are installed, and the redesign of products before they are first produced in the society. Perhaps more important still is the whole area of post-investment innovation. We know little about this phenomenon in the industrialised societies. At least, however, we know that it exists. Moreover, an increasing number of people are coming to believe that it is an important contributor to increases in productivity and economic change. Our own research in Thailand suggests that there it does not exist — or at least is hardly detectable. The frequency of technical changes within industrial plants — other than the multiplication or replication of previous technique — appears to be very low. Increases in the productivity of the resources committed in past investments do occur. However these increases in productivity are largely accounted for by increasing utilisation of existing capacity and by increasing skills of the labour force in operating essentially unchanged techniques. The increase owes little or nothing to anything resembling innovation.

If this diagnosis is reasonably valid and reasonably generalisable it reveals a situation of some very considerable importance. We have already suggested that the cumulative process of minor and incremental innovation and technical improvement is important in two ways. Firstly it probably constitutes in itself a very large part of the economic change process which we describe as "technical progress", and with which we are familiar in the DC context (sometimes!) Secondly, and perhaps most importantly, it is probably the basis of autonomous "technical dynamism". It is probably because of, by way of, and out of this process that many of the more radical and significant steps of technical progress occur. This incremental innovation process may be a necessary condition for success in more significant and perhaps research or science-intensive innovation — not necessarily the greater rather than lesser success in any particular innovation, but for success in terms of the general frequency of incidence of innovation. Moreover, given the importance of *learning by doing* in building up all types of technical change of capabilities, it is probably through this process that the capabilities are developed to manage, execute and interact with the larger steps of both initiating production with new techniques and of innovating on the basis of substantially new technology.

Thus we suggest that the apparent absence, or very limited occurrence, of this type of post-investment, minor, and "incremental" innovative activity may be of very considerable social signifcance. As suggested in Section 2 this type of innovation process may be very different — qualitatively different — from the innovation process normally considered.

The bias in innovation studies towards the "hardware core" of technological innovation is, we suggest, similarly unhelpful. For example, Ranis [39] describes the innovations which had the most significant impact on LDC development as "technological assimilations". Within these he distinguished three types of labour-using, adaptive technological changes: those relating to the "machine proper or core activity"; those relating to the "intermachine within-plant process, or machine-peripheral activity"; and those relating to the "total production process, including organisational variants by plant and stage of processing, or plant related activities". Ranis suggests that as Japan, Korea, and Taiwan in particular (and to a lesser extent West Pakistan, India, Mexico and Kenya) moved into the substitution of export of traditional goods by that of more manufactured goods, the most important innovations were not as much in the "core activity" as in machine-peripheral activities and in total production integration.

In these types of innovation ("minor", "incremental" and "peripheral") "inputs" to the process other than those from science, research, and the most recent technology assume very considerable significance — problem-solving, integrating, organising and developing procedures and different organisational forms. One example from Thailand can be used to further illustrate this point. For a number of years in Southern Thai-

258

land technological change efforts to improve the simple processes by which smallholders treat rubber latex failed to have any effect. The "decisive event" (to use a familiar terminology) in eventually effecting this technical change had nothing at all to do with the techniques of the core activity — processing latex into sheets. Nor had it very much to do with transferring technical knowledge. Only when a new organisational technique was developed for marketing smallholders' rubber sheets did the smallholders begin to change their "core" processing techniques.

This sort of situation may be of considerable significance. Many LDC's are increasingly becoming concerned less with their "modern" sector and more with the "traditional", small-scale, and often rural, production sectors. This raises an important point. The closer one moves to the "traditional" and small-scale production systems, the more closely interwoven into the detailed fabric of society becomes that technology. The social and technical systems of the work and production is less separated from the other social structures within which it exists. In addition, the more delicately balanced are the relationships between production technique and social structure. Even quite minor changes in technique can generate large and critical implications for the social fabric within which it is embedded. The study by Sharp [40] of the introduction of steel axes to Australian aboriginals is a classic, if extreme, example of this. Possession of stone axes has been intimately woven into the tribal social structure and trading relationships. When young men were given the much more efficient steel axes the impact on both social and trading relationships was profound.

In cases of imbalance and inconsistency between technical and social change, either (a) the social structure prevails and the innovation is totally rejected, or ineffectively absorbed or (b) the innovation prevails and generates costly social disruption.

Thus, the more one is concerned with technical innovation for, or technology transfer to this type of production sector, the more important may be those components of the innovative activity which are concerned with organisational structures and social relationships. Again, the closer one moves to smaller scale and more traditional production systems, the more circumscribed is control by the individual producing institution over the related stages of production and over the social context of its techniques. Thus the less is the ability of the production institution itself to execute the necessary adjustments to its surrounding social, technical and organisational structures. Therefore in this type of situation it is likely to become more important that concern about the social and organisational aspects of innovative activity is closely incorporated into the innovation process itself — alongside concern with the hardware and with technique. Thus flows of knowledge and information, other than those relating to the hardware core of the technique, may be major components of the "package" of knowledge that is, or should be, transferred in relation to innovation.

This is closely related to our discussion in Section 2 about the narrowness of the prevailing view of what constitute the significant variables to explain the phenomenon of innovation. We discussed the importance of the managerial and technical capabilities in the production system, as one example of those aspects of the institutional environment of the central part of an innovation process which are usually assumed as parameters. We suggested that these characteristics were probably critical for initiation and absorption in the production system, and with respect to "minor" innovation they were probably important determinants of whether and how the central part of the innovation process itself was done.

Before discussing whether we can sensibly analyse innovation processes in the context of developing countries while assuming the existence of these capabilities, we shall try to throw a little more light on what we mean by "managerial and technical capabilities". As a starting point we shall take a distinction often made by analysts of industrial behaviour — such as by Penrose [41]* or, in a slightly different way, by Ansoff [42] between "operating" and "change" activities. The meaning of the

* In our opinion this seems to be a sadly neglected book. It is concerned with the fundamental questions about technical and other change in firms — why it happens at all and why it takes particular forms and directions — rather than with the types of marginalist questions we have mentioned above. In seeking answers Penrose tries to get to the institutional "guts" of the firm. Perhaps the neglect of the book is due to its (perhaps inevitable?) avoidance of fashionable, quantitative analysis of the results of firm behaviour and of the processes of decision-making. It seems to fall into an academic limbo lying somewhere between history, economics and sociology — a limbo in which many academics profess interest, but into which few have penetrated effectively.

distinction is obvious enough and we shall focus on "change" activities and on the change-resources needed to effect them. It is in the availability of "change" resources in the firm that Penrose locates the growth mechanism of firms. It is here that the dynamism of the industrial system lies, and it is the "nature" of these change resources that determine the "nature", direction and persistence of that dynamic. Within general change resources we distinguish those concerned with change that is intensive in the use of "technical knowledge". We have found it convenient to subdivide this type of technical change into six categories of capabilities:

(1) for executing "major" innovative activity;

(2) for effecting the host of necessary "adjustments" that ripple outwards through the production system from the point of introduction of innovation;

(3) for executing "minor" innovation;

(4) for decision-making about, rather than effecting of, technical change — particularly the processes of search, identification, specification and evaluation that initiate innovative activity;

(5) for effecting technical change which involves replication of techniques that have already been used, but which are perhaps "new" to the firm or to some entity smaller than the universe. In addition to these, there exist on the border between operation and change those capabilities;

(6) For operation-optimising — i.e. for pushing technical efficiency to, and maintaining it at, the limits imposed by the installed and utilised techniques of production.

The first of these — capabilities for "major" innovation — we locate within the distinct institutional structures concerned with effecting innovations. We turn our attention here to the remaining five.

These capabilities are usually (in DC's) located within the production oriented parts of the firm, rather than being separated off in institutions explicitly concerned with change — in Research Institutes, management and technical consultancies, R and D divisions etc. Usually the primary task of personnel with these other four types of capability is maintaining day-to-day operations, but periodically they turn their attention to change activities. For example, the plant manager and/or production engineer will at times turn from daily operations to become involved in decision-making about technical (and other) change. Similarly the engineering and/or maintenance departments will become involved in minor innovations and improvements, or in initiating activities such as plant layout design for expanded facilities, equipment specification or even its manufacture. In a similar way production foremen or supervisors, or quality control departments, for example, may become involved in effecting "minor" technical changes. These personnel, together with production managers and production operatives will constantly/periodically be under pressure to squeeze more out of the given system — to optimise production. In general, the point is simply that the production-oriented structures of the "typical DC firm" may be rich in "change" resources. Such resources may seldom be institutionalised in a way which sets change as their primary objective, but nonetheless they are in fact frequently involved in technical change.

The contrast in the LDC's is stark. The "typical LDC firm" is poverty stricken with respect to those resources. In the mass of firms in the small-scale sector (employing perhaps fewer than fifty workers) it is hard to find these resources. However one might expect to find them in the "larger" firms in the more rapidly expanding and more technologically advanced sector of industry. We did not.

If one looks within these firms, one finds a skeletal, emaciated form of the change-resource-rich DC structure of the firm. Plant managers and production engineers often have very little of the deep technological experience which allows effective technical decision-making. Even when such experience does exist one finds two types of constraint on its use for these types of change. First there is frequently a very limited degree of division and specialisation of labour. Often the manufacturing manager has management responsibility also for personnel and engineering (perhaps also for sales and finance). Beneath him in the organisation one may drop straight to production foremen. Secondly, and partly in consequence of the limited specialisation of function, the problems of day-to-day management seem to occupy a high proportion of available time of those who might be change-oriented. Attention to change, even if all other factors are favourable, just has to be put off.

Engineering and maintenance facilities again tend to be "thin" on experience, "light" in staff, and heavily involved in day-to-day demands. Quality control facilities, if they exist, very often add up to little more than on-line "checking" capabilities. Product design or product improvement departments or sections hardly ever exist. Where they do, for example, in some electronics firms, their concern is almost exclusively with the "art" aspects rather than the technical aspects of design (for example, in designing next year's cabinet for the un-changed, technical "guts" of the portable radio). Production supervisors and foremen often have very limited technical ex-perience. They and the production operatives seem totally oriented to basic operation. Again and again questions we asked management about the objectives of training at these levels induce responses about operation — and in detail about basic operation — of the plant. Any "atmosphere" of change, of "stretching" the system or even of optimising seems to be absent — or at best rather "thin".

In general then we suggest that in the LDC's this whole intra-firm "sub-culture" of technical change capabilities and at-titudes hardly exists. We suggest that in DC's not only does it exist, but it plays key roles in the innovation process. This paper is not the place to explore *why* it does not exist, but some implications of its absence might be briefly noted.

Given our earlier discussion most of the implications are ob-vious. If production operations tend not to be optimised to the point where they push against the limits of the techniques used, one of the main sources of "demand" for innovative ac-tivity is absent — be it for "major" and "significant" or "minor" and "incremental" innovations. At best, constraints imposed by the *apparent* limits of capacity are overcome by replications of techniques. The more limited is the level of "minor" innovative activity, the lower is the probability that this "backdrop" of ongoing change will generate either the in-dications of needed "major" innovation or the opportunities to pursue more "radical" innovative approaches. Even if such in-dications and opportunities do objectively exist at some level, the limited capabilities to take the initiating actions of search-ing, specifying, and deciding lowers the probability that they will be perceived and exploited. These limitations with respect to innovation initiation, together with those relating to the capability to absorb innovation,* mean that, even if capabili-

---

* This limited ability to effect minor adjustments in the system to accommo-date and optimally exploit changes introduced elsewhere in the system is im-portant not only with respect to the introduction of innovative changes. The introduction of replicative changes in the system often set up similar ripples of requirement and opportunity for complementary (perhaps minor) technical

ties for executing the central innovative activities do exist, there is little for them to relate to in the production system.

If the central innovative activities are pursued and the results "pushed" towards the production system, the limited absorption capability lowers the probability of actual adoption or increases the probability of sub-optimal utilisation — in turn increasing the probability both of subsequent rejection of the innovation and of subsequent lowered interest in further innovative efforts.

Perhaps the most important implication of the poverty of the interlinked capabilities for change within the production system stems from the probable existence of an important feedback process — learning by *doing*. It seems most likely that these types of change capability are expanded and developed to higher levels of capability by being exercised. See, for example, Solo [44] for a discussion of an economy's absorptive capacity for technology, and of how this seems dependent on a "learning by doing" process. To the extent that limited capacities for some types of change capability that do exist are limited — to some degree — then "doing" and hence "learning" is curtailed. At best this leads to a very slow rate of growth of those capabilities which constitute a large part of the dynamic power of industrial systems. Alternatively this leads to a vicious circle of continuing stagnation and dependence on "outsiders" for whatever (mainly replicative?) technical changes are introduced into the system.

In summary, then, in this section we have illustrated some of the critical differences in the context for innovation and technology transfer between developed and (some) developing countries. The innovative technical change processes that are of greatest economic and social relevance in the developing countries are likely to draw on knowledge that, on average, is much "older" than in the case of developed country innovation, which, for a variety of reasons, tends to draw heavily on most recent "vintages" of knowledge and information. The

---

change elsewhere. The limited capability to identify and exploit these "ripples" probably accounts in part for the very limited effectiveness of the "backward linkage" mechanism which has been held by some e.g. Hirschman, [43] to be a most important motor of industrial growth and dynamism in developing countries.

dynamic significance of "minor and incremental species" of innovative technical change is probably greater in developing countries than it appears to be (even allowing for our ignorance about it) in developed countries — where it is probably considerable, but underrated. As we discussed in Section 2, these "species" probably differ in many fundamental respects from the species which have been most studied, and upon the knowledge about which we tend to base our views of how innovation as a whole happens. Beyond this, even with respect to "major" innovations drawing heavily on relatively "new" knowledge, the importance of the transfer to utilisation of knowledge about parts of the system peripheral to the "hardware core" is probably greater in developing than in developed economics. As an extension of this, we suggested that the importance of innovations which had little or no "hardware core" component were probably more important. Finally we suggested that, again even with reference to "major" innovations, factors concerned with the institutional environment of the innovation process (e.g. managerial and technical capabilities within the production system) could not be regarded as parameters in the analysis of innovation — even if that analysis was concerned with explaining marginal differences in innovative behaviour or in success, rather than with explaining the overall incidence of any such behaviour at all.

4. Some Conclusions

We have had three purposes in mind in setting some aspects of the prevailing models and methodologies of technology transfer and innovation research alongside some of the features of the context of innovation which we observed in developing countries (primarily Thailand):

(1) to illustrate the need for substantial change in basic questions, underlying model and utilised methodologies if research on technology transfer and innovation in *developing* countries is to explain the most important problems — perhaps if it is to explain anything at all;

(2) to suggest that research on innovation in *developed* countries might profitably break outside the prevailing paradigm and ask different questions, necessitating the use of different models and methodologies;

(3) to draw attention to the possibility that the implementation of practical efforts to do something about technology

transfer and innovation may (a) be based on wildly erroneous and misleading views about what is involved, and may (b) be directed towards the solution of problems that are relatively trivial and marginal to the issues of greatest social and economic relevance.

In the guise of dealing with the first of these points, we can simultaneously deal with the first two. Those who are primarily interested in the second can simply select from our comments on research in developing countries whatever seems relevant to a different approach to research on technology transfer and innovation in industrialised societies.

As we outlined in Section 2, research in this field has been dominated (not exclusively) by questions of either relatively marginalist or relatively partial types. For example, much of the work has been concerned with a relatively narrow class of innovative efforts and with why they have been relatively "better" or "worse", successful or unsuccessful. Alternatively the interests of particular groups have prompted questions about how science flows to production, or about how research is linked to "application" in innovation. As we have suggested, for certain purposes, in certain places and at certain times, these are important questions. But they by no means exhaust the range of important questions in those places at those times, and may be less important or totally unimportant for other purposes at other places in other times.

We find it rather curious that relatively little research on innovation and technology transfer has been guided by such basic questions as what "it" is, why it exists and why it does not exist. We believe that in developing countries research in this area is important, but that it would be most appropriate if it was guided by questions of the following types. (For developed countries select according to preference.) Are there substantially different types of significant innovation and technical change? In what does their significance consist? In what situations do they occur? Why? Why do they not occur in those situations in which one might expect them, or in which the social and economic returns to their occurrence would be high? Those interested in, for example, the apparently limited innovative performance of industrial sectors of the UK economy might find this a more pertinent question than any number that might be asked about innovations that did occur. What forms of knowledge are drawn on from where, and how, to effect *all aspects* of each of the different types of innovation? What factors contribute to the transfer of each of these forms of technology for different types of innovation? How do the factors which explain the existence, or not, of innovative activity affect these various transfer processes?

To approach these types of question with the guidance of models that are dominated by concepts of one form or another of a continuous flow process would be unduly restricting — however elaborated with multiplicity and interaction of stimuli and "inputs". We would suggest that, in place of *flow* concepts, the basic models might more usefully be dominated by a *stock* concept. As we hopefully indicated in Section 1, greater flexibility is allowed if the dominating, central component of a model about transferring technology is defined in some way as a *stock* of technology. Subsidiary to this are the necessary flows of knowledge (transfers of technology) from the stock to innovative technical change. Even more subsidiary, and perhaps not even necessary at all in some cases, are the flows by which the stock is augmented and the creative systems which generate such flows. If, after starting with a stock-centred model, one finds it necessary in some situations to elaborate this with a complex of flow-systems contributing to the stock then it is obviously desirable to explore those input flow-systems. However, one need not *define* the problem area in terms of such systems, and if one does, the result is likely to constrict the directions of research.

To the extent that research starts from the types of questions we outlined above, it is likely to seek ways around some of the methodological biases we noted in Section 2 — relating to the selection of phenomena for observation and to the differentiation between variables and parameters. However, problems are likely to persist unless quite fundamental shifts are taken in the dominant methodological approaches. Three points seem to be worth mentioning:

(1) Serious attempts to develop inter-disciplinarity will be necessary to break away from the confines of "core-hardware" focus in the selection of innovation phenomena, the "hardware" focus in the identification of knowledge flows and the exclusive focus on the "central" innovative activities to the exclusion of what goes on around those central activities — particularly with respect to the critical initiating and absorbing activities within the production system. To the extent that innovative activity is explored exclusively by those in the techno-economic disciplines, it is likely that research will continue to

267

be dominated by the selection of "hardware" innovations and flows of "hardware-related" knowledge, and by the relative exclusion of explanations relating to the complex of "institutional factors" surrounding the central activities of innovation itself.

(2) There would seem to be a basic step in the development of knowledge through research that has been bypassed in this field – at least as a deliberate, explicit activity. A procedure that is almost standard in most fields of exploration in the natural sciences, in many relating to technology and in some in the social sciences, is the initial identification, description and classification of the phenomena within the bounds of the field of enquiry. Given such a taxonomy, enquiry proceeds to detail within it, but the existence of the taxonomy is a constant reminder to researchers that they are dealing with a part of the elephant not the whole of it. Much of the confusion in the "innovation literature" seems to stem from a failure to perceive that apparently contradictory results relate to different parts of the elephant. The neglect of some important "species" of innovation phenomena can, as we have complained above, probably be explained by the simple fact that an exhaustive taxonomy has not been drawn up to indicate the existence and importance of yet other vital components of the complete "innovation animal". We suggest that the articulation of an appropriate taxonomy of the phenomena within the field of "innovation studies" should be developed as a priority.

(3) The dominating approach to technology transfer and innovation research has been retrospection. However valiant and ingenious are the efforts to overcome the inherent limitations of this approach, it must almost inevitably bias phenomena-selection towards the more "significant" and notable, knowledge-flow identification towards the recorded and documented, and variable-selection towards the rationalised and remembered. Questions about the whats, hows and why's of *change* are commonly posed for research in the natural and medical sciences and in relation to technology. A not uncommon procedure is to observe change as it happens and to record – often exhaustively – what appears to be relevant and even what initially appears irrelevant. The social sciences, of course, are somewhat limited in their ability to set up controlled, experimental change processes for observation, but there are far fewer limits on the ability to observe and "monitor" change *as*

268

it happens. We believe that a much more frequent use of such a "longitudinal" research method is essential if research on the complex process of innovative *change* is to avoid some of the limitations we outlined in Section 2.

Even if a revised set of basic questions is adopted, if stock-centred models are developed, and if methodological approaches outlined above are used, there is likely to be still a need to take explicit steps to "dig into" the sub-stratum of characteristics within the production system which can justifiably be taken as parameters in some situations and for some types of question, but which probably become critical variables in other situations or for other types of question. This is particularly so in the developing country situations and for the types of questions that seem most important in that context.

Changes along these lines in the approach to research on innovation and its related transfers of technology seem necessary if the field of study is to cover those areas of omission which seem particularly important in the context of developing countries and which are probably also important in many industrialised country contexts. Of course, to the extent that research is led (forced?) to operate within the existing paradigm structure by the interests and power of particular groups outside the research-executing community, then that also is an issue that must be faced.

Whether we need to be very worried about areas of omission, and whether we need to be very worried about the speed at which research is shifted to cover these areas are questions which lead to the third point in this concluding section. If innovation research is an academic exercise, which has little bearing on what happens in the practice of innovation, then what it omits and what it explains are simply matters of concern to those who worry about the nature and content of academic, intellectual enquiry. If the results of such research are used in any way to assist practice in the areas to which the research refers, but can contribute nothing to practice in the areas not covered, then again we need not be too worried. Indeed, we can even be satisfied that what is done has some social relevance and that probably no harm is being done. If on the other hand the restricted results of such research do not contribute to changing existing practice which is irrelevant or even harmful and counter-productive, or if they contribute in some way to practice in areas of action in which the results are partially or wholly inapplicable, then we need to be much more concerned.

We believe that this, in fact, is the situation in many developing countries. Views about what innovation is and how it happens, which reflect the dominating paradigm which we discussed in Section 2, seem to be the main guidelines for *practice* in at least two types of situation:

(1) at the macro level of planning for technical change and establishing institutions to effect it, as well as in the allocation of resources to the expansion and development of these institutions;

(2) at the more micro level of the management and review of established LDC institutions.

This, of course, is not too surprising since much of the "analysis" for planning, advice, and recommendation for action is provided by "experts" from the industrialised countries who naturally draw primarily on their practical experience, which has usually been acquired in the context of science and research-intensive activity in which a high incidence of "significant" innovation occurs, and which in itself constitutes a "peak" based on a rich and complex, but usually unnoticed, substratum of technical and managerial capabilities and activities within the production system. The local counterparts of the "experts" usually themselves have their training, and perhaps work, experience in this same context.

These situations seem to have at least four important consequences:

(1) The overall balance of resource allocation to activities for exploiting technology becomes heavily weighted towards the types of activity which play critical roles in some types of DC innovation, but which, we suggested in Section 3, are probably less effective and less important in the developing country context.

(2) Such investments often generate little or no discernible returns in terms of innovative change in the production system. This tends to discredit the whole class of investments to which the words science or technology are attached.

(3) It is not uncommon that the "right" thing is done for the "wrong" reason — as when a scientific research institute is set up following persuasive arguments that the resources allocated will "*soon*" have a significant impact on the production system and generate substantial returns. When the impact and the returns do not materialise within a space of time that the policy-maker considers as "soon", future resource allocations

to the activity are threatened, the progress of the activity is disrupted by uncertainty and by changing objectives, and once again future allocations to activities with similar generic labels are discounted and threatened.

(4) In response to problems of these types it is common to turn again to overseas experts for advice on rectifying the situation. Predominantly the "advice" is drawn from the experience, and perhaps research-derived knowledge, of how to marginally adjust and "manage better" the types of innovative process and related activity which are at the centre of the paradigm we discussed in Section 2. Our experience of the effects of the remedial treatment is more or less what we would predict on the basis of the discussion in Section 3.

It is for these types of reason, if for no others, that we believe there is an urgency about the need to re-orient research on technology transfer and innovation, and to break outside the constraining paradigm we outlined in Section 2. We also suggest that this is not solely a matter of concern for research in developing countries. As we noted above, much of the guidance for action about effecting technical change is provided by advisers from the developed countries. For good or ill this is likely to persist in some degree. It might at least be for better if there existed a body of knowledge derived from their familiar developed country context that was more appropriate for the context in which their advice is used.

Many of the revised set of basic research questions that we outlined earlier can be asked in the developed country context, and research there can proceed on the basis of different models and methodologies. Such research might help to correct the dominance over practice of what we believe to be a misleading, and only marginally relevant view of what is involved in effecting innovation in developing countries. If, in addition, it was to throw light on some important problems facing developing societies, so much the better.

References

[1] Freeman, C. and Pavitt, K., "Economics of Research and Development", Ch. 7. in I. Spiegel-Rosing and D. de Solla Price (eds.) *Science Policy Studies in Perspective*, 1977.

[2] Mansfield, E., *Industrial Research and Technological Innovation*, Norton, New York, 1968.

[3] Rosenberg, N., *Factors Affecting the Payoff to Technological Innovation*, National Science Foundation, 1975.

[4] Grilliches, Z., "Hybrid Corn: An Exploration in the Economics of Technological Change," *Econometrica*, 1957, pp. 501-522.

[5] Grilliches, Z., "Hybrid Corn and the Economics of Innovation", *Science*, 1960. pp. 275-280.

[6] Schon, D.A., *Technology and Change – the New Heraclitus*, Oxford, Penguin, 1967.

[7] *Frascati Manual*, OECD, 1970.

[8] Ziman, J., *Public Knowledge*, Cambridge University Press, 1968.

[9] Langrish, J., Gibbons, M., Evans, W.G., and Jevons, F.R., *Wealth from Knowledge – Studies of Innovation in Industry*, London, MacMillan, 1972.

[10] Blackett, P.M.S., "Memorandum to the Select Committee on Science and Technology", *Nature* 219, (1968), 1107.

[11] Gruber, W.H., and Marquis, D.G. (eds.), *Factors in the Transfer of Technology*, MIT Press, Cambridge, Massachusetts, 1969.

[12] Office of the Director of Defense Research and Engineering, *Project Hindsight Final Report*, Washington, D.C., 1969.

[13] Burns, T., "Models, Images and Myths", in W.H. Gruber and D.G. Marquis (eds.), *op. cit.*, pp. 11-23.

[14] Kreilkamp, K., "Hindsight and the Real World of Science Policy", *Science Studies* 1, (1971) 43-66.

[15] Greenberg, D.S., "Hindsight: DOD Study Examines Returns on Investment in Research", *Science* 154 (1966), 873.

[16] Sherwin, C.W. and Isenson, R.S., "Project Hindsight: A Defense Department Study of the Utility of Research", *Science* 156 (1967), 1571-1577.

[17] Globe, S., Levy, G.W., and Schwartz, C.M., *Science Technology and Innovation*, Report prepared for National Science Foundation, NSF – 0667, Columbus, Ohio, Battelle, 1973.

[19] Thompson, P., "Traces: Basic Research Links to Technology Appraised", *Science* 163 (1969), 374-375.

[20] Globe, S., Levy, G.W., and Schwartz, C.M., *The Interactions of Science and Technology in the Innovative Process: Some Case Studies*, NSF – 0667, Columbus, Ohio, Battelle, 1973.

[21] Hollomon, J.H., in Tybout, R.A. (ed.), *Economics of Research and Development*, Columbus, Ohio State University Press, 1965, p. 253.

[22] Rothwell, R., *SAPPHO Updated – Project SAPPHO, Phase II*, University of Sussex, Science Policy Research Unit, 1973.

[23] Achilladelis, B., Jervis, P., and Robertson, A., *Project SAPPHO: A Study of Success and Failure in Industrial Innovation*, Report to the Science Research Council, Science Policy Research Unit, University of Sussex, 1971.

[24] Gibbons, M. and Johnston, R.D., *The Interaction of Science and Tech-*

272

nology, Final report of a study carried out for the Economic Benefits Working Group of the Council for Scientific Policy, Manchester, Manchester University, 1972.

[25] Gibbons, M. and Johnston, R.D., "The Roles of Science in Industrial Innovation", *Research Policy*, 3 (1974) 220-242.

[26] Smith, C.S., "Materials", *Scientific American* 217, (1967), 69-79.

[27] Baker, N.R., Siegman, J., and Rubenstein, A.H., "The Effects of Perceived Needs and Means on the Generation of Ideas for Industrial Research and Development", *IEEE Transactions on Engineering Management* 14, (1967), 156-163.

[28] Price, Derek de Solla, "The Structures of Publication in Science and Technology", in W.H. Gruber and D.G. Marquis, *op. cit.* pp. 91-104.

[29] Toynbee, A.J., "Introduction: The Genesis of Civilisations" in *A Study of History*, (12 Volumes), New York, 1962.

[30] Mensch, Gerhard, "Institutional Barriers to the Science and Technology Interaction", in H.F. Davidson, M.J. Cetron, J.D. Goldhar, *Technology Transfer*, Noordhoff, Leiden, 1974.

[31] Hill, S.C., "Australian Engineers and Environmental Action", *Australian Journal Institution of Engineers*, 45(9), (1973), 25-28.

[32] Hill, S.C., "Professions: Mechanical Solidarity and Process (– or, 'How I learnt to live with a primitive society')", *Journal Sociological Association of Australia and New Zealand*, 9(3), 1973.

[33] Hill, S.C., Fensham, P.J., and Howden, I.B., "The Education of Ph.D. Scientists in Australia and its Implications for their Employment", in *Monograph No. 8*, Australian Academy of Science, Canberra, 1974.

[34] Hill, S.C., Fensham, P.J., and Howden, I.B., "Ph.D. Education in Australia – the Making of a Professional Scientist", *Monograph No. 7*, Australian Academy of Science, Canberra, 1974.

[35] Greenberg, D.S., *The Politics of American Science*, Penguin, London, 1969 (first published as *The Politics of Pure Science*, 1966).

[36] Freeman, C., *The Economics of Industrial Innovation*, Penguin, London, 1974.

[37] Senker, P.J., *The Application of Numerically Controlled Machines to Toolmaking*, Science Policy Research Unit, mimeo, Research Report, 1974.

[38] Bell, R.M., Cooper, C.M., Kaplinski, I.R. and Sabyarakwit, W., *Industrial Technology and Employment Opportunity: A Study of Technical Alternatives for Can Manufacture in Developing Countries*, ILO, Geneva, 1976.

[39] Ranis, G., *Some Observations on the Economic Framework for Optimum LDC Utilisation of Technology*, Yale University: Economic Growth Centre, mimeo, 1972.

[40] Sharp, L., "Steel Axes for Stone Age Australia", in E.H. Spicer (ed.), *Human Problems in Technological Change*, Russel Sage Foundation, New York, 1952.

[41] Penrose, E.T., *The Theory of the Growth of the Firm*, John Wiley, New York, 1959.

[42] Ansoff, H.I., *Corporate Strategy*, Penguin, London, 1968.
[43] Hirschman, A.O., *The Strategy of Economic Development*, Yale University Press, Newhaven, 1958.
[44] Solo, R., "The Capacity to Assimilate an Advanced Technology", *American Economic Review Papers and Proceedings*, May 1966, pp. 91-97; reprinted in N. Rosenberg, *The Economics of Technological Change*, Penguin, London, 1971.

INDEX

275

278